W9-ADF-874

LITERATURE AND
GERMAN REUNIFICATION

This book is the first systematic attempt in English to examine the literary consequences of German reunification. Placing the concept of the *Kulturnation* at the center of its analysis, the book explores the ways in which literature both responds to and helps to constitute notions of German national identity. Previous studies of postwar German literature have tended to avoid the problem of nationhood: this is one of the few books in any language to treat contemporary Germany as a cultural and national unity. The book discusses German literature from the early 1980s through the late 1990s, with a primary focus on the way in which authors of the 1990s have sought to cope with and respond to reunification and emerging questions about history, politics, and identity. Larger questions are addressed about the role of both the nation and a national literature in the context of economic and political globalization.

Stephen Brockmann is Associate Professor of German in the Department of Modern Languages at Carnegie Mellon University, Pittsburgh. He is co-editor, with Thomas Kniesche, of *Dancing on the Volcano: Essays on the Culture of the Weimar Republic* (1994), and, with Frank Trommler, of *Revisiting Zero Hour 1945: The Emergence of Post-War German Culture* (1996).

CAMBRIDGE STUDIES IN GERMAN

General editors
H. B. Nisbet, University of Cambridge
Martin Swales, University of London
Advisory editor
Theodore J. Ziolkowski, Princeton University

Also in the series

SEÁN ALLAN: *The Plays of Heinrich von Kleist: Ideals and Illusions*
0 521 49511 3

W. E. YATES: *Theatre in Vienna: A Critical History, 1776–1995*
0 521 42100 4

MICHAEL MINDEN: *The German "Bildungsroman":*
Incest and Inheritance
0 521 49573 3

TODD KONTJE: *Women, the Novel, and the German Nation 1771–1871*:
Domestic Fiction in the Fatherland
0 521 63110 6

LITERATURE AND
GERMAN REUNIFICATION

STEPHEN BROCKMANN

CAMBRIDGE
UNIVERSITY PRESS

PUBLISHED BY THE PRESS SYNDICATE OF THE UNIVERSITY OF CAMBRIDGE
The Pitt Building, Trumpington Street, Cambridge CB2 1RP, United Kingdom

CAMBRIDGE UNIVERSITY PRESS
The Edinburgh Building, Cambridge CB2 2RU, UK   http://www.cup.cam.ac.uk
40 West 20th Street, New York, NY 10011–4211, USA   http://www.cup.org
10 Stamford Road, Oakleigh, Melbourne 3166, Australia

© Stephen Brockmann 1999

First published 1999

Printed in the United Kingdom at the University Press, Cambridge

Typeset in Baskerville 11/12½ pt [CE]

A catalogue record for this book is available from the British Library

Library of Congress Cataloging in Publication data

Brockmann, Stephen.
Literature and German reunification / Stephen Brockmann.
p.   cm. – (Cambridge studies in German)
Includes bibliographical references and index.
ISBN 0 521 66054 8 (hardback)
1. German literature – 20th century – History and criticism.
2. Politics and literature – German – History – 20th century.
3. Literature and society – German – History – 20th century.
4. German reunification question (1949–1990) in literature.
5. Germany – History – Unification, 1990. I. Title. II. Series.
PT405.B684   1999
830.9′358–dc21   98–53641
CIP

ISBN 0 521 66054 8 hardback

to my mother,
Karen Brockmann

Contents

Acknowledgments		*page* xi
Introduction: locating the nation		1
1	Searching for Germany in the 1980s	22
2	A third path?	45
3	Literature and politics	64
4	Literature and the Stasi	80
5	The rebirth of tragedy?	109
6	The defense of childhood and the guilt of the fathers	137
7	The time and the place of the nation	163
Notes		199
Works cited		225
Index		239

Acknowledgments

I am grateful to many people for their support and encouragement during my work on this book. Rita Wegner, Thorsten Hinz, and Frank Linke have been important partners in Leipzig and Berlin, while Mabel Lesch-Rey and Claus and Erika Keiper have helped me further west. Kurt Drawert has given me insights in both the East and the West. Professor Erhard Schütz at the Humboldt Universität has been remarkably helpful to me during several research visits to Berlin, while Professor Klaus Schuhmann provided vital support to me in Leipzig; I am also grateful to Professor Jochen Vogt in Essen. In the United States, I owe a debt of gratitude to Professors Frank Trommler and David Bathrick, who have provided consistent support and help to me throughout my work on this book. To Professor Keith Bullivant I am grateful for giving me the opportunity, in his book *Beyond 1989: Re-reading German Literature Since 1945*, to develop some of the ideas which ultimately became part of chapter one of this book. Professor Hinrich Seeba helped to start the ball rolling on this project many years ago, while Professors Jost Hermand, James Steakley, Peter Uwe Hohendahl, Marc Silberman, Siegfried Mews, and Neil Donahue have all given me valuable advice along the way. To Professors Sabine Hake at the University of Pittsburgh and Vibeke Petersen at Drake University I owe particular thanks for their comments and suggestions on earlier versions of the manuscript as well as for their friendship and support. At Carnegie Mellon University I am grateful to my colleagues Christian Hallstein and Anne Green in the German program for their encouragement; and to Peter Stearns and Dick Tucker in the College of Humanities and Social Sciences for their support. I also owe a debt of gratitude to Geraldine Kruglak and Joan Stein at the Hunt Library, who have given me invaluable help in tracking down materials. I am grateful to the many inquisitive students I have had and continue to have in my courses on contemporary German culture; it is partly their questions that I have set out to explore in this book. The Alexander von Humboldt Foundation, German Academic Exchange Service, and the National Endowment for the Humanities have provided generous financial support during my work on this project, and I was also the beneficiary of a Falk Grant and a Faculty Development Grant at Carnegie Mellon University. Bill and Judy Craig and Paul and Chuck Brockmann have been unfailing in their encouragement, and Johnny and Danniel Ward-Packard have been good friends to me throughout. Without my first language teacher, Karen Brockmann, I could never have completed the project, and it is to her that I dedicate this book.

Introduction: locating the nation

When, in August 1995, the German news magazine *Der Spiegel* featured a cover story – and attack – by the critic Marcel Reich-Ranicki on Günter Grass's recently published novel *Ein weites Feld* [*Too Far Afield*], it was confirming once again the central importance of literature in the German national imagination. Although the argument is not universally accepted, I am by no means the first observer to point out the tremendous importance of literature in Germany during the current conjuncture. In his study *The Future of German Literature*, Keith Bullivant devotes considerable acuity to demonstrating that literature, particularly in the West German Federal Republic, has played and, in the reunified Germany of the 1990s, continues to play, a political role that would be unthinkable, for instance, in Britain. Notwithstanding the strategic protestations of German writers to the contrary, Bullivant argues, "it is the British, rather than the Germans, who have lacked an ongoing intellectual discourse, within which imaginative writers played their part."[1] Indeed, Bullivant, along with many others, ascribes to a West German writer like Heinrich Böll the role of "conscience of the nation," and he argues that other West German writers have at times played a similar role.[2] Even the sometimes "vicious attacks on writers by conservative politicians and newspapers" in Germany are, Bullivant suggests, "perhaps the clearest indication of the seriousness with which these writers' views were considered."[3] Much of Bullivant's work is devoted to a critique of those intellectuals inside Germany who have sought to attack the role of German writers in the nation's political life in the post-reunification context.

Although Bullivant does not extend his argument about the pre-1989 "vicious attacks" of German politicians to the similar post-reunification diatribes of some intellectuals, the same point could be made here as well: the very vehemence of intellectual attacks on the

I

political role of writers in Germany is an indication of the continuing importance of German writers in the nation's political life. To take the example of Günter Grass and Marcel Reich-Ranicki, it is hardly credible that *Der Spiegel* would have placed this story on its cover had the editors not been convinced that Reich-Ranicki's attack was important news with real consequences for the nation. Whether the editors were for or against Grass's book did not seem to matter: what mattered was that they believed the book to be important. As obvious as this observation may seem, it needs to be reemphasized in an academic context characterized by discussions of "the declining cultural status of literature."[4]

In his study *Die literarische Republik: Westdeutsche Schriftsteller und die Politik* [The Literary Republic: West German Authors and Politics] (1982), Helmut L. Müller made a similar point about the tremendous importance of literary discourse in West Germany, arguing that in many instances West German writers help to create the terms of political discourse within which politicians must justify themselves: "precisely the 1970s clearly showed how great the influence of literary intellectuals is," the largely strategic contrary protestations of writers notwithstanding.[5] As Müller notes, writers "can play a substantial role in determining the political discussion, even if or precisely because they are not in alliance with the powerful." He argues that "the mutual action and reaction of *Geist* and *Macht*, of literature and politics, has helped form the picture of the Federal Republic."[6]

Within the context of East German literature, David Bathrick has made a convincing case for the political role of writers in the German Democratic Republic. His recent monograph *The Powers of Speech* revolves around the concept that in a Communist country that lacked an open public sphere, writers and their works took on a specific political function by enabling discussion and reflection, sometimes in allegorical form, on political and social problems that would otherwise have been ignored. Where other avenues of discourse were blocked because of the Communist regime's repression of open political dialog, literature assumed a privileged role in enabling a more oblique form of communication. As Bathrick suggests, the "very centrality" of literature for East German politicians "helped facilitate the development historically of critical discourses and the articulation of alternative political views within the larger polity."[7] Moreover, the ambiguity of literature gave it a privileged place in a socialist public sphere, since "it was literary discourse as discourse that opened up possibilities for a more mutually conceived dialogue between author and reader, literature and the public."[8] Wolfgang Emmerich has argued that the political importance of literature in the GDR gave it "a largely premodern" status that differentiated it from its western counterpart.[9] Like Bathrick and Emmerich, Bullivant also stresses "the unquestioned moral authority which critical literary intellectuals acquired throughout the 1980s in the GDR, when they essentially constituted the only alternative discourse to that of the party and its media,"[10] and he makes the revealing point that in many ways, and in spite of massive political and economic differences between East and West Germany, writers in the two countries enjoyed a substantially similar prestige and authority – a point implicitly contested by Bathrick, who argues that "as an institution, the writer in the GDR bore little resemblance to his or her counterpart in a capitalist society."[11] It is of course true that the institutionalization of literature in the Communist GDR proceeded very differently from the processes in the Federal Republic. But in the seriousness with which they treated their writers, the capitalist and the Communist German state did to some extent parallel each other. Bathrick himself has suggested that "regardless of the very different experiences and institutional structures out of which they came, western writers . . . and GDR dissident writers . . . came to inhabit similar positions as moral leaders of invisible constituencies."[12] As Helmut Peitsch has pointed out, such parallels were partially concealed by the cold war enmity between the FRG and the GDR, which led intellectuals in the two German states to imagine their counterparts as radically different and usually prevented the recognition of overarching similarities.[13]

Confirming Peitsch's point, neither Volker Wehdeking in his study *Die deutsche Einheit und die Schriftsteller* [German Unity and Writers][14] nor Emmerich in the revised version of his authoritative *Kleine Literaturgeschichte der DDR* [Concise Literary History of the GDR] inquires into the similarity of the political role of literature in the two Germanys prior to reunification or in the single Germany of the 1990s.[15] As Emmerich writes self-critically in a 1993 article, "the context of national literature" was virtually ignored by scholars of the 1970s and 1980s, who were all too intent on "divisions and differences" between the two German literatures and failed "to point out connections and even commonalities."[16] Emmerich calls this overarching national context "one that may seem obvious but which in fact was not obvious at all, not even in the West."[17] Wehdeking virtually ignores the many literary debates of the early 1990s, concentrating instead almost exclusively on the analysis of individual literary texts. Emmerich devotes himself to a demonstration of the convergent tendencies between West and East German literature during the decade and a half prior to reunification, while eliding the issue of a similar or convergent function of the two literatures at the political level.[18] While he is well aware of the political function of East German literature within GDR society, he is not concerned with comparing that function to the function of literature in West Germany. Indeed, both Emmerich and Wehdeking seem to take for granted that literature and literary intellectuals enjoy profound political importance; they are less interested in asking why that should be the case. It seems possible that the resonance of literary discourse in Germany may be a deep-seated phenomenon easily taken for granted, indeed reified, by those who have become used to it – something, to repeat Emmerich's words, that "may seem obvious but which in fact was not obvious at all."

Peitsch's book *Vom Faschismus zum Kalten Krieg* [From Fascism to the Cold War] is an example of a recent work that places the political role of German literature at the center of attention, and which directly addresses both the Federal Republic and the GDR. However Peitsch's analysis of convergences is highly ambivalent. While he acknowledges parallels, he is, like most other scholars, reluctant to explore those convergences from an overarching national or historical perspective. Moreover, even Peitsch does not seek to make comparisons between the situation in the two Germanys and the situation in other countries. In spite of his emphasis on "Literaturverhältnisse" (literary relations), Peitsch seems more interested in unpacking the political messages encoded in and around discussions of German literature than in analyzing the relationship between literature and politics itself. If confronted with the *Spiegel* cover attacking Grass, such an approach might analyze and criticize Reich-Ranicki's conservative message rather than inquire into the implication of both writer and critic in one and the same discursive context affirming the national importance of literature. There would, of course, be nothing wrong with such an analysis, and indeed Oskar Negt has already gone some way toward providing it.[19] But in addition to analyzing the content of messages, it is important to understand the context of which those messages are a part. Reich-Ranicki's criticisms would have had a substantially different impact if they had been uttered by an unknown scholar on the back pages of a regional daily. Appearing in the context it did, however, the attack on Grass was nevertheless also, paradoxically, a reconfirmation of Grass's preeminent cultural-political status as a writer in Germany. In discussing the many debates about German literature in the post-reunification context, few scholars have noted this paradox.

There is a related paradox in the position of a left-liberal academic critic like Peitsch. While Peitsch is concerned with what he sees as the right-wing, authoritarian connotations of most concepts of German national identity, he is nevertheless intent on preserving the prestige of critical literary intellectuals like Günter Grass, a prestige which is, however, itself dependent on the concept of national identity. If Grass were not perceived as in some way a representative of German national culture, he would not appear on the cover of "the German news magazine," and no one would be interested in attacks against or interventions for him. Grass's power and prestige are connected precisely to his role as "conscience of the nation." Where there is no sense of national identity, however, there can be no "conscience of the nation." The powerful political role of postwar German literature is a direct result of its significance not for some unspecified collective but for German national identity. That Peitsch does not seem to be aware of this paradox is indicative of a fundamental problem in left-liberal German criticisms of national identity. German leftists tend to be uncomfortable with, indeed mistrustful of, concepts of the nation, but they would nevertheless like to preserve for literature a progressive political role. How that role could possibly be articulated in an intellectual space outside or above the nation is almost never made clear. Peitsch seems to recognize the dilemma when he notes that apolitical definitions of the writer's role in German society have tended to imply "the renunciation of the representatives of the nation"; however, because Peitsch is himself reluctant to invoke concepts of national identity, the dilemma is not articulated further.[20]

The relative absence or negative judgment in recent literary criticism of the concept of the *Kulturnation* (cultural nation) is a striking indication of the difficulty critics seem to have in addressing this issue. Peitsch, Wehdeking, and Emmerich all fail to mention

Friedrich Meinecke, the distinguished historian who initially formu-
lated the concept of the *Kulturnation* in the early twentieth century;
and in their attempts to define the relationship between literature
and politics even K. Stuart Parkes, in his book *Writers and Politics in
West Germany,* and Keith Bullivant are silent about Meinecke's
invocation of a German cultural unity that preceded and prefigured
German political unity. The relative absence of the *Kulturnation* in
recent scholarship is all the more striking because the fact of postwar
German division and ultimate reunification would seem to be a
prime example of the long duration of such forms and concepts.
Meinecke had meant to describe Germany's cultural and literary
coming-to-consciousness of itself over the course of the nineteenth
century – the path from cultural to political unity – but his ideas
would seem applicable at least in part to the story of reunification
over a century later, in which first writers and later politicians came
to recognize the socially constructed reality of the German nation.
Since the first publication of Meinecke's *Weltbürgertum und National-
staat* [*Cosmopolitanism and the National State*], the concept of the
Kulturnation has had a substantial impact on the way Germans have
thought about the relationship between politics and culture
throughout the twentieth century.[21] If the concept and its history are
now conspicuously absent from scholarly discussions of German
culture and reunification, then it would seem that the concept itself
may be a sore spot, perhaps even a taboo: a disquieting object
around which German culture may revolve, but which frequently
remains unspoken or even unobserved.

The concept of the *Kulturnation* implies that because of its political
division Germany was, for centuries after the political solidification
of its chief European rivals France and England, a fragmented,
indeed non-existent political entity in the middle of Europe, and that
because of this fragmentation Germans could experience national
identity and unity only in and through culture. What brought
Bavarians, Prussians, Swabians, and Saxons together in the first half
of the nineteenth century was not a common political home but
rather the sense of a German culture that existed prior to and
independent of any political nation-building. "In France, it was the
middle class and the men of letters together that created the new
national idea," writes Meinecke, but "in Germany it was almost
exclusively the men of letters," and hence "the national spirit
emerged as a by-product of the intellectual efforts of the great poets

and thinkers of the time."[22] In Germany the *Kulturnation* preceded the political nation, or, as Meinecke calls it, the *Staatsnation*. Rogers Brubaker has recently reiterated Meinecke's central claim by suggesting that the concept of nationhood in Germany developed "as an essentially ethnocultural fact, prior to and independent of the state."[23] For a country experiencing the humiliation of the Napoleonic invasions of the early nineteenth century, national culture became a way of creating an identity inaccessible to and above politics. Friedrich Schiller expressed this idea in 1801, arguing that

The German Empire and the German nation are two different things. The majesty of the German never rested on the head of his prince. The German has founded his own value apart from politics, and even if the Empire perished, German dignity would remain uncontested. This dignity is a moral greatness. It resides in the culture and in the character of the nation that are both independent of her political vicissitudes . . . While the political Empire has tottered, the spiritual realm has become all the firmer and richer.[24]

Schiller's 1801 speculation about the demise of the German Empire became true in 1806, when the Holy Roman Empire ceased to exist. As a result of that disaster, Johann Gottlieb Fichte echoed Schiller's thoughts, suggesting that "after recent events a German nation can probably exist only in the republic of letters."[25] It is during the late eighteenth century that we find Johann Gottfried Herder defining a national identity based on common language, tradition, and customs; and it is precisely during the late eighteenth and nineteenth centuries, as a sense of German national consciousness began to emerge, that historians and philologists began the intensive study and discoveries which led to a new understanding of German national history and hence of the German nation itself: the discovery of more than a thousand years of history dating all the way back to Arminius; the study of medieval epics like the *Nibelungenlied*, *Parzival*, and *Tristan*; and collections of folk tales like the Grimm brothers' *Kinder- und Hausmärchen* [*Fairy Tales*] and Clemens Brentano and Achim von Arnim's *Des Knaben Wunderhorn* [The Boy's Magic Horn]. Aleida Assmann has suggested that in the process of German cultural nation-building, "the past is combed through for events and experiences that can serve as characteristics of identity and be established as markers of a common memory."[26] All of these discoveries – and inventions – helped to shape Germans' understanding of themselves as a culturally cohesive nation in spite of the ongoing fact of political division. Contemporary German Studies scholars have largely accepted this view of cultural nation-building. Describing the same phenomenon, Russell Berman has noted that in Germany, "literature became a privileged topic precisely because it was viewed as the vehicle that provided an ideal and cultural unity to the nation."[27] Anton Kaes has likewise suggested that with the decline of traditional folk myth and religion in the nineteenth century, literature became a vehicle for "the presentation, communication, and preservation of national identity," serving as a "collective memory over many centuries" and helping to articulate and preserve "the wishes, fears, and hopes of the Germans."[28]

None of this is particularly controversial, and few scholars would care to challenge the idea that the *Kulturnation* played a role in German nation-building well into the twentieth century, precisely as Meinecke contended. But what remains largely unspoken among literary scholars is the idea that the concept continues to have validity in the postwar period – and this in spite of the fact that politicians like Willy Brandt and writers like Grass and Günter de Bruyn have repeatedly invoked the concept in their own spheres. The Cold War antagonisms that Peitsch identifies have probably played a role here: neither of the two Germanys wanted to imagine itself as implicated in a larger cultural unity with the enemy that it continued to reject and revile. Precisely because of the essential similarity between the two Germanys, each state had to conceive of itself as fundamentally different at every level from its counterpart. The unspoken assumption or wish among scholars seems to have been that the German *Kulturnation* died along with the *Staatsnation* in 1945, as if Theodor Adorno's 1950 declaration that "culture in the traditional sense of the word is dead" implied that traditional notions of German cultural nation-building were therefore also dead.[29] And yet Adorno precedes his remark with a cautionary warning: if culture is indeed dead, no one knows about it, because "the word has not yet gotten out . . ." But if no one *knows* that it is dead, then what does it mean to proclaim the death of a socially constructed reality like *Kultur*? Adorno's words identify a paradox whose complexity seems to have been lost in the intervening years.

The idea that the German *Kulturnation* could simply have disappeared in 1945 would imply the continuing validity of a long since discredited belief that 1945 was a German "zero hour," a radical break with previous history, and that what followed after 1945 was somehow completely new and hermetically sealed off from contamination with what had gone before. As Bullivant writes, this myth was eventually "nailed" by left-liberal scholars in the 1960s and 1970s seeking to confront the ongoing legacy of the difficult German past.[30] However, part of that legacy was precisely the undead *Kulturnation*. That culture generally and literature specifically could be viewed after 1945 as guarantors of continuing German unity was demonstrated repeatedly in the postwar years, perhaps most memorably by Thomas Mann's public refusal to respect the border between East and West Germany during the Goethe celebrations of 1949, when Mann proudly declared in both Frankfurt and Weimar: "Who should represent and guarantee the unity of Germany if not an independent writer, whose real home . . . is the free German language, untouched by zones of occupation?"[31] A more pointed declaration of the writer's role in guaranteeing the unity of the *Kulturnation* would be hard to find.

That a nation can exist as a cultural unity in addition to or in place of politics is unique neither to Meinecke nor to Germany. In a speech delivered at the Sorbonne in March of 1882, Ernest Renan defined the nation first and foremost not as a geographic, racial, military, or dynastic unity, but rather as "a soul, a spiritual principle" characterized on the one hand by "the possession in common of a rich legacy of memories" and on the other by "present-day consent, the desire to live together, the will to perpetuate the value of the heritage that one has received in an undivided form." Out of this mixture of the "rich legacy of memories" and "present-day consent" comes the nation itself as "a large-scale solidarity, constituted by the feeling of the sacrifices that one has made in the past and of those that one is prepared to make in the future."[32]

Renan's definition gives voice to the fact that a nation is defined above all by a commonly recognized tradition which gains political force in the present. "To have performed great deeds together, to wish to perform still more – these are the essential conditions for being a people," he declares.[33] The French historian's definition suggests that national identity itself is dependent upon story-telling. Renan is perfectly open about the fact that this story-telling does not always imply historical accuracy, breadth, and consistency. As Renan writes: "Forgetting, I would even go so far as to say historical error, is a crucial factor in the creation of a nation, which is why progress in historical studies often constitutes a danger for [the principle of] nationality."[34]

Culture is the primary way in which nations without political boundaries locate and identify themselves. While Renan makes it clear that even for politically unified nations culture is of vital importance, and while Meinecke identifies the concept of the *Kulturnation* at work in the *Staatsnationen* of England and France, both suggest that in the absence of a unified state, culture takes on paramount importance. Germany is Meinecke's case in point. Even though Germany's birth as a nation-state did not occur until 1871, Germans prior to unification had long since been aware of a common language and tradition. Renan refers to this awareness as "the work of a general consciousness, belatedly victorious over the caprices of feudalism."[35] In the absence of political unity the factors of language and tradition, as fundamental elements in Renan's "general consciousness," become doubly important in the process of nation-building.

Meinecke's concept of a *Kulturnation* is useful as a way of understanding not just the German division of the early nineteenth century but also the divided Germany of the postwar years. As I seek to show in the first chapter of this book, and as scholars such as Parkes, Peitsch, Müller, and Wehdeking have also pointed out, German literature in the late 1970s and 1980s increasingly began to address questions of German national identity, as if prefiguring the move toward political unification at the end of the decade, in much the same way that Meinecke saw Ernst Moritz Arndt and Fichte as both prefiguring and moving toward the 1871 unification of the German *Reich*. When, over a century later, the official state treaty on reunification declared that during the period of post-1945 German division "art and culture were . . . a basis of the continuing unity of the German nation," politics made a bow to culture in a way of which Meinecke and Mann would no doubt have approved.[36]

And yet, as I demonstrate in chapters two and seven of this book, many German writers during the decades leading up to German reunification rejected or denied the possibility of national unity. Indeed, the primary intellectual opponents of German unity in 1990 were writers like Grass and Christa Wolf. Moreover, large numbers of younger West German writers professed themselves uninterested in the eastern part of Germany specifically and questions of national unity and identity more generally. How does this widespread resistance to national identity square with a concept of writers as the privileged articulators of national identity? What is the location of the German nation for German writers? Is it, as August Heinrich Hoffmann von Fallersleben suggested in a mid-nineteenth century song which ultimately became the German national anthem, "über alles" (above everything)? Or is it, as many younger German authors have seemed to suggest, completely unworthy of notice?

I would suggest that the path toward solving these apparently insoluble problems goes back to 1945 and the destruction of the German nation, which ultimately led to the very rejection of the national of which I have been writing, and to the invocation of a "zero hour" as a radical historical caesura. As Parkes notes, postwar German writers' engagement in politics did not emerge out of a historical vacuum. Rather, "German intellectuals' distrust of power has to be seen in its historical context: the total misuse of power in the Third Reich."[37] Because of the nation's crimes against humanity from 1933 to 1945, it became understandably difficult, if not impossible, for many German writers to maintain a positive view of their own nation. "Humanity shudders in horror at Germany!" declared Thomas Mann on May 8, 1945.[38] Ernst Wiechert's 1945 description of the German people as "lonelier than any people has ever been on this earth . . . branded as no other people has ever been branded" contains a kernel of objective and subjective truth that German writers after 1945 could hardly ignore.[39] Mann and Wiechert speak eloquently of their discomfort with the nation, and their laments were to be followed by a host of other literary reflections on the problematic German nation that have continued into the present. It is true that the political crimes of the German nation made a recourse to the supposedly sacrosanct realm of *Kultur* even more appealing in 1945. As Franz Werfel declared during that year, it was only the representatives of German *Kultur* "who will be [Germans'] witnesses in eternity," helping to "take the shame away" for Germany's crimes.[40] But given the horrific nature of those crimes, the relationship between *Kultur* on the one hand and *Nation* on the other could no longer be unproblematic in the postwar period. Andrei Markovits and Simon Reich are therefore surely mistaken in their insistence that "German culture had weathered Nazism intact," even while their focus on the way in which German collective memory has inhibited the exercise of political power in the postwar period suggests a particularly strong link between cultural and political factors in Germany.[41]

The term widely used to describe literature in general and specific figures like Böll in the postwar German context – "conscience of the nation" – is revealing, suggesting that far from embodying an unproblematic national unity, many German writers after 1945 became a kind of national superego, chastizing and seeking to punish the nation for its crimes. The use of the term superego here is consistent with Freud's speculative late theory of the mind, including his insistence on the parallel development of the individual human psyche and of civilization itself. As Freud argued, "Civilization . . . obtains mastery over the individual's dangerous desire for aggression by weakening and disarming it and by setting up an agency within him" – the superego, defined as "a portion of the ego, which sets itself over against the rest of the ego" – "to watch over it, like a garrison in a conquered city."[42] Likewise, "the community, too, evolves a super-ego under whose influence cultural development proceeds," so that "the super-ego of an epoch of civilization has an origin similar to that of an individual."[43] What Freud suggests for the individual superego can, in his framework, easily hold true for the collective superego as well: that its demands upon the ego are so punitive that they frequently lead to the disintegration of the individual or the collective. As Freud notes, self-preservation is not the primary goal of the superego. Even though its harsh punishment of the ego, if carried to an extreme, can lead to self-destruction, the superego carries on with its punitive measures. For Freud, this tendency toward a hypertrophy of guilt is the primary paradox of human civilization, and it is the origin of our profound "discontent."

If German culture generally and German literature specifically came to play the role of a German collective superego after the disaster of the Second World War, this implies that all of the punishment meted out to Germany by the Allies, as well as all of the feelings of German rage against the Allies which could not be acted out in the postwar years, were internalized in that collective superego and acquired a masochistic, self-punishing edge. It implies, to repeat Freud's words, that postwar German culture generally and literature specifically came to "watch over" Germany, "like a garrison in a conquered city." The *Kulturnation* became the prison warden of the *Staatsnation*. If this is the case, then it is no wonder that so much German literature of the postwar period is so dark and brooding. Nor is it any wonder that German politicians again and again complained about the unreasonable demands of German literary intellectuals. In the post-1945 period literature, the very cultural sphere which, prior to 1945, had been centrally concerned with affirming the positive existence of the nation, became its punitive task-master.

The fact that what Peitsch calls the "renationalization" of German political discourse in the 1980s occurred at the same time as a renewed discussion of central problems of the German past is surely anything but a coincidence. Throughout the 1980s, from the debates about a German *Sonderweg* (special path) through the fiftieth anniversary of Hitler's rise to power in 1983; Ronald Reagan and Helmut Kohl's visit to the Bitburg military cemetery in 1985; the *Historikerstreit* (Historians' debate) about the uniqueness of the Holocaust in 1986; the controversy surrounding Bundestag President Philipp Jenninger's speech commemorating the fiftieth anniversary of the pogrom against German Jews known as the "Reichskristallnacht" (Night of Broken Glass) in 1988; to the opening of the Berlin Wall one year later on the same date; it was clear that German attempts to reformulate a more positive conception of national identity were carried out in and through attempts to relocate history in the German national imagination. Ernst Nolte's 1986 declaration that the German past "hangs over the present like a sword of judgment" was clearly true, even if Nolte's attempt to escape from that sword of judgment proved futile.[44] What Nolte was articulating was the fear that German history, and left-liberal German intellectuals' instrumentalization of that history, was preventing the nation from healing and achieving a "normal" national identity. As Nolte's ally Michael Stürmer argued, in Germany "the future is won by those who are able to harness memory, coin concepts and interpret the past."[45] During the 1980s that reconfiguration of the German past was clearly intended as a normalization of the nation. Kohl himself stressed his desire for German normality at the moment of economic and currency union in the middle of 1990. Asked what his major hope for the united nation was, he replied: "That things will normalize. That's the most important thing for us, that we become a wholly normal country, not 'singularized' in any question . . . that we simply don't stick out. That's the important thing."[46]

As problematic as Kohl's desire for German normalization may have been, however, it is important to note that there is nothing inherently right-wing or left-wing in concepts of normality. Kohl's desire for "a wholly normal country" that does not "stick out" could hardly be further from the fanatical nationalist raving of a Hitler. If Kohl's invocation of German normalization is nationalism at all, it is a very subdued and modest form of nationalism. In its desire for normality, Kohl's 1990 statement in fact sounds remarkably like a distant echo of Bertolt Brecht's alternative German national anthem, the "Children's Hymn" of 1950:

> Grace spare not and spare no labour
> Passion nor intelligence
> That a decent German nation
> Flourish as do other lands.
>
> That the people give up flinching
> At the crimes which we evoke
> And hold out their hands in friendship
> As they do to other folk.
>
> Neither over nor yet under
> Other peoples will we be
> From the Oder to the Rhineland
> From the Alps to the North Sea.
>
> And because we'll make it better
> Let us guard and love our home
> Love it as our dearest country
> As the others love their own.[47]

Brecht's relocation of the German nation places it neither "über alles" nor beneath contempt but rather among and in the midst of other nations, as one of many. Brecht's invocation of a Germany that is similar to "other lands" and "other folk," that will be "neither over nor yet under other peoples," and that will be loved by Germans just "as . . . others love their own" countries is a compassionate plea for German normalization. As common as they were among German leftists during the struggle against Hitler, such expressions of patriotism had become exceedingly rare among left-liberals in Germany by the 1980s, and their relative absence spoke volumes about German leftists' negative attitudes to any kind of national identity, even a "normal" one. That such sentiments were instead left to Helmut Kohl probably goes a long way toward explaining Kohl's political success and longevity in the 1980s and

1990s, as well as the relative ineffectiveness of the German left in national politics. When, in September 1998, Kohl was finally defeated by a Social Democratic and Green coalition led by Gerhard Schröder, the left's political success after sixteen years of opposition could be attributed at least in part to a new, less tortured attitude toward German national identity.

And yet even among German leftists, Brechtian sentiments of national pride were not completely repressed in the politically correct 1980s. Wolf Biermann has a telling anecdote about a rainy 1983 visit he made to the university football stadium in Columbus, Ohio to watch the Buckeyes play against the Longhorns. The singing of the American national anthem made a profound impression on Biermann:

But then all seventy thousand – there really is such a thing! and without a cramp in their ass – sang with a full chest the national anthem of the USA. No: to be more specific, sixty thousand nine hundred and ninety-nine people stood up, laid their hands over their American hearts, and sang their song. But I stood by smiling stupidly, and tears poured down my cheeks.

Biermann interprets the event and his own reaction to it in the following way:

It was nothing. Just the deeply-felt, the naked and idiotic envy of a little German. They can do this, I thought, in spite of Vietnam and the Bay of Pigs, in spite of the CIA in Chile and in spite of the genocide of the Indians, in spite of the Ku Klux Klan . . .[48]

What is not explicitly spelled out but nevertheless implied in Biermann's ruminations is that he, as a German, is unable to but wishes that he could take pleasure in the positive feeling of national identity that he ascribes to his American hosts. Appropriately, Biermann ends his reflections with an invocation of Brecht's "Children's Hymn," suggesting that "perhaps we [Germans] will one day succeed [in creating] the country that would correspond to the song."[49] Biermann was thus wishing for correspondence between the *Kulturnation* and the *Staatsnation*. And yet Biermann's left-liberal allies still have trouble in locating that elusive Germany.

The negative view of national identity that many German writers and intellectuals have had in the postwar period is entirely understandable in light of twentieth century history. But, as I have tried to show, the negation of national identity is paradoxical because it tends to eliminate the basis on which political engagement becomes possible. Likewise, right-wing critics' attacks on German writers are also paradoxical, because in attacking the preeminent political role of German literature they are attacking the foundation of the *Kulturnation*, which, at another level, they seek to uphold. German leftists are comfortable with a politically engaged, activist literature, but they resist concepts of national identity. Conversely, right-wingers revere concepts of nationhood and identity while they disdain political engagement in literature. Both positions seek to separate the unity between *Kultur* and *Nation* implied by Meinecke's concept.

In 1982, Helmut Müller rejected the "obsolete conception of the Bismarckian nation-state" as a "backward-looking utopia of the nineteenth century," arguing that "the burden of political barbarity, for which the Germans were responsible in the past, ought to be seen as the problematic reverse side of the coin of the concept of the *Kulturnation*."[50] Müller's assertion identifies Hitler's Third Reich as the primary reason for Germans' postwar discomfort with concepts of national identity at both the political and cultural levels; and it relegates the idea of German national unity to the distant past, not the present or the future. In spite of increasing discussions among German writers during the late 1970s and 1980s about questions of national identity, such rejections of the national among scholars were typical right up to the moment when German reunification proved them wrong. However the left-liberal discomfort with concepts of German national identity has continued even into the post-reunification period. Peitsch's approach to the problem of the *Kulturnation*, for instance, shows how some intellectuals, for very good reasons, continue to resist or reject concepts of German national identity. Like many other critical intellectuals, Peitsch identifies the movement among some left- and right-wing intellectuals during the late 1970s and 1980s toward a renewed concept of German national identity as largely negative, arguing that in spite of the differences between right-wing and left-wing proponents of German national identity there are "problematic" points of intersection which lead "to an effect of mutual strengthening." Peitsch argues that "conservative rhetoric about a reunification in peace and freedom, right-wing agitation against Yalta and re-education, and Green-alternative demands [for a solution to the German question] agree with each other in the 'renationalization' of public discourse."[51] Along with

Jürgen Habermas and many others, Peitsch associates concepts of national identity primarily with the problematic continued strength of irrationalism and a rejection of core Enlightenment values: "What needs to be discussed is the social need for irrationality."[52] This is the voice of cultural criticism as nay-sayer to the nation.

I am far from denying Peitsch's central point about the problematic nature of German – or any other – national identity. The fifth chapter of this book is in fact largely devoted to what I see as a problematic rebirth of irrationalist cultural critique inside the re-unified Germany. What I am concerned with, however, is the apparent continued taboo on discussions of national identity, which results in a wide variety of political intentions and viewpoints being negatively equated solely because they share a common interest in the nation. It is simply not true, I submit, that concepts of national identity necessarily invite right-wing extremism. The real danger seems to me to be the opposite: to allow the idea of national identity to be monopolized by right-wing hooligans. In the modern western world, the nation is, for better or worse, the primary sphere of political existence, and to cede that sphere entirely to one's opponents would seem both self-destructive and irrational. Fortunately, not every critic wishes to make this concession. As Peitsch points out, there was a lively discussion about national identity on the German left during the 1980s. The fact that the partial "renationalization" of German cultural life in the 1980s tended to transcend political spheres would seem to re-enforce the view that there is no necessary left- or right-wing ideology associated with concepts of national identity. Were all the German left-wingers who tried to reclaim the concept of the nation for themselves during the 1980s simply fools unable to recognize that they were playing with ideological fire, or had they recognized the importance of the nation for a reinvigorated German left? That Peitsch does not address this question in his critique of "renationalization" undermines his argument.

The rejection of German national identity among left-liberal critics in Germany has largely been reflected within my own professional sphere, American German Studies, which has, since the mid-1980s, largely constituted itself as a critique of a previous *Germanistik* viewed polemically as handmaiden to German nationalism. In its effort to reflect similar trends in the academic study of American culture, American German Studies has, during the 1980s and 1990s, turned increasingly to the exploration of marginalized and subaltern identities, moving away from the question of German national identity. In contrast to an exclusive focus on non-mainstream identities, Hinrich Seeba has suggested that the problem of German national identity should be at the center of a critical German Studies as an "intercultural critique of identity formation."[53] Peitsch has also placed the question of German national identity at the center of his project. I would agree with both scholars that the problem of German national identity should indeed be central to the project of a critical German Studies, but I believe that the "critique" needs to start not with an a priori rejection of the nation but, on the contrary, with an acceptance of its continuing existence and importance. As liberating as it is intended to be, self-consciously deconstructive work runs a danger that is exemplified by the following statement from Seeba: "The Berlin Wall has come to symbolize in the most drastic form the illusionary nature of German national identity."[54] Such a statement seems to fetishize the physical and to imply that the socially constructed non-physical is nothing but a figment of the imagination. Published in the spring of 1989 in the major American *Germanistik* journal, Seeba's declaration was proved false only half a year later, when it was the Berlin Wall itself which was literally deconstructed, while German national identity appeared surprisingly resilient. It was the supposedly drastic and irrefutable physical monstrosity – the wall as a reified Lukácsian *thing* – that disappeared, not the social construct that it had supposedly revealed as illusory. The German nation was clearly not as moribund as its well-intentioned scholarly grave-diggers had assumed. However, American German Studies has yet to address the implications of 1989 for its own theoretical and historical understanding, and it is still largely caught up in a reflexive rejection of concepts of the national. While his celebration of the nation is no doubt exaggerated, Russell Berman's insistence that "it is in the nation, and in the nation alone, that freedom emerges in history" is a useful historical reminder of the positive aspects of nation-building within a scholarly context dominated by condemnation and scolding. As Berman insists, "nationhood consequently should be seen . . . as a crucial component of life beyond reification."[55]

In spite of my criticism of one isolated but representative statement, my own approach in this book will closely follow Seeba's emphasis on the formation of German identity and on "literary fiction as the site of vicarious satisfaction" for German identity.[56]

The chief difference between Seeba and myself is that while Seeba views German identity as itself "fictional," I view it as "real," if by "real" is meant "having consequences in the world we live in." Perhaps a more satisfactory way of stating the same thing is that in the world of social constructions the boundary between the real and the fictional is not impermeable. Moreover, Seeba's approach to German identity formation is largely negative, whereas mine is cautiously positive, treating liberal nationalism as the most realistic and effective sphere for progressive political action in the present conjuncture. I treat national identity as a socially constructed fact that sometimes has positive and sometimes has negative consequences. It is true that nations have historically been oppressive, but so have all other social formations in which human beings have lived.

Throughout my arguments here, I treat literature as a privileged sphere for reflection on German national identity. By "literature" I mean primarily the prose writing of literary intellectuals and am much less concerned with lyric poetry and drama, although I do not ignore these genres entirely. The reason for my primary focus on prose is only secondarily pragmatic, i.e. the result of a need to limit and make manageable a large amount of material. At a more fundamental level, I would agree with George Steiner that, since the nineteenth century, prose literature, and particularly the genre of the novel, has been the primary mode for literary communication with larger social implications and resonances. As Steiner writes, "since the time of the industrial revolution, the writer in essence, the man who typifies even at first glance the profession of letters, is the novelist."[57] With the "death of tragedy," drama has largely been confined to a non-literary sphere, while lyric poetry has devoted itself to the personal and the private. It is mostly in prose literature that western societies confront larger social problems from the vantage point and with the prestige of what one might call, using concepts developed by Peter Bürger with respect to art in general, the "institution literature."[58] It is anything but a coincidence that when the critic Frank Schirrmacher attacked and summed up the history of West German literature in 1990 – Keith Bullivant's monograph on the future of German literature is largely a response to that attack – he focused on writers of prose fiction, virtually ignoring lyric poetry and drama. The same is largely true of many other observers both before and after reunification, from Helmut

Peitsch and Volker Wehdeking to Stuart Parkes and Bullivant himself.

It is not my purpose in this book to inquire into the reasons for the preeminence of prose literature. Such an inquiry is well beyond my present capabilities and would interfere with the largely thematic focus of this book. In his seminal *Theory of the Novel*, György Lukács suggested that the novel is the quintessential expression of the lonely human individual severed from connection with the totality.[59] Steiner suggests that the novel is the primary form of cultured entertainment for the literate bourgeoisie, while Benedict Anderson connects that literacy with the process of nation-building itself.[60] It is certainly true that the rise of the novel as a literary genre coincides with the rise of the modern nation-state, and that the relatively belated breakthrough of the novel in Germany in the nineteenth century corresponded to a relatively belated breakthrough of the German nation-state, which Helmuth Plessner once famously called "the belated nation." Moreover, if the novel is the literary expression of psychological fragmentation and lack of immanence, of mourning for a lost totality, then it would seem precisely to fit the situation of a fragmented, "wounded" Germany.

My primary concern in this book, however, is not with particular genres or generic questions but rather with the political and national discourses entered into by writers in and through literature, both at the level of specific works and at the level of literature as an institution. I am dealing with the intersection between particular literary works, the institution literature, and discourses on German national identity; as such I will occasionally make reference to lyric poetry or drama if those two genres can be of use in illuminating or explaining the implications of this intersection. As Frank Trommler has accurately noted, the development of postwar German literature coincided with an emerging political authority for German writers that was more or less independent of specific literary genres or even works.[61] Because he wrote novels, the novelist became an authority, and Germans did not have to read the novels themselves in order to acknowledge that authority. The fact that Grass is the author of *Die Blechtrommel* [*The Tin Drum*] and *Ein weites Feld*, among other works, is the basis of his continuing authority in Germany, but those who acknowledge that authority are not necessarily readers of the two novels. The literary institution consists only partly of the works of individual authors; those works serve as the basis for an authority that goes beyond them. It is only a relatively small elite in Germany that actually reads such works; but this is neither a new state of affairs nor particularly surprising. The same could be said of a great many other non-literary documents (e.g. the American constitution) that are nevertheless politically important. In ascribing to literature a central role in the creation of German national identity, I am of course taking issue with the widespread belief even among some writers and literary scholars that in a post-Gutenberg universe literature has lost its cultural significance. This is an issue to which I will return in the final chapter of this book. For now I will limit myself to asserting that, as the 1995 *Spiegel* cover and many other phenomena indicate, literature continues in spite of many changes to play a profound role in helping Germans to locate the place of their nation in history. Exactly what that place will be is of course an open question – but then, the future always is.

CHAPTER I

Searching for Germany in the 1980s

What Franco Moretti once said of German culture in general was especially true of the political situation after 1945: "Germany is a sort of Magic Stage, where the symbolic antagonisms of European culture achieve a metaphysical intractability, and clash irreconcilably. It is the centre and catalyst of the integrated historical system we call Europe."[1] Historically, the post-1945 division of Germany was not new, since the country had been divided into many different smaller principalities prior to the first unification of 1871. What was new with the emergence of the Federal Republic of Germany (FRG) and the German Democratic Republic (GDR) in 1949 was not so much the fact of disunity as the division into only two states directly opposed to each other, each claiming to represent the best of the German tradition, and each with the support of one of the world's two superpowers. This stark opposition gave German division an ominousness it had never possessed before. The feeling of foreboding that emerged from Germany's and Berlin's new situation is given voice in a plethora of cold war spy novels, especially John le Carré's renowned *The Spy Who Came in From the Cold* (1963).

How did German literature react to the German division? Based on the long history of the German *Kulturnation*, one might have expected that, in the face of political division, writers would stress the importance of German unity; and indeed many writers did. In the West figures such as Hans Werner Richter argued forcefully against the division of Germany, and in the East Johannes R. Becher enshrined the phrase "Germany, united fatherland" in the GDR's national anthem. This phrase was later to become a slogan for the East German crowds demanding reunification in the late fall of 1989, although most of the younger demonstrators probably did not know the provenance of their slogan, since the words to the anthem had been banned from official use in the GDR for over a decade precisely because of their reference to national unity. A towering figure such as Thomas Mann traveled back and forth between the two Germanys in the early years of the cold war arguing for unity and stressing the indivisible nature of the German cultural heritage.

And yet the division into East and West Germany was not the first and only division for German writers. Many German writers had been separated from their country since Hitler's seizure of power in 1933. Those who came back to Germany generally returned with the intention of building a better, more democratic Germany – which for a great many of them meant a socialist Germany that would avoid the crises of capitalism that, they believed, had contributed to the disaster of 1933. The late 1940s and 1950s were a time of intense ideological opposition between the East and West in Germany, and most writers in the GDR and the FRG tended to go along with and reflect that opposition. While in the 1950s the two German states publicly proclaimed the goal of national reunification, at the same time the two German literatures were very far apart. In the West the 1950s saw an upsurge of nonpolitical, abstractly humanist literature, while in the East writers operated under the dicates of a "socialist realism" which saw writers as "engineers of the human soul," in Stalin's terrifying terminology.[2]

Over the course of the 1960s, the ideological credibility won by the Soviet Union because of its rapid industrialization and victory over Nazi Germany was largely lost as it became increasingly evident that the East bloc had entered a long period of stagnation relative to the economies of the capitalist West. With the liberal West at the height of its postwar economic boom and the East bloc seeking to correct the many failings of its command economy via cautious liberalization, economists and political scientists began to speak of a "convergence" between the two systems, suggesting that the West was becoming increasingly Social Democratic, while the East was gradually moving from Stalinism toward more political and economic freedom. The father of this theory was the Dutch economist Jan Tinbergen, who, in a 1961 article, argued that the various changes occurring in the two systems were "in many respects converging movements," and that "the systems begin to influence each other more and more," suggesting that ultimately the two systems would move toward an optimum mix of free market and command elements.[3] Tinbergen's suggestion spawned an entire branch of comparative economics known as "convergence theory."[4]

The concept soon spread beyond the relatively narrow realm of economics to become part of broader cultural debate about postwar industrial society. Soviet dissidents such as Andrei Sakharov referred precisely to the theory of convergence in suggesting that "the development of modern society in both the Soviet Union and the United States is now following the same course of increasing complexity of structure and of industrial management," and that there would be a general "socialist convergence" in the future.[5] Sakharov and others argued for a democratization of socialism while at the same time maintaining the superiority of the socialist system over its ideological and economic competitor.

By the 1970s, when the disappointing performance of Soviet and East bloc economies had led growing numbers of economists to doubt the validity of convergence theory as an economic model, others welcomed the theory as part of a more general climate of détente, ideological moderation, and coexistence in the face of common problems. In a 1975 open letter to the Soviet writer Konstantin Mikhailovich Simonov, Alfred Andersch described convergence as the theory "that our two technocracies will ultimately even out the differences between our social systems and create a unified, computerized human model."[6] Andersch's definition is particularly useful because it shows that by the mid-1970s the idea of convergence had gone far beyond a relatively specific set of predictions about economic organization and performance to encompass entire societies and the human beings within them.

The emerging rapprochement between East and West over the course of the 1960s also brought the literature of East and West Germany closer together. The relative political freedom inaugurated in the East bloc in the era of détente meant that writers could begin to deal more freely and openly with unresolved problems in socialist society, while the triumph of the protest movement in the FRG in the 1960s made West German writers more critical of capitalist short-comings as well. In the GDR the rise to power of Erich Honecker in 1971 was accompanied by the new leader's declaration that there were to be no more "taboos" in literature and the admission that even developed socialist society in the GDR was plagued with contradictions and problems.[7]

Six years earlier, at the eleventh plenum of the Central Committee of the Socialist Unity Party in December 1965, cultural figures had been severely attacked by the party leadership. These attacks had shocked several of the GDR's writers so severely that they began increasingly to distance themselves from party doctrine while at the same time seeking to move their writing away from the controversial realm of politics and toward less problematic areas such as myth and legend.[8] The most famous example of the new questioning and distancing in GDR literature preceded Honecker's rise to power: Christa Wolf's 1968 novel *Nachdenken über Christa T.* [*The Quest for Christa T.*], which ushered in a growing openness about personal problems, especially the role of women in socialist society. This new emphasis on the personal coincided with a growing recognition in West Germany that "the personal is the political" – one of the major refrains of the feminist movement. These words were to become representative of the "new subjectivity," a social shift in both Germanys during the 1970s away from purely political problems to lifestyle issues. In the FRG, the shift away from politics was known as the "Tendenzwende" (change of tendencies). Both Helmut Peitsch and Ulrich Schmidt have identified the "Tendenzwende" as a crucial expression of West German political disillusionment.[9]

What is noteworthy in the context of German literary development in the postwar period is that it is precisely the late 1960s and 1970s, during the heyday of both convergence theory and détente, including the German *Ostpolitik* pioneered by Willy Brandt, that East German literature began to break out of the socialist realist aesthetic of the 1940s, 1950s, and early 1960s and to win acceptance in the West as part of a larger German cultural project – as contributing not just to GDR literature but to German literature as a whole. German literature began, paradoxically, to "converge" at precisely the moment that the two political systems were tending to acknowledge the permanence of German division. During this period East German literature was to become less specifically East German and more humanistic. As Wolfgang Emmerich has noted, East German literature began to lose its uniqueness during this period.[10] Peitsch has suggested that as a result of Brandt's emphasis on the concept of a German *Kulturnation* that transcended political borders, many writers and scholars during the 1970s began to look for cultural convergence, whereas they had previously stressed cultural differentiation.[11] By 1987, Alexander von Bormann was suggesting that the conception that there were two separate German literatures was itself an ideological relic "from the time of the Cold War, in which people liked to assert that soon Germans would not be able to talk to each other any more."[12]

Christa Wolf, as the most famous East German writer, is also the best example of literary convergence. Not only did her *Nachdenken über Christa T.* become a major event in the West as well as the East, but her subsequent publications, particularly *Kindheitsmuster* [*Patterns of Childhood*] (1976), *Kein Ort. Nirgends* [*No Place on Earth*] (1979), *Kassandra* [*Cassandra*] (1983), and *Störfall* [*Accident*] (1987), were literary events of significance in both the East and the West. Since Wolf's development was so symptomatic of a more general literary convergence – and since she was to emerge at the center of the first post-reunification literary debate – it is useful briefly to summarize her major literary accomplishments from the 1960s to the 1980s.

Wolf's debut novel, *Der geteilte Himmel* [*Divided Heaven*] (1963), which described a young woman intellectual's idealistic attempt to integrate herself into socialist factory production, had dealt explicitly with GDR content. It would have been difficult to read *Der geteilte Himmel* as anything other than a coming to terms with socialist society. Emerging from the "Bitterfelder Weg," a state-supported literary-political movement in the GDR which sent writers into factories to work side-by-side with members of the proletariat, *Der geteilte Himmel* addressed problems of production in socialist society against a backdrop of intense East–West ideological confrontation. *Nachdenken über Christa T.*, however, opened itself up to a more modernist and multi-layered reading. While it was certainly a confrontation with socialist society, the novel was also a depiction of a young woman's nonconformism in the face of rigid social constraints. Such nonconformism was just as possible or impossible in any modern industrial social structure as in the GDR. Critics could and did read *Nachdenken* as a work primarily concerned with general human problems rather than the specificity of socialist society. As Fritz J. Raddatz wrote in a 1969 review for *Der Spiegel*, this novel was not exclusively "socialist."[13] Noting that the novel defended private life against the encroachments of public reality, the critic Thomas von Vegesack suggested that Wolf was part of a more general humanist revolt in the GDR.[14] Meanwhile Marcel Reich-Ranicki noted Wolf's proximity to German-language writers outside the GDR: "Wolf has assiduously explored recent German fiction, and she has learned much from all the writers, from Johnson, Böll, and Frisch, and perhaps also from Grass and Hildesheimer."[15] Reich-

Ranicki's statement was tantamount to an admission that, because of Christa Wolf, the best East German literature now satisfied the aesthetic criteria of even the most exalted Western authors. Reich-Ranicki's treatment of Wolf was a prefiguration of the reception of much of the best East German literature in the Federal Republic for the next two decades. If Western critics concluded that such literature met their own standards, it became redefined more as German than as specifically GDR literature. The lop-sided terms of this critical appropriation, in which power rested primarily with critics in the West, itself prefigured the modus operandi for the absorption of the GDR state into the FRG at the end of the 1980s.

The predominance of a humanist worldview in Wolf's work was even more obvious in the author's next major work, *Kindheitsmuster*, which focused on the problem of Germany coming to terms with the Nazi past. The 1933–1945 experiences of Nelly, the young subject of *Kindheitsmuster*, occurred well before the foundation of the GDR in 1949 and could have happened to almost any German girl born around 1929, no matter where she happened to find herself after 1949. While the narrative voice in *Kindheitsmuster* was clearly a GDR voice, her subject was Germany as a whole, not the land of postwar division. Wolf's subsequent books *Kein Ort. Nirgends* and *Kassandra* dealt with a past that was even further removed: the former with two figures from early nineteenth-century German romanticism and the latter with the mythical Trojan prophetess. While these books clearly can and must be read within a specific GDR context, they also appeal to more general German and human problems. Finally, *Störfall* returned to very current events – the 1986 explosion at the Chernobyl nuclear reactor – but it did so in a way which made the border between East and West Germany virtually irrelevant. Neither nuclear radiation nor most other ecological problems respect such political and ideological borders, and hence the problems of instrumental rationality discussed in Wolf's text were in no way system-specific. *Störfall* was to be the primary German literary response to the Chernobyl disaster, as popular in the West as it was in the East.

From the appearance of *Der geteilte Himmel* in 1963, Wolf had excelled at a personal, intimate kind of narration that many critics hailed as specifically female; her stories and novels were frequently autobiographical and almost always dealt with a woman's attempt to come to terms with her own individuality and with the people and society around her. *Störfall*, for instance, had literally told the news of

one woman's late spring day in 1986: "I switched off the TV, locked
the front, then the back door, did the supper dishes, put the cold cuts
in the refrigerator."[16] This quotidian passage from a novella about
the problem of nuclear technology in modern society is typical of the
way in which Wolf interweaves the personal with the political in her
novels, stories, and essays. It was to a large extent this ability to
combine the personal and the political that helped to make Wolf a
crucial link between East and West German literature in the era of
"new subjectivity."

As much as it points to important commonalities between East
and West German literature during the 1980s, however, *Störfall* can
also be used to illustrate an ongoing difference. In a society with no
open public sphere for debates about politics, a writer such as Wolf
provided, through her books, stories, articles, and public readings, a
forum for discussion and debate about matters which frequently
went far beyond the purely literary. To continue with the example of
Störfall, Wolf's 1987 novella made it possible for East Germans to
recreate at least in the privacy of their armchairs and via literary
means the public debate about nuclear energy which had occurred
in West Germany; through the life and thoughts of one woman as
she attempted to cope with the "news of the day," East German
readers could address important debates about technology and
society.

The fact that *Störfall* was able to function in the GDR as a fill-in
for a necessary but missing political discussion demonstrates that in
East German public life a writer such as Wolf was not "just" a
creator of elegant literary entertainments. She became an essential
medium for social communication. Wolf herself took on aspects of
the seer or the prophet that she had depicted in her novel about the
fall of the walled-in city of Troy. As important as this role was in the
context of the authoritarian GDR, it was to become problematic
after German reunification. And yet Wolf's political role within
GDR society was neither incomprehensible nor unknown for writers
in the West, many of whom had at times sought for themselves a
similar role. The political importance of literature in East German
society was not solely a function of GDR authoritarianism; it
contained important elements of a long German tradition.

This abbreviated summary of Wolf's production from 1964 to
1987 is not intended to be exhaustive. It is clear that during this time
Wolf made a transition from relatively limited socialist-realist narra-

tive and content to a more open and humanistic approach. This
transition made it possible for Wolf to be received in the West as
both a GDR writer and a representative of larger German, feminist,
and human concerns. The transition involved a number of different
factors: 1) a change in Wolf's texts toward a more critical and open
narration and content; 2) the recognition inside the GDR that the
advent of fully developed socialist society had not eliminated all
social or personal contradictions; and 3) a growing willingness on the
part of critics and readers in the West to look beyond system-specific
differences at similarities and convergences in modern industrial
society, including a wealth of difficult problems such as ecological
devastation, individual integrity, instrumental technology, and the
role of women. All of these developments occurred in a context
characterized by détente and its scholarly correlate convergence
theory, as well as by a general feeling in the late 1970s that the age of
ideology had come to an end.[17] Moreover, the transition in literature
of the GDR and its reception in the West occurred at precisely the
time of the so-called "new subjectivity" in West Germany, an
increasing confrontation with the National Socialist past, and disillusionment with the reformist politics of the Social-Liberal coalition
government installed in the West in 1969. The path taken by Wolf
was also open to other GDR writers, especially women authors who
began to join a larger discussion among feminists internationally:
Irmtraud Morgner, Helga Königsdorf, Maxi Wander, Brigitte
Reimann. A decidedly non-feminist writer such as Heiner Müller,
however, showed a remarkably similar development: from the GDR-
specific "production plays" of the 1950s (socialist realist theatre
about factory work, especially the fulfillment of state-imposed
production norms) to pessimistic meditations on modern catastrophe
in the 1970s and 1980s.[18] And Christoph Hein's spectacularly
successful 1982 novel *Der fremde Freund* [*The Distant Lover*] became
successful in West Germany largely because its tale of alienation and
spiritual numbing transcended East–West dichotomies and appealed
directly to the state of human beings in the modern age. As David
Roberts has suggested, Hein's "diagnosis of sickness relates to the
process of civilization, i.e., the dialectic of enlightenment, which
cannot be reduced in the specific history of the GDR."[19]

Given these considerations, there were good reasons for Hans
Mayer to declare in 1979 that "there is a movement of convergence
in German-language literature of our day." Mayer stated that "the

convergences are obvious" and "amazing," and he spoke of contemporary German literature as a "concrete totality."[20] Likewise
Frank Trommler suggested five years later that there was only one
German literature irrespective of state boundaries.[21] Working with
specifically literary criteria, as opposed to national-political ones,
Trommler identified areas of commonality and convergence in all
German-language literatures. While Trommler's declaration seemed
provocative given the history of cold war criticism and the institutionalization of literary studies in the 1980s, it seems much more
reasonable in a post-reunification framework. As Trommler wrote in
1984: "The thesis of the two separate German literatures now
reveals its historical-political function and limitations."[22] During the
1970s and 1980s, as the permanence of German political division
came to appear increasingly self-evident, German literature moved
in the opposite direction, as if literature were following the role
Meinecke had laid out for it in guaranteeing a German cultural
unity in the absence of a unified state. What primarily characterized
the literature of the 1970s and 1980s was its lack of ideological
specificity. "It is the same suffering individual . . . of whom the
literature in the GDR and the Federal Republic speaks," wrote
Heinrich Mohr in 1980, suggesting that the literary spheres in the
two German states had become a single "inner-German commu-
nications system."[23] Because of these internal literary developments,
it was not unrealistic for the 1990 state treaty on German reunification to ascribe to culture an important role in preserving national
unity during the years of German division.

The era of détente that had coincided with the convergence of the
two German literatures in the 1970s came to an end in 1980 because
of larger geostrategic tensions related to the Soviet invasion of
Afghanistan and the NATO decision to station medium-range
Pershing II and cruise nuclear missiles on West German soil. The
resulting friction between an ongoing internal German détente and
increasing superpower confrontation led to a remarkable revitaliza-
tion of the German national question, expressed in the form of the
largest German postwar mass movement: the peace movement of
the early 1980s, in which thousands of people marched on the streets
of West Germany against the NATO armament decision. The peace
movement was not limited to West Germany; in the GDR as well,
Germans protested against both NATO and Warsaw Pact nuclear
weapons, and some, like the dissident physicist Robert Havemann,

explicitly connected their agitation for disarmament with calls for German reunification.[24] This upsurge in German national feeling, identified by Peitsch as a "renationalization," was directly related to German discomfort with larger international developments that seemed to threaten not only German-German cooperation but world peace. German national thinking was informed by two simple facts: 1) the growing realization among Germans that even after thirty years no peace treaty had been signed to end the Second World War, which meant that Germans still lacked full political sovereignty and might not have any choice in accepting foreign nuclear missiles; and 2) the simultaneous realization that their country, lying at the fault line of the cold war, would be the first to be destroyed in any nuclear war, even a "limited" one.

German writers responded to the threat of the "new cold war" of the early 1980s in a major show of support for the peace movement. Writers like Heinrich Böll and Walter Jens marched in antinuclear demonstrations and even participated in acts of civil disobedience at nuclear weapons sites in West Germany. Within the realm of literary politics the peace movement spurred a new focus on the German *Kulturnation* and the role of writers as prophets and seers in a spiritual Germany that transcended the merely political border between the GDR and the FRG. This new focus was embodied in two widely publicized all-German writers' conferences in East and West Berlin in 1981 and 1983, called the "Berlin Encounters for the Furtherance of Peace."[25] As Parkes has written, the fact "that such gatherings took place at all . . . was a major new development" in literary politics.[26] Quite aside from the discussions and debates that occurred at these writers' conferences themselves, the very fact that East and West German writers were coming together to discuss questions of war and peace in such a highly public context spoke volumes both about the writers' ultimate sense of belonging together and about their view of their role in German society. Parkes identifies the writers' sense "of a common purpose" in the struggle for peace, while Peitsch has suggested that in both Germanys writers saw themselves as part of a literary opposition to the political status quo.[27]

Several years later, the film director Werner Herzog invoked the status of writers as guarantors of German unity in the face of political opposition when he suggested that "it is only culture and language that really hold us together," and that in the long run only writers "can save Germany."[28] This renewed concept of the *Kulturna-tion* as the compensatory site of national identity also emerges from Günter Grass's 1980 declaration that "the only thing in the two German states that can be proven to be pan-German is literature."[29] Indeed, the specific intent of the writers gathered in Berlin during the conferences of the early 1980s was to overcome political tensions through cultural rapprochement and to achieve at least a minimal "convergence" on the question of peace. However in the German context convergence was necessarily linked to the national question and the problem of reunification. Although Peitsch has criticized the national turn among some German literary figures of the 1980s as a flight from political responsibility, it would seem that what was occurring was in fact a move toward a different politics of national reaffirmation, not a departure from politics altogether. Nevertheless, in the context of a literary culture that still understood itself primarily as the nay-saying "conscience of the nation," this reaffir-mation of national identity was bound to cause controversy and elicit criticism.

The two major works of German literature to come out of the peace movement and the Berlin writers' conferences were Christa Wolf's *Kassandra* and Günter Grass's *Die Rättin* [*The Rat*] (1985). Both of these works are protests against the threat of nuclear war and pleas for an overcoming of the differences between East and West. What is particularly revealing about both is that they do not take sides in the East–West debate. Instead, they argue from a third position which rejects the confrontation between the other two. The critique of the cold war is clearest in *Kassandra*, in which Wolf returns to the oldest motif in Western literature, the battle between the Greeks and the Trojans depicted in Homer's epics, not to celebrate the male heroes of those epics, but rather to meditate on the fate of the Trojan princess Cassandra, condemned by the god Apollo always to tell the truth but never to be believed. Although daughter to the Trojan king Priam, Cassandra is equally critical of both Greece and Troy, and she refuses to be pressured by war-time paranoia into unthinking support for her father or his peons. At one level *Kassandra* is an allegory of the cold war between the West and the East, with the Greeks as representatives of the triumphant West and the Trojans as representatives of the defeated East. However, Wolf's interest lies not so much in the exploits of the Greeks and Trojans as in the possibility of a non-confrontational way of life that transcends the East–West conflict. In *Kassandra* the vision of a community that goes beyond the bipolar East–West division is embodied in the feminist collective of which Cassandra becomes a part. While this collective is ultimately disbanded with the fall of Troy, it remains real as a memory of a different form of life, of a "third path." For Wolf the seeming ideological differences between Troy and Greece (and between the East bloc and the West bloc) are outweighed by a fundamental convergence at the level of patriarchal domination.[30]

Grass's fantastical dream-novel *Die Rättin* tells the story of a post-apocalyptic world in which the nuclear catastrophe feared by so many Germans during the early 1980s has already occurred and the only mammalian survivors are rats, who are able to form a community of solidarity and peace so unlike the warlike communities of human beings. Central to Grass's critique of human stupidity is the ecological devastation of the planet earth, represented in the book by the German forest. This devastation eliminates not only the physical conditions for the survival of the human race but also its spiritual center. As the place of mystery occupied by so many figures in German fairy tales, the forest is a cultural as well as an agricultural and ecological value.

German literature of the early 1980s is full of the fear of nuclear war and a sometimes desperate critique of the United States and its leaders, an anti-Americanism rightly criticized at the time by Andrei S. Markovits.[31] A typical example of such anti-Americanism is a 1985 poem by the veteran Austrian leftist writer Erich Fried entitled "Conversation Between Two Great Statesmen in Heaven or in Hell:"

> "Maybe
> I ought
> to have
> remained
> a painter,"
> said the one.
>
> "And I
> an actor,"
> said the other.[32]

The point of the poem is on the one hand a direct comparison between Adolf Hitler and Ronald Reagan underlined by the fact that both are in either heaven or hell together; and on the other hand the suggestion that the world would have been better off if the two artists, however untalented, had stuck to their original professions. While such a comparison may be offensive to both American sensibilities and the historical record, it is fairly typical of the edgy atmosphere in Central Europe during the early 1980s.

Probably the most controversial German literary critique of the United States and its President in the early 1980s was Rolf Hochhuth's 1984 play *Judith*, which addressed the moral question of whether political murder is acceptable in order to prevent greater harm. Hochhuth prefaced his play with a quotation from the biblical *Judith*: "Bring to pass, O Lord, that his pride may be cut off with his own sword,"[33] and used the story of the Jewish princess Judith, who sleeps with the Persian tyrant Holofernes and then cuts off his head, as the basis for both his title and the two main strands of the play. *Judith* tells the story of two different political assassinations, the first of which is based on historical reality, and the second of which is therefore suggested to be at least a real possibility: respectively the murder of the German General Commissar of Belarus in 1943 and that of the President of the United States in the early 1980s. In the first plot, the heroine Judith murders the German official as an act of protest and defiance against the ongoing Holocaust of the Jews in Eastern Europe. In the second plot, the heroine (also named Judith) uses the chemical weapon being developed by the United States for a future war to kill the murderous President at whose request it is being manufactured. Judith has tried to reason with the President and stop his experiments with chemical weapons, but to no avail. The President scorns the peace movement and believes only in war. Trying to explain her act after the President's assassination, Judith refers to the Biblical injunction to beat swords into ploughshares, one of the most important images of the German peace movement:

> I stood next to him, as he mocked those
> who, even in this country, want to
> beat their swords into ploughshares.
> And when he slapped away Arthur's professor
> like a stupid fly, the chemist
> who opened his eyes
> to what he had ordered
> to be produced . . . Swords into ploughshares . . .
> His arrogance, as he quoted that.
> That those in favor of disarmament are simply fools, supplicants

who never shoot – this habit of thought
of the power-sick:
has an end – since I made an end of *him*.[34]

Hochhuth's play was highly controversial because of its perceived anti-Americanism, justification of political assassination, and equation of American foreign and military policy with Nazi genocide. As an overtly political work seeking directly to influence the German debates of the 1980s, *Judith* was in no way a major work of literature, in spite of Hochhuth's somewhat pretentious affectation of free verse. Nevertheless, the play is a relatively accurate representation of German discomfort with the United States in the early 1980s.

Another important literary reflection of German politics in the early 1980s was Stefan Heym's 1984 novel *Schwarzenberg*. Heym's novel was based on a little-known but nevertheless true piece of history. In 1945, when the Soviet Red Army was sweeping through Germany to the West and the American army was moving toward the East, the two armies met at the Elbe river and, with their Allies, occupied all of Germany except for a small portion of land twenty kilometers wide and twenty kilometers deep along the Czechoslovak border southwest of Chemnitz and southeast of Zwickau. This area, named after its major town, Schwarzenberg, remained free of occupying armies for about a month in the spring of 1945. Communists and Social Democrats in Schwarzenberg organized a mini-revolution against the Nazis and set up a free, democratic socialist government. This brief experiment in socialist democracy becomes for Heym the memory of a German utopia. Schwarzenberg represents the possibility of a democratic, socialist Germany that rejects adherence to either of the two superpowers. Heym begins the novel with a quotation from Schiller's poem "The Commencement of the New Century" that directly speaks to the early 1980s:

> Two mighty nations strive, with hostile power,
>   For undivided mastery of the world;
> And, by them, each land's freedom to devour,
>   The trident brandish'd is – the lightning hurl'd.
>
>   . . .
>
> Although thine eye may ev'ry map explore,
>   Vainly thou'lt seek to find that blissful place,
> Where freedom's garden smiles for evermore,
>   And where in youth still blooms the human race.[35]

Within the context of Heym's novel it becomes clear that

Schwarzenberg is precisely that free and "blissful place" which Schiller could not find on his maps, and that a neutral, free Germany could fulfill in the future the unfulfilled promise of Schwarzenberg in the past and present. At this point Heym is close to the utopian dream of a free and unified German *Kulturnation* propagated in the late eighteenth and early nineteenth centuries.

In 1984 Peter Schneider published a long story entitled *Der Mauerspringer* [*The Wall Jumper*] in which the divided state of Germany became the primary theme. Schneider's book was a series of stories about people who had traveled from the one Germany to the other, sometimes quite literally by jumping over the Wall. The stories were held together loosely by a framing architecture in which the first-person narrator, who resembled Schneider himself, told about his own experiences in West and East Berlin, and in particular his troubled personal relationships with a close male friend and a female lover from the East. The book was a kind of German comedy of errors, in which primarily ideological misunderstandings worked to conceal the fundamental similarity among Germans on both sides of the wall. The narrator's final statements on German identity closely resembled Schiller's eighteenth-century declaration on the same subject: "If I were asked where it [Germany] lies, I could only locate it in its history and in the language I speak." Schneider's reflections on German identity were a clear declaration in favor of the *Kulturnation*:

If my fatherland exists, it isn't a state, and the state of which I am a citizen is not a fatherland. If I respond to queries about my nationality by saying without hesitation that I'm a German, I am clearly opting not for a state, but for a people that no longer has a state identity. At the same time, however, I assert that my national identity does not depend on either of the German states.[36]

Schneider suggested that the two German governments in East and West were so slavishly devoted to their respective superpowers in Moscow and Washington that they had forgotten the larger unity guaranteed by language, culture, history, and tradition. This unity was possible only when individual Germans recognized their own lack of completeness. Each of the individual stories in Schneider's book is therefore incomplete; it is only the entirety of the German stories that gives a true picture. As the narrator says, "Every story lacks something that the next one has; but then the next story is missing something from the one before."[37] The narrator ultimately suggests that the real problem of German unity is not political but rather psychological: "It will take us longer to tear down the Wall in our heads than any wrecking company will need for the Wall we can see."[38] These words of 1984 were to prove prescient for the relations between West and East Germans after 1990.

One of the most determined literary proponents of German unity in the 1980s was Martin Walser, whose controversial spy novella *Dorle und Wolf* [*No Man's Land*] (1987) was a tragicomedy about German division and a plea for unity. In this novella Walser told the story of an East German spy and virtuoso piano player named Wolfgang Zieger (nickname: Wolf) who moves to West Germany, acquires West German citizenship, marries a West German named Dorris (Dorle) and works his way up to a high position in Bonn in order to pass on technological and scientific information to his bosses in East Berlin. Wolf's motivation is primarily patriotic, but not in the conventional bipolar sense of the 1980s. Wolf considers himself to be neither an East nor a West German but rather a citizen of the lost German whole. Refusing to pay fealty to either of the temporary states which existed in the 1980s, Wolf devotes his loyalty to a Germany no longer – or not yet – existent. His activity as a spy is an ingenious way of working to destabilize German division. Given the East's seemingly hopeless scientific-technological backwardness, Wolf hopes that his illegal technology transfers will decrease the harshness of German division by bringing the two Germanys together technologically. For him spying is simply a patriotic attempt to keep the more backward part of Germany closer to the more advanced part. In a divided Germany characterized by mutual contempt and historical forgetfulness, Wolf seeks to preserve the memory of what has been lost:

In the West, Wolf had discovered how much of the East had been lost here. He had experienced the growing coldness toward everything the two parts had in common, as well as the crass want of understanding, the overweening insensitivity and arrogance toward what was happening in the GDR. The two parts reverberated with mutual want of understanding. Each wanted to outdo the other in rejection. Each wished to lay claim to more historical justification, thereby relegating the other to proportionately less. Each vied with the other as an ardent shield-bearer for the camp to which it had been allocated. Each wanted to be a model student in its own school. In this way each had developed hostility toward the other as the most vital ingredient of its self-awareness. And this was what Wolf wanted to remedy, in a precarious field – that of armaments.[39]

Just as in Schneider's *The Wall Jumper*, *Dorle und Wolf* presents the personal as the political and the political as the personal. However Walser's apparent longing for Germany is much more acute than Schneider's. Dorle is a West German, while Wolf is an East German, and their marital union is already an image of a future reunified Germany. Moreover, Wolf experiences the division of Germany as an elemental split in his own psyche. German national division has created in Wolf a schizophrenic self-perception. Thomas Steinfeld and Heidrun Suhr have suggested that in *Dorle und Wolf* the abstract idea of a unified national "We" takes over the center "of the . . . individual, as an element of personal identity."[40] And yet it would be more accurate to say that in *Dorle und Wolf* the seemingly abstract becomes the concrete, or that the imagined becomes the real. In Walser's novel, the powerful force of eros itself, which Freud had identified as the primary force in human civilization, is directed toward an overcoming of German division. The coming together of man and woman is imagined on the same plane with the coming together of the German East and the German West. Wolf's description of the divided Germans recalls what is probably the most famous account of love in Western literature: Aristophanes' description of the origin of the sexes in Plato's *Symposium*, in which male and female were originally part of a single, attached body and sexual desire is explained as a longing for the restoration of a lost whole. According to Aristophanes, "each of us is a mere fragment of a man," and "we're all looking for our 'other half.'"[41] Walser's description of divided Germans differs from Aristophanes' description of man and woman, however, in that the knowledge of fragmentation has been lost, thus rendering a future coming together even more problematic. In a train station in Bonn Wolf observes his fellow passengers and imagines that he recognizes in them a lack of wholeness that corresponds to his own intense feelings of lack. As Wolf sees it, German division has entered into the very bodies of the West German people:

The other travelers on the platform, in their compactness, neatness, smartness, and purposefulness suddenly seemed to him like half-people. A mass of half-people were pushing their way back and forth.[42]

Of course it was precisely as half-people that Aristophanes had described man and woman in the *Symposium*. But in that account, men and women were constantly in search of each other, always trying to regain their missing wholeness. Because contemporary West Germans have lost the sense of their own incompleteness, Wolf believes that they lack the erotic drive to push for personal and national reunification. Part of the horror of German division is that the half-people walking around the train station are completely unaware of their own inadequacy. They mistakenly believe themselves to be whole:

They don't know what they lack. And not one of them would say, if asked, that he lacked his Leipzig half, his Dresden part, his Mecklenburg extension, his Thuringian depth. They appear lost in one extreme. And the ones over there are trapped in the other. This is more divisive than that hateful stroke across the map. One should proclaim it loudly on a station platform. But he didn't have the courage. Yet he was surprised that no one shouted: We are half-people![43]

Although Walser's attempt to create a strict parallel between the individual and the nation remains unconvincing, Wolf's recognition here is a subtle one. It is not just the fact of division that is problematic; what is equally problematic is people's lack of awareness of that division. What is necessary for the process of healing to begin is a recognition of sickness. Walser's picture here was an explicit critique of what the author saw as West German attempts to repress the fact of national division.[44] Significantly, the bearer of the knowledge of German incompleteness is an East German, not a West German. In Walser's view, West Germans, as citizens of the more successful and prosperous German "half," are less likely to understand the need for national unity than East Germans, who live in a much less successful, much poorer half-state and for that reason are more capable of recognizing their neediness.

Botho Strauß expressed a similar concern for German division in a long poem entitled *Diese Erinnerung an einen, der nur einen Tag zu Gast war* [This Memory of One Who Was a Guest for Only a Day] (1985). For Strauß, German division was less a problem of personal or geographical division than of historical memory. Far from being the schizophrenic product of German division, the poem's lyric voice is unified by national memory, which remains undivided even in a present characterized by separation. The voice asks, "was I, then, not born in my fatherland?" and laments the fact of German division, because it goes against the grain of historical memory. Germany's unified cultural heritage belies the reality of its present division:

No Germany known during my lifetime.
Two foreign states only, which forbade me
ever in the name of one people to be the German.
So much history, thus to end?

One must sense: the heart of a Kleist and
the division of the land. One must think: what a reunion
if one, in us, were to open the stage of history!

Perhaps whoever is German learns to supplement himself.
And every tiny piece of understanding
is like one cell in the national fabric,
which always contains the blueprint of the whole.[45]

Whereas Walser had been concerned with the effects of German division at the personal level, Strauß's concern went from the personal to the large-scale political, with each personal act of understanding contributing to the national project. Significantly, the rhetorical opposite of the "separation of the country" is drawn from the realm of literary culture as the traditional guarantor of German identity above and beyond political barriers: "the heart of a Kleist." It is also noteworthy that Strauß chooses not Goethe, the Weimar classicist, but rather the despairing, riven Kleist as the embodiment of "the division of the land." Strauß uses a biological metaphor to illustrate the relationship of individual Germans to each other in the larger context of the nation: each German individual is a cell, and the nation itself is a unified organism, however torn. The word "Geweb," used to refer to the nation, can mean both biological tissue and woven fabric and is hence connected to the Latin meaning of the word "text." Significantly, the poem's voice refers to both Germanys as being "foreign," suggesting that, like Walser's Wolf, Strauß recognizes himself not as a citizen of either one or the other, but rather as part of the missing German whole. Indeed, the fact that the two extant German states "forbade me / ever in the name of one people to be the German" suggests that East and West were in fact unpatriotic and anti-German.

As the development of West German society and the West German economy accelerated, the Federal Republic left the East German society and economy ever further behind. It was precisely the recognition of this growing gap between the two Germanys that had led Walser's fictional Wolfgang Ziegler to become a patriotic spy. The success of the postwar West German economic miracle had made possible a modernization of the FRG's villages and cities, the emergence of automotive culture, and a dominance of new media such as television. In the course of this rapid modernization, the signs of the destruction caused by the Second World War had largely been eliminated, and along with those signs had disappeared many traces of an older, more bucolic, less hurried German lifestyle. In the GDR, economic difficulties associated with the country's less efficient system of production had meant the preservation not only of war ruins but also of architectural and cultural traditions. As Wolf Biermann suggested two years before the Wall came down, "the GDR-Germans have not become as Russian as the West Germans have become American."[46] In a post-1989 book the author Andreas Neumeister agreed. Referring to the former GDR as "the area of the Reichsbahn" ("Reichsbahngebiet") because the old pre-1945 Imperial German train service ("Reichsbahn") had continued to exist in Germany after the war only on the territory of the GDR, he wrote: "Germany is at its most German in the area of the Reichsbahn."[47] This statement expresses the widespread belief among West Germans that because the GDR's status as poor brother to the FRG had made rapid economic change less possible there, the other Germany had remained more uniquely German.

The first West German emissary to the GDR after the two governments extended partial diplomatic recognition to each other with the "Grundlagenvertrag" (Basic Treaty) in December of 1972 was the Social Democratic journalist and diplomat Günter Gaus, who served as the head of the "ständige Vertretung" (permanent representation) of the Federal Republic of Germany to the German Democratic Republic from 1974 to 1981 and became one of the most important theoreticians of the German Question during the 1970s and 1980s. Gaus suggested that the GDR was largely characterized by an apolitical "Nischengesellschaft" (society of niches) in which people sought to live undisturbed by larger political issues. Within the space of these niches many older German "prewar-bourgeois" (vorkriegsmäßig-bürgerlich) traditions had, he argued, been preserved. Gaus suggested that "in some good and bad habits and traditional values, the GDR is . . . the last bourgeois state on German soil."[48] The relatively slower pace of modernization in the GDR had, according to Gaus, allowed for "the conservation of behavior patterns that, since about 1950, have been ever more rapidly leveled out, melted away, and internationalized in our part of the country."[49]

What Gaus was suggesting ran counter to the conventional understanding of the Communist system as a radical attack on conservative values. It also contradicted the Communist party's own understanding of itself as a progressive force for social change. In Gaus's view, Communist domination in the GDR had, paradoxically, resulted in the preservation of traditional, conservative German values. As Gaus wrote, "a number of factors have meant that traditional family structures, positive and negative attitudes toward one's social surroundings, behavior patterns, sentiments, and resentments have to this very day been preserved more strongly over there than over here."[50] It was capitalist society that was revolutionary because of its progressive destruction and elimination of traditional social values. Gaus explicitly urged observers of the German-German relationship to go beyond the level of verbal ideology to the level of day-to-day social relations and interactions. There, he argued, observers would see that the GDR was the more truly traditional German state. Gaus wrote that West Germans who traveled to East Germany experience a shock of recognition that comes from the national past:

To West German eyes, much of the way of life in the GDR appears, in a strangely moving way, . . . prewar-bourgeois. That is what a fifty-year-old man says . . . a man who has occasionally felt a kind of throbbing of memory against his heart during his trips to the beautiful countryside over there, when he happened to pass through a village in Mecklenburg or a small town in Thuringia. As he thought more about it he realized that even though he had never been there as a child, he had transformed the external impression into the epiphany of an automobile trip with his parents in the 1930s: through another village and another small town, and yet the very same – and here I have to say: German – small-town feeling.[51]

Gaus's narration of the West German's memory of traveling with his parents and the recognition that the East German landscape more closely resembles the landscape of a fifty-year-old's childhood are remarkably similar to Botho Strauß's invocation of the East German university city Jena and the memory: "did I not see it early / and walked with my father along the bank of the Saale and Unstrut."[52] Karl Heinz Bohrer suggested in January of 1990 that "this depth dimension of the one-time 'Zone' has always appeared to West German visitors . . . as an exotic attraction in which a romantic Germany, long since lost in the West, resurfaces like a remembered dream in the cities and landscapes of Thuringia,

Brandenburg and Saxony."[53] Bohrer's sentiment was echoed two years later by a fictional psychologist in Irene Dische's 1993 novel *Ein fremdes Gefühl* [A Strange Feeling], who makes the following declaration to a somewhat old-fashioned West German patient: "Maybe you would like the East better, if you were to take a look around there. Have you ever been over there, in those tiny villages? It's beautiful there, untouched, it's still like before the war."[54] One year later the theater critic Peter von Becker had a character in his first novel *Die andere Zeit* [The Other Time] ruminate about eastern Germany: "In the gray-brown patina or 'scar tissue,'" of everyday reality in the drab GDR "was . . . preserved a sense of history, something deeply German, not yet cleaned away by the international, uniform color of the West."[55] Gaus's picture of East Germany from the West German perspective was echoed ironically from the GDR itself in Hein's *Der fremde Freund* [*The Distant Lover*], in which a West German character, visiting the East, rhapsodizes about the GDR's nineteenth-century qualities:

The West German gave a nervous laugh. Then he remarked that everything here was like the nineteenth century, marvellously intact, like a forgotten village. Like some country invented by Adalbert Stifter.[56]

Probably the most important public invocation of the German national question by a West German writer during the 1980s was a speech given one year before the collapse of the GDR by Martin Walser. In that speech, which was highly controversial at the time because of its insistence on reopening a "German Question" that most political pundits considered closed, Walser set up a dichotomy between an East German life that had preserved much of its German integrity and a superficial, fast life in West Germany in which much of history and tradition had been forgotten. Using the GDR poet Wulf Kirsten as his example of a purer, more original language posited to exist in East Germany, Walser suggested that life in the West was characterized by "speed, conformism, loss," as well as by "the judgmental, the idea," and "made-for-television apocalypse." Walser declared that language in West Germany was "addicted to judgment, addicted to statement." In contrast, the GDR language which Kirsten represented "does not judge. It carries things forward. Against forgetting."[57] As if anticipating the central importance accorded to preservation in subsequent debates about "what remains" of the GDR, Walser summarized his ideas by

suggesting: "I believe that in the GDR something has been preserved for us."[58] What had been preserved in the GDR was, for
Walser, precisely a slower, less frenetic pace of life, an awareness of
history and tradition, and a more authentic Germanness now lost in
the West. For this reason Walser insisted that the German Question
was still very much open, declaring, "I refuse to take part in the
liquidation of history," and that "We must . . . recognize the FRG
just as little as we recognize the GDR."[59] Walser's terminology once
again invoked a history of German national idealism in which the
nation was less a concrete political entity than a utopian cultural
space where tradition and history preserved elements of salvation
from an unhappy politics. "We must keep open the wound called
Germany," declared Walser.[60] It was precisely their lack of wholeness, their wounded condition, that enabled Germans to experiment
with cultural and historical possibilities not readily apparent in the
status quo. If for Strauß it had been "the heart of" the tortured
Kleist that embodied Germany's problematic national identity,
Walser suggested that Germany itself existed as a wound, as something by its very nature incomplete and imperfect and therefore
incapable of healing. Walser's speech was at one and the same time a
call to remember the division of Germany and try to overcome it
culturally and a reminder that, beyond all political categories,
German identity itself was necessarily fragmentary. It was in
accepting that mystical vulnerability, Walser believed, that Germans
could preserve and relocate their unity in the *Kulturnation*.

CHAPTER 2

A third path?

The events of October and November, 1989 forced a fundamental rethinking of postwar German cultural history and initiated major philosophical, political, sociological, and literary debates which are still continuing. What happened in Europe in the fall of 1989 was not just political and was certainly not confined to the eastern half of what used to be the divided continent; it was the total breakdown of a linguistic and ideological system at once bipolar and regressive which had governed European affairs since the end of World War Two. If many of Germany's writers and intellectuals reacted to German reunification as if they had completely lost all sense of proportion and bearing, it is because to a large extent they had. For over forty years, they had been living in an infinite bipolar regression, in a language and ideology machine which seemed to function in perpetual motion. The machine may have been inhuman and cruel, but it was one's own. It was what one knew. There is little doubt that Germany and the world will be feeling the shock waves from this collapse for some time to come.

At the center of "the German Question" as it emerged once again in the fall of 1989 were two fundamental problems: the problem of German nationhood on the one hand, and the problem of socialism on the other. Within the German context these two questions were interconnected because of Germany's troubled twentieth-century history. Germany had experienced both of the major forms of twentieth-century totalitarianism: National Socialism and Stalinism. Partly as a reaction to Hitler's anti-Communism and as a result of the Soviet victory in World War Two, German intellectuals had assigned to socialism a prestige that was uniquely part of the country's own trauma with itself and its Nazi past. Nowhere else in the world did Communism as antifascism have the same kind of intellectual and moral prestige. Moreover, the trauma of Germany's National Socialist past had made many Germans unsure of their country's moral right to national unity and sovereignty. It was not just British, French, and Italian intellectuals who were afraid of German reunification. German intellectuals themselves were afraid of it, too, because reunification seemed to them to throw into question all of the achievements of the Second World War: the victory over fascism, the validation of socialism, and, in the West, the achievement of a democratic polity. Reunification, as the political solution to the German Question, seemed to many intellectuals to mean the dissolution of socialism as the dream of a better, non-alienated society and at the same time the threat of renewed German racism, nationalism, militarism, and unchecked consumerism.

As the chronology of reunification worked itself out, the most shocking thing about it to most of the participants was the sheer speed with which events were moving. As one character in a subsequent novel muses, "time had been struck with mad cow disease, and it began to go crazy. No one could stop it."[1] On October 7, 1989, the GDR had celebrated its fortieth anniversary with the requisite speeches and torchlight parades; less than a year later, the new "zero hour" came at precisely midnight between October 2 and 3, 1990, when, from one second to another, all of Germany became unified and West German laws became applicable to the former GDR. At that second Germany once again became a sovereign and unified nation-state for the first time since May 8, 1945. A person uncorking a champagne bottle in the German Democratic Republic at 11:59 p.m. on October 2 drank the champagne a minute later in the Federal Republic of Germany. A division which most people then alive had grown up with, taken for granted, and never seriously believed would be overcome in their lifetimes, was suddenly gone. This speed left intellectuals and politicians scrambling just to keep up with events, and in the scramble all the old certainties of politics and ideology not only in East but also in West Germany seemed just as unstable as the partition which had disappeared overnight.

The extent to which German intellectuals were unprepared for the events which took place in the second half of 1989 was demonstrated by a prominent article published in the middle of the year by Peter Schneider. Shortly after the Hungarian government declared that it would begin eliminating the fortifications on its Western border to Austria, Schneider wrote the lead article in *The New York Times Magazine*.[2] The author of *Der Mauerspringer* had by this time become the leading German expert American news organizations turned to in seeking advice on the state of German mentalities. In his cover story for *The New York Times Magazine*, Schneider now addressed the state of German affairs at the end of the cold war, arguing that over the course of almost half a century of postwar history Germans in the West and in the East had grown so far apart from each other that they had virtually nothing left in common. Paradoxically, Schneider suggested that it was only the existence of the Berlin Wall that gave Germans the illusion of a common national identity: the Wall as a physical barrier between the two Germanys had prevented Germans from recognizing the extent of their own mental and spiritual alienation from each other. The very existence of the Berlin Wall suggested the East German government's need to suppress by force an otherwise existing sense of unity. If for some unexpected reason the Wall were to come down, Schneider argued, "ironically, the two Germanys would lose the only thing still unifying them." However, Schneider argued confidently, the Wall was *not* going to come down. In fact, the writer went on, the end of the cold war suggested the need for the two Germanys to face existing realities and accept the permanent political division of the nation. Schneider wrote: "The wall will truly come down only when Germans face a basic reality: there is no 'human right' of German reunification and there will continue to be two German states. Rather than dreaming of some utopian reunification, West Germans should push for the democratic rights of their East German fellows and of all East Europeans. Only if such rights evolve can there ever be a normal border between the two Germanys."[3]

It is perhaps misleading to focus on one writer's inaccurate predictions, because such an exclusive focus might falsely imply that writers were uniquely susceptible to being mistaken. Nothing could be further from the truth. At the time that it was published, Schneider's remarks were without doubt the consensus of enlightened expert opinion both in the United States and in Europe. That same summer West Germany's former chancellor, Helmut Schmidt, suggested that the Wall would continue to exist until well into the twenty-first century, and Erich Honecker, the seventy-eight-year-old East German leader, declared that the Wall would last for another hundred years. During the summer of 1989 no one was suggesting that Schneider (or Schmidt or Honecker) was wrong and that only half a year later the Wall would lie in ruins and the two Germanys would find themselves on the road to what Schneider had termed "some utopian reunification." Writers were no more mistaken than the rest of the country's elites.

Nevertheless, in the months that followed, German writers, and particularly GDR writers, were swept into the vortex of historical events which proved them anything but seers and prophets. GDR writers were particularly susceptible to this problem because, in spite of the many well-documented protests and disagreements between them and the Communist regime, they were often associated, fairly or unfairly, with the dictatorship then coming to its end. As much as they criticized the East German regime itself, many of them clung to the dream of a democratic socialism that would overcome the exploitation and alienation they believed predominant in the capitalist economic systems of the West. Like the idealistic leaders of many of the citizens rights groups spearheading the revolution inside the GDR, East German writers frequently believed that what they were witnessing during the autumn of 1989, far from being the collapse of the East German state, was simply the overthrow of post-Stalinist structures of domination and the victory of democratic socialism. As demonstrations against the Communist Politburo escalated during the late summer and early autumn, many writers and intellectuals saw the revolution in the GDR as above all a *socialist* revolution aimed at actually realizing the promises of socialism that had been ignored for the last forty years. Such dreams of a socialist transformation of the German Democratic Republic reached their high point on November 4, 1989, only five days before the opening of the Wall, when over half a million people demonstrated at East Berlin's Alexanderplatz. Because of the Berlin crowd's vociferous support for radical reform, this demonstration seemed to reinforce intellectuals' mistaken belief that what was happening in East Germany in the fall of 1989 was the first successful democratic socialist revolution in German history.

It was to a large extent the naive idealism of such writers and intellectuals which later made them susceptible to charges of political ingenuousness or, worse, adherence to an authoritarian and discredited socialist system. In a speech at the Alexanderplatz demonstration, Christoph Hein declared that it was high time for the structures of GDR society to become "democratic and socialist."

His invocation of a utopian socialism accurately reflected the dreams of many other East German writers:

Let us create a democratic society on a legal basis that is subject to challenge. A socialism that doesn't make a caricature of the word. A society which is commensurate with humanity instead of subjugating humanity to its structures.[4]

As he spoke to the demonstrators that day, Stefan Heym spoke out "for freedom and democracy and for a socialism worthy of the name." Like Hein, Heym rejected the authoritarian post-Stalinism of the GDR's aging leaders but insisted on the continuing promise of democratic socialism: "Socialism, not the Stalinist kind, the true socialism that we finally want to build for our benefit and the benefit of all Germany."[5]

In her own speech Christa Wolf invoked a great dream: "Imagine there was socialism and nobody ran away!"[6] Over the course of August and September, as the waves of refugees from East Germany had risen inexorably, the internal opposition had defined itself precisely as "Hierbleiber" (ones who stay here), as opposed to "Ausreiser" (ones who leave). The concept of "staying here" implied the desire *not* to exchange the socialist authoritarianism of the GDR for the successful capitalism of the FRG, but, rather, to work inside the GDR for a socialism "worthy of the name." "Staying here" meant staying in the GDR, which, in turn, meant that the GDR would have to continue as a separate German state, a legitimate socialist alternative to the capitalist FRG.

Since, in spite of hecklers, most of the people in the crowd enthusiastically cheered the writers' statements, including the calls for a democratic socialism, it is understandable that the writers believed themselves in touch with the dreams of the East German people. The fact that these writers played such a prominent role in the GDR's largest and freest mass demonstration spoke volumes about their own and the GDR's understanding of the relationship between writer and society. As one character in a 1994 novel declares somewhat ironically with respect to the former GDR,

The more state, and I mean the dictatorial state of a German Democratic Republic, the more literature. The deeper the politicians stuck their heads into the sand of their own misorganization, the higher we hung the banners of fantasy and fiction in the clouds of utopia, which are so high that they just manage to brush against the sun chariot of Phoebus . . .[7]

In less flowery language, Bathrick has expressed the exalted position of the writer in East German society by suggesting that, "more than any other public institution, the literary writer [in the GDR] served as spokesperson for issues of moral, philosophical, social, and above all political significance – a role that far transcended the social function traditionally accorded the realm of belles lettres in Western capitalist societies."[8] The very desire of the Communist regime to censor and regulate literature in the past had been a testament to its firm belief in the importance of literature. Armed with an almost metaphysical power, writers such as Wolf, Heim, and Heyn, had agitated for a better, more democratic political future.

Once that future had come, however, East German writers and intellectuals were to experience Western intellectuals' freedom coupled with the full force of their relative insignificance in the face of a popular culture interested largely in different values. John Erpenbeck has expressed this paradox in the image of an East German intellectual accorded complete freedom to write anything he wants without censorship after reunification – but without readers. Examining an unpublished post-1989 article, the formerly famous personage in Erpenbeck's novel *Aufschwung* [Boom Times] (1996) realizes that "he could not have written or even thought [these thoughts] previously. There he had profited from reunification." But this profit has come at a great price: "Previously, people would have torn this manuscript from his hands, today no one was interested in it. There he had suffered because of reunification."[9] Ironically, the new freedom of literature had come at the price of a perceived loss in political and social significance. The speeches given at the Alexanderplatz on November 4, 1989, occurred at a golden moment for writers when their dreams of a freer and more open public sphere appeared to have been achieved, but when writers had not yet lost the moral and political authority granted to East German writers only because of GDR authoritarianism. That golden moment came to an end less than a week later, when the East German Politburo under Erich Honecker's successor Egon Krenz issued travel guidelines which allowed East Germans unrestricted access to the capitalist West, thereby ushering in the fall of the Berlin Wall, and, ultimately, of the GDR itself.[10] It was as if the SED had decided to let the state go down with the party itself, making party theoretician Otto Reinhold's thesis that without socialism there was no need for a separate GDR a self-fulfilling prophecy.[11]

Some German writers suspected a cynical conspiracy. In his novel *Ein weites Feld*, whose publication coincided with the fifth anniversary of German reunification, Grass suggested that the GDR's leaders had let the Wall fall in order to prevent the advent of a "third path," the utopian social and economic concept longed for by so many writers and dissidents in the GDR. As the GDR's dreamers envisioned it, the third path was to combine the best aspects of socialist distribution and capitalist production, and it would avoid the perceived extremes of eastern authoritarianism on the one hand and western exploitation on the other. One of the major characters in *Ein weites Feld*, a Stasi officer, declares:

We had to act, yes, because the thing with the Third Path was even more dangerous . . . That doesn't exist anywhere, a Third Path! Not here, and not under capitalism either. Our counterparts in the West saw things the same way. So we simply opened it up, yes, the Wall . . . Abracadabra! And it was open. Yes indeed! We were the ones who did it. We wanted to create a new situation. Now they were the suckers, the ones with their Third Path. They could forget about that.[12]

These words give voice to the widespread belief among dissident intellectuals that the opening of the Wall was an attempt to forestall the coming of democratic socialism and to maintain authoritarian control. Of course, in viewing the opening of the Wall so negatively, German writers were putting themselves in direct opposition to ordinary Germans, who perceived the demise of the hated structure as an unparalleled national and human triumph.

Most writers did not seem to be aware of the ironic fact that the moment of their greatest victory was also the beginning of a long-term defeat. Later on, Wolf Biermann acknowledged the irony that the real losers in the GDR's revolution were the revolutionaries themselves:

We are the real losers, a handful of leftist intellectuals. In the name of real Marxism and true socialism we had dug ourselves into the fight with party leaders. But our opponents of yesterday have long since disappeared into the sunset. And we, a tiny group of more or less upright people, cringe at the grave and chew over the body of Communism.[13]

These leftist intellectuals stood in a long tradition of utopian dreaming and hopes for a better world. Was that dream now over? Had the alternative movements in East and West throughout the 1980s resulted solely in the triumph of Western capitalism? Or did

German reunification present, as the dissident Robert Havemann had believed in the 1980s, a new kind of opportunity for leftists?

In the first week of December, alarmed by the growing signs of disintegration inside the GDR, Christa Wolf and a group of other prominent East German intellectuals banded together to put out a statement entitled "Für unser Land" [For Our Country]. They declared:

We still have the chance to develop in a relationship of equals with all European states a socialist alternative to the Federal Republic. We can still reflect our antifascist and humanistic ideals from which we proceeded long ago.[14]

This declaration clearly showed the entirely negative light in which many East German writers viewed the opening of the Berlin Wall and the possibility of national reunification. Shortly after the publication of this document, Stefan Heym declared himself confounded by the change that had come about after the October Revolution. In an article for *Der Spiegel* published at the end of December, Heym used overwhelmingly negative language to describe the East German crowds reveling in West Berlin:

The very same people who had risen up and taken their fate into their own hands . . . became suddenly a horde of frenzied shoppers . . . on the hunt for glitzy trash. What expressions on their faces as, with cannibalistic lust, they rooted like pigs through display tables intentionally placed in their paths by Western shopkeepers . . .[15]

Heym complained bitterly about what he saw as the manipulators in the Federal Republic, tempting the GDR with the carrot of consumerism and threatening it with the stick of economic retaliation until, in the end, the smaller, poorer country simply collapsed and surrendered to its tormentors. He called the Federal Republic a "Freibeuterstaat" (pirate country) and declared, just as the SED's theorist Reinhold had before him, that socialism was the sole raison d'être for the GDR; without socialism, the GDR had no further purpose. Was the dream of socialism now dead? Heym asked rhetorically, and answered his own question with a tentative no: "There is a hope there against all probability, a hope to which one could cling."[16] Heym did not make it clear exactly where this hope was or how he proposed to bring it into reality. At this point he was so out of touch with the ordinary citizens whom he had compared to "pigs" that his words said more about his own "dreams and ideals" than about the real state of affairs in East Germany.

In the wake of the autumn revolution in the GDR, Wolf Biermann made a triumphant return to East Germany and gave a hugely successful concert in Leipzig, where the demonstrations against the SED regime had grown larger from Monday to Monday during September and October of 1989. In that concert Biermann also sang out in favor of democratic socialism and against reunification. One of the texts he sang included the following verses:

> Don't sell us out to Krupp and Thyssen
> Mercedes-Benz and Deutsche Bank . . .
> We want to make our own mistakes –
> and not just repeat the mistakes of the West
> Don't sell the whole bankrupt firm
> We are the people! We're staying here!
> The only thing that'll be sold to the West:
> The Wall in pieces as a souvenir.[17]

Biermann's words here were surprisingly similar to the sentiments of the East German writers' declaration "For Our Country." In another song Biermann further stressed his socialist beliefs by suggesting that "the West is not / the yolk of the egg either," and that "the dream of the Commune / it was only sleeping and is / a long way from dead."[18] For Biermann, as for so many other writers, the revolution in the GDR was a revolution for, not against, socialism.

In an article for *Der Spiegel* entitled "The Writers and the People," the novelist Monika Maron launched a counterattack, charging that GDR intellectuals had become isolated not only from the real hopes and fears of ordinary human beings but also from their everyday living conditions. Maron suggested that even oppositional intellectuals formed part of a privileged elite which was now being rejected by the vast majority of GDR citizens.[19] And yet Maron's critique was problematic for two reasons: because it implied that it was the role of intellectuals to agree with and cheer on "ordinary people"; and because it also implied that any criticism of "ordinary people" was wrong and elitist. In a country which had, half a century earlier, witnessed anti-Nazi writers and intellectuals similarly accused of being out of touch with what the Nazis called "gesundes Volksempfinden" (the healthy feeling of the people), and where, for instance, the modernist poet Gottfried Benn had famously accused exile writers of being unable to "feel the concept of 'the people' – a concept so alien to them – grow within themselves, not as a thought but as a living experience, not as an abstraction but as condensed nature,"[20] such an anti-elitist critique conjured up historical shadows of which Maron herself did not seem to be aware.

Maron's criticisms were nevertheless an important intervention in the debate, and they foreshadowed the controversy that was to emerge in the summer of 1990 around GDR writers' privileged position. But at the end of November and the beginning of December, 1989, it was by no means clear that Maron and Heym were right in assuming that the East German majority opposed socialism. November had, after all, seen the November 4 demonstration at the Alexanderplatz as well as the November 9 opening of the Wall. A *Spiegel/ZDF* opinion poll taken in the first week of December, 1989, produced startling results: 71% of the 1,032 respondents from all over East Germany declared themselves in favor of sovereignty for the GDR, while only 27% came out in favor of German reunification. Evidently there was a good deal more East German national identity in the GDR and a good deal less enthusiasm for the Federal Republic than most Westerners then assumed. Even by the end of the year, it was still not obvious that reunification was inevitable or that most of the citizens of the GDR supported it. Given this uncertainty, it was understandable that many intellectuals in the GDR opposition – now suddenly catapulted into influence and prominence after many years of fruitless protests – continued fighting for what they had wanted all along: democratic socialism. Their desires partook of a powerful utopian urge that had long been part of the socialist movement, even if Marx and Engels themselves had criticized such utopianism.

Whether or not there had ever been any hope of a "third path," by January of 1990 it was clear that any such hope had disappeared. The GDR had, in essence, capitulated to the Federal Republic by opening its borders without restrictions to West Germans in late December, and the various events which were to follow – GDR Prime Minister Hans Modrow's icy reception by Helmut Kohl in Bonn in February 1990; the election of CDU conservative Lothar de Maizière to replace the Communist Modrow as Prime Minister in March; the decision to unify the currencies and economies of the two Germanys by July 1; Germany's political reunification on October 3 – all seemed to have the inevitability of foregone conclusions. Once the border was gone, reunification had become *selbstver-ständlich*, self-understood: it was as obvious and ordinary a condition now as its opposite had been only one year earlier. What for Peter Schneider had been "some utopian reunification" in the early summer of 1989 was, by the spring of 1990, a political fact recognized even by children, and it was, now, a continued political division that came to seem utopian.

In the wake of its great disappointment, the East German intelligentsia grew quiet, as if it had lost its voice. What mattered now was what happened in Bonn, not what happened in Leipzig or Berlin. A vacuum had emerged in the GDR. This vacuum began to be filled in January from the Federal Republic. As the debate inside the GDR on *whether* or not to reunify collapsed in the face of unfolding events, the debate was taken up by intellectuals in West Germany. East German intellectuals' disappointment at the turn of events in the winter of 1989/90 in the GDR was transformed into the makings of a major debate among *West* German intellectuals about the nature and pace of reunification.

The GDR had always played a special role for West German intellectuals, many of whom viewed the Germany to their East as the land that time forgot. While the West had been culturally American-ized, the East had not been Russified; instead, it had gone into a long process of decay. But its ruins were of archeological value for time travellers from the West. Their admittedly problematic and rather kitschy vision of the GDR as a somehow more authentically traditional and therefore truer Germany was to have an important impact on the intellectual debates which followed.

It was the potential loss of this special, "sleeping-beauty" existence of the GDR that Martin Ahrends, an East German writer who had left for the West a decade earlier, mourned in a movingly elegiac but also cleverly ironic essay published in early November of 1989. Ahrends referred again and again to metaphors of Sleeping Beauty and her 100-year slumber behind the hedge of thorns in the German fairy tale. For Ahrends the fairy tale became a metaphor for life in the GDR, with the Berlin Wall as the modern-day incarnation of the hedge of thorns that "surrounded and covered the entire castle, so that it was no longer visible."[21] Behind this hedge, life was stark, but simple. It allowed time for quiet contemplation, for deep and genuine friendships, even for a more sensuous and relaxed love. The prince's kiss meant an awakening to freedom but also to care and toil, to the same hectic, superficial existence that Ahrends found in the Federal Republic. In the fairy tale, after the prince "leaned over and gave [Sleeping Beauty] a kiss . . . the fire in the kitchen flared up, flickered, and cooked the meat. The roast began to sizzle again, and the cook gave the kitchen boy such a box on the ear that he let out a cry, while the maid finished plucking the chicken."[22] In other words, work defined as economic production begins again. "Waking up" means the loss of a beautiful dream:

Not to have to walk the treadmill of capital, not to have to produce, sell, consume, take care of things ASAP: that, too, is the freedom of the East. Armies of hard-working entrepreneurs, trade representatives, advertising experts were not needed here behind the hedge of thorns. Their entrepreneurship, their imagination, their fighting spirit, everything having to do with the macho ambition that lies sleeping in the primeval brain – all of that lay fallow. It was an untilled field, covered over with the most beautiful weeds, which bloomed impressively, able to reproduce themselves without interruption. Weeds that were not needed and which, if they did not suffer too much from their existence as weeds, lived happily, spreading wildly, self-satisfied, useful to no one.[23]

Ahrends even went so far as to claim that the almost "pre-industrial" mentality of the GDR might give its citizens a head start in the search for "post-industrial" forms of life which the new, unified Germany and even the world would ultimately have to acquire if it was to overcome the severe ecological problems of the twenty-first century.

Meanwhile Karl Heinz Bohrer, a professor of German literature at the University of Bielefeld and the saturnine editor of the prestigious journal *Merkur*, weighed in at the beginning of 1990 with a contribution to the reunification debate entitled "Why We Are Not a Nation – And Why We Ought to Become One." Bohrer ridiculed what he viewed as the chiliasm implicit in the concept of a third path, as well as the idea of the GDR as a Sleeping Beauty protected by a hedge of thorns. Instead, he argued that German reunification promised to fill a missing space in German national consciousness, and that the re-emergence of the German nation after almost half a century of dormancy might result in a welcome new cosmopolitanism. Finally Germany would have a national identity, and this identity would make it possible to do away with the moralistic Protestantism Bohrer saw in much of contemporary West German political culture. Unlike Heym, Ahrends and other contemporary

East German or former GDR intellectuals, Bohrer did not lose any time thinking about GDR identity; his concern was with his own half of the divided Germany, and like so many other West Germans he took for granted the utter lack of importance of the GDR. Bohrer's arguments about the re-emergence of the German nation were to provide a foundational discourse for the triumphal conservatism that emerged on the German right in the wake of reunification. This conservatism was to play an important role in German debates about the 1991 Persian Gulf War and German military policy in the former Yugoslavia.

The major West German intellectual opposing reunification was Günter Grass. In a series of blistering lectures and essays throughout most of 1990, Grass argued that Germany's nationalist past precluded any thought of reunification now or in the future. Grass returned to themes which had formed the center of the historical debates about National Socialism conducted with such vehemence in West Germany during the 1980s, in particular the 1986 debate known as the *Historikerstreit*. According to Grass, the essence of Germany's nationalist past could be summarized by the single word Auschwitz:

We will not get around Auschwitz. We should not even attempt such an act of violence, no matter how much we might wish to do so, because Auschwitz belongs to us, it is a permanent scar on our history, and it has, on the positive side, made possible an insight which might run like this: now, finally, we know ourselves.[24]

This is the voice of the literary intellectual as spokesman for the German collective superego, punishing the nation for its evil behavior in the past. Grass was suggesting that at the core of German identity was Auschwitz, and that German self-knowledge required a recognition of this fact and, consequently, permanent political division. He argued that the insight of self-recognition, so valuable after Germany's Nazi past, was now threatened by a forced reunification which would once again call forth the ghosts of the past, including, ultimately, pan-German irredentism and the call for the return of Germany's lost Eastern territories, particularly in Poland. German unity, the writer suggested, had been one of the preconditions for Auschwitz; without German unity, Auschwitz would not have happened. Therefore, Germans ought not to have the same right to self-determination that other peoples had, especially if that self-determination meant the fulfillment of what Grass referred to as a "forced trend" created by the "buying power of the West German economy – everything can be bought for hard D-Marks, even unity."[25] In Grass's view, reunification was turning what had originally been a democratic revolution in the GDR into nothing more than a revolution from above, an authoritarian restoration based purely on the ugly rule of the richest bidder. As a result, all the energy and vision created by the first successful democratic revolution on German soil was being squandered. Reunification was not the result of any genuine national feeling, Grass contended; rather, any such feeling was the artificial byproduct of the naked rule of money. What had begun as a national and international discussion about the nature of democracy, the best way to organize a nation-state, about the German past and Germany's neighbors,

has been reduced to the level of marks and pfennigs. Money has to stand in for the lack of an overarching idea. Hard currency is supposed to make up for poverty of spirit.[26]

While Grass's arguments had no effect on the actual course of events leading to German reunification on October 3, they were nevertheless powerful evidence of intellectual dissatisfaction with that course of events, suggesting that many German literary intellectuals were reluctant to give up their role as "conscience of the nation."

In a similar vein, Jürgen Habermas contended that Kohl's policy of rapid reunification threatened to destroy the tendencies toward a "postconventional," i.e. postnational identity which Habermas claimed to have perceived in West Germany prior to reunification. The West Germany of one year earlier, Habermas argued, had indeed been tending toward a non-nationalist "Verfassungspatrio- tismus" (constitutional patriotism), the rule of law and democratic procedure, and it had begun to leave behind previous ethnic and national arrogance. Now, in Habermas's view, all these achievements were threatened. Pride in Germany's democratic constitution might well soon be replaced by the one unifying factor capable of bringing together the vast disparities inside the two Germanys: the D-Mark.[27]

Both Grass and Habermas focused critically on the purely economic nature of current German nationalism, but both failed to point out that, if their analysis was correct, then this was a historic change, since previous German nationalisms, particularly in the period around the First World War, had claimed for the German spirit precisely a noneconomic motivation, assigning to the West the role of crass capitalist materialism and to Germany a spiritual and cultural mission completely foreign to purely economic concerns. Anti-materialist and anticapitalist rhetoric had previously been a major part of the ideology of German nationalism; if, at the time of German reunification, such rhetoric had now become a part of anti-nationalist discourse, while nationalist discourse happily asserted its own materialism, then what was happening was nothing less than a sea change in German ideology: the acceptance in Germany of "normal," Western standards of economic pride. The reunified Germany of today was being criticized by Grass and Habermas for precisely the same economic success that previous German national-ists had used to criticize in England; over three-quarters of a century after World War One, Germany had become a super-England, a stronghold of unashamed European capitalism.[28] As Hans Magnus Enzensberger suggested, Germans had "turned . . . into what they once accused others of being: a nation of shopkeepers."[29] From the very beginning, Chancellor Kohl's project had been the restoration of German "normality" in the Federal Republic; the events of autumn 1989 gave him the chance to make that restoration complete and end Germany's special status even in the political sphere. Small wonder that in arguing that "joylessness is the godfather of German unity," Grass was to create historical associations with previous German nationalists, such as the philososopher and academic Paul de Lagarde, who, in a similar critique of Bismarck's Second Reich, had argued: "There has never been a creation as joyless as this one."[30]

Among Grass's many fears during 1989 and 1990 was the belief that the political reunification of the German *Nation* would come about at the expense of the German *Kulturnation*. This concern was clearly expressed when Grass talked about an "understanding of the nation" as an "expanded cultural notion of our time," bringing together "the multiplicity of German culture without having to proclaim nation-state unity."[31] If, moreover, East Germany had, in the years from 1949 to 1989, come to represent a certain kind of culture lost in West Germany; if it had been the guarantor of cultural uniqueness, a kind of intellectual nature conservancy where strange and exotic species from long ago had continued to flourish, just as East German border areas and military preserves, closed to human habitation, had in fact become centers for the preservation of rare

and endangered species of plants and animals – then the reunification of Germany, if it simply meant the swallowing up of East
Germany by West Germany, did indeed pose a major problem for
West German identity also. West Germany suddenly lost its ideological Other, the specific location of its utopian hopes and its
dystopian fears.

Even arguing in favor of reunification, Bohrer nevertheless
declared that what East Germany had in store for it was the
intellectual discovery of America: hamburgers, consumer culture,
disposable packaging, the entire panoply of Western materialism
denoted in West Germany by the concept America. At the same
time Bohrer criticized the materialism of West Germany, arguing
that his country had

succumbed increasingly to the illusion that economic prosperity and
pedestrian malls, the superiority of the D-Mark and a house to the north of
Rome could serve as symbols of identity for an internationally oriented,
happy economic bourgeoisie without political ambitions.[32]

West Germany, Bohrer's argument went, was a materialist consumer
society without any spiritual or moral foundation. The paradox of
Bohrer's position was that, while he believed the GDR's collapse
would lead to East Germans' discovery of America forty years late,
he also believed that reunification would somehow also lead to the
development or reclaiming of the specifically spiritual territory of the
Nation which others saw as being preserved in East Germany
precisely *because* of its failure to Americanize. Bohrer, however, did
not seem to be aware of the contradiction inherent in his own
position.

Others feared that, quite to the contrary, the fall of East Germany
would mean the end of any culture specifically German and the
implication of all of Germany in the general international cultural
leveling associated with America. Gaus pointedly asked: "Will the
spiritual flattening of the television era . . . call to life a society in
which those who have been generally deprived of a voice in their
own affairs consume their own deprivation as a kind of entertainment?"[33] Whether or not it is a conscious reference, Gaus's critique
of the western media recalls Walter Benjamin's declaration that "the
logical result of fascism is the introduction of aesthetics into political
life," and that under fascism mankind's "self-alienation has reached
such a degree that it can experience its own destruction as an

aesthetic pleasure of the first order."[34] The implication of this parallel is that the world of western media necessarily tended toward fascism.

The Marxist Gisela Elsner saw the advent of television culture in the very revolution that had brought an end to the GDR regime itself. For her, the entire spectacle of October and November lived and breathed in the aura of the nightly television news, so that the "heroes" (Christoph Hein) demonstrating in Leipzig on Monday nights could always get home in time to see themselves on television – a self-reflexive self-consumption for which, she believed, the entire demonstration had been planned in the first place.[35] Helmut Hanke, an East German dissident generally skeptical of claims of East German cultural uniqueness, nevertheless agreed that what would emerge out of reunification would be a generalized mass consumer television culture. State support for the arts would decline, he argued, and the various niches made possible for oppositional artists in the GDR would gradually disappear. All artists would have to compete on the open market, under the naked rule of capital.[36] Likewise, the major concern of many East German artists in 1990 was that, as "the history of the GDR is coming to an end," so too the culture made possible inside the GDR was coming to an end, and with it the jobs of many artists.[37]

The negative correlation between *Macht* and *Geist* (power and spirit) in the ideology of the *Kulturnation* has led many German intellectuals, even today, to believe that, in Germany, culture and politics are irrevocably opposed to each other, and that political unity necessarily implies a cultural and human downfall. Germany's great cultural achievements, the argument goes, have all occurred at times of political disunity and powerlessness; and all of Germany's great crimes have, conversely, occurred in times of power and unity. Vestiges of these beliefs are evident in the German debate on reunification that occurred in the early 1990s. Underlying the criticism that Chancellor Kohl was trying to force a Bismarck-style unification-from-above onto a passive and willing nation, creating a national unity by dictat where none existed in fact, was the fear that this reunification might have results just as horrendous as those of the earlier, Bismarckian unification. Grass's feeling that no one was listening to him calling from the station as the German locomotive rolled toward probable disaster is, in this sense, surprisingly similar to Friedrich Nietzsche's feeling, in 1873, that he was a man out of season and out of touch with general public opinion in Germany. Grass and Nietzsche are connected to each other by their self-perception as "untimely" intellectuals opposed to the political trends of their day. In their opposition to reunification and negative perceptions of West German consumerism, many German intellectuals during the early 1990s unconsciously mimicked the anti-political critiques of German intellectuals a century earlier.

An extended quote from Nietzsche reveals that the debates about culture and nation in 1989–1990 carried powerful historical resonances. In this passage from the *Unzeitgemäße Betrachtungen* [*Untimely Meditations*], Nietzsche is referring to the triumphant Franco-Prussian war of 1870–1871 and the subsequent formation of the second German Reich:

Of all the terrible results which the last war with France is bringing in its path, perhaps the worst is a wide-spread, even general misunderstanding: the misunderstanding of public opinion and of all public opinion-makers that German culture, too, achieved a victory in that battle . . . This insanity is insidious in the highest degree . . . , because it is capable of transforming our victory into a complete defeat: into the defeat, yes, even extirpation of the German spirit in favor of the "German Reich."[38]

When East Germany's then Prime Minister Hans Modrow went to Bonn to meet with Chancellor Kohl in the middle of February, 1990, he was told by his host that East Germany would be allowed "to share directly in what the citizens of West Germany have built up and achieved in decades of continuous work." The clear implication was that, unlike their West German cousins, East Germans had not built up and achieved anything. According to Kohl, the centerpiece of the work of the West Germans was the Deutsche Mark, "one of the world's strongest, most stable and widely accepted currencies and . . . the basis of our prosperity and our economic prowess," as the Chancellor put it. Kohl defined the achievement of West Germany in purely economic terms. Modrow responded by pointing out that, while his country was certainly in need of economic assistance, East Germany nevertheless had managed to preserve certain "spiritual and cultural values" which the West should not ignore.[39] In spite of their disagreement, both leaders concurred in defining West Germany's achievement in economic and East Germany's achievement in cultural terms. The implications for this split when East Germany ceased to exist were left unstated: the end of the traditional German culture thought by so many western intellectuals to be represented by the GDR and the victory of German economics embodied in the FRG. If reunification meant a triumph of economics over culture, it should not be surprising that many German writers on both sides were less than delighted with the end of German division. Nor should it be surprising that the first important intellectual attack on the GDR was on a major cultural figure: Christa Wolf. It was, after all, in the realm of culture, not in the realm of economics, that the GDR was considered to be strong, and it was in precisely this realm that the major intellectual debate of 1990 occurred. As Markovits and Reich suggest, "culture was one of the few areas in which East Germany had something to offer united Germany."[40] The victory of the western economic system was by this time already a foregone conclusion, but in the year of German reunification there was still a powerful belief in East German cultural accomplishments, if not superiority. The attack on Wolf began to shake the foundations of that belief and tended to suggest that the GDR could point neither to economic nor to cultural greatness in self-justification.

When, one year prior to the collapse of the Wall, Walser had made his controversial call for a new discussion of the German Question, his major reason was that, without the GDR, the Federal Republic was spiritually incomplete, lacking in that sense of history which had been preserved in the GDR. Walser argued that, inside the GDR, it had been more possible to live with things as they were in themselves, rather than with words and symbols. In the GDR, history had been preserved; in the FRG, history had been bulldozed over to make way for the next shopping mall. The major question for cultural life in Germany after the collapse of the GDR and the reunification of the country was whether reunification represented a fusion of the strengths of both countries or, rather, the loss of whatever strengths had existed in the GDR and the FRG and the fusion of the two countries' weaknesses instead. If the Federal Republic was incomplete without the GDR, did reunification mean a healing of Walser's "wound called Germany," or, rather, the permanent loss of a necessary part of cultural identity? What was left of the cultural history of the postwar period? It was singularly appropriate that the most talked-about German book of 1990 carried the title: *What remains.*

CHAPTER 3

Literature and politics

> But now the men are gone
> To the Indies,
> From that breezy spit of land
> And hillsides of grapes, where
> The Dordogne descends
> Toward the majestic Garonne
> And the two flow out
> As one wide sea. But memory
> Is taken and given by the ocean,
> And the eyes of love do not waver in their gaze,
> But poets establish what remains.
>
> Friedrich Hölderlin, from "Remembrance"[1]

In the summer of 1990 Christa Wolf published a short book entitled *Was bleibt*. Because of its publication only a few months prior to German reunification, its focus on the political life of a writer in East Germany, and the savage attacks that were immediately directed against it, the book and the debate it gave rise to became a kind of ground zero for German literary reunification, embodying and prefiguring many of the debates that were subsequently to emerge about the complex relationship between literature and politics in Germany. If Wolf's novella was a first attempt to locate the position of the writer politically at the moment of reunification, the attacks on *Was bleibt* offered a completely different view of the relationship between literature and politics in a reunified Germany. As the novella's title suggested, Wolf seemed to be arguing for an essential continuity between the antifascist political commitment of the postwar past and the possible literary developments of the future. Wolf's critics argued instead for a radical break and a new beginning, a "zero hour" that would be analogous to the radical discontinuity associated in German culture with the end of the Second World War in 1945.

The relatively innocuous and mundane subject matter of this short book contrasts wildly with the fuss that was made about it after its publication. The novella relates one day in the life of a writer in East Berlin, from the time she wakes up in the morning to the time she goes to bed in the evening. "I brushed my teeth, combed my hair, employed various sprays unthinkingly, albeit conscientiously, got dressed, same things as yesterday, slacks, sweater . . ."[2] During the course of the day the woman, who bears more than a passing resemblance to Wolf herself, mostly remains in her apartment, thinking and writing. She also receives a visit from a younger woman writer. Toward the end of the day she visits her husband in hospital and then goes to give a public reading to a large audience. This is hardly the stuff of which revolutions and book burnings are made.

As innocuous as its plot may sound, *Was bleibt* soon became the eye of a major literary storm. The very writer who had previously seemed to embody the best of East German culture now came, in the minds of some critics, to embody all the faults of the old regime. What critics objected to was less the personal depiction of one day in an author's life than the picture of the East German secret police, the Staatssicherheit or Stasi, that the book touched on. If the 1987 *Störfall* had used one day in the life of its female narrator as a way of reflecting on problems in high-technology modern society, *Was bleibt* used a similar narrative construct partly as a way of reflecting on life in an authoritarian society in which the secret police were gradually beginning to dominate not only individual people's lives but also society itself. Such a reflection on the secret police was not entirely new for Wolf. In *Kassandra* she had allowed the figure of Eumelos and his Trojan praetorian guard to stand in for the Stasi; ultimately Eumelos becomes a kind of dictatorial usurper, replacing the open power of the state with a hidden, subversive power that contributes to Troy's destruction.[3] However as critical as it was, *Kassandra* had still treated the Stasi problem allegorically; it was possible for readers to fail to notice contemporary references in a book about the Trojan War and treat its material purely as one woman writer's feminist reappropriation of a 3,000-year-old myth at the root of Western civilization. In *Was bleibt* such a reading was impossible, since the references to the Stasi were no longer allegorical but direct and the material patently autobiographical. Wolf never used the words "Stasi" or "Staatssicherheit"; instead she referred to her tormentors as "three young gentlemen . . . sitting for hours on end in a white Wartburg directly opposite our window."[4] Nevertheless, Wolf's readers could not fail to recognize who the "young gentlemen" were: agents of the East German secret police. With the publication of *Was bleibt*, Wolf made a significant departure from the humanistic, convergent literature of the late 1960s through the 1980s and returned to specific GDR themes and problems. In a sense, *Was bleibt*, published at the end of the GDR's political existence, thus marked the beginning of a new GDR literature, now for the first time free to address directly and without the use of allegory the problems and failings of GDR society. And partly because of its return to specifically East German themes, *Was bleibt* provoked a literary debate that had implications for the future of all literature in a reunified Germany.

The book's reception was complicated, however, by the fact that Wolf had written the first draft of *Was bleibt* long before its 1990 publication date, namely in 1979, at about the same time that she was beginning her work on *Kassandra*. The late 1970s were a difficult time for many East German writers. After Wolf Biermann's forced exile from the GDR in 1976, a number of East German literary figures joined together to issue a letter of protest against the singer's removal, and Christa Wolf became one of several prominent writers to sign her name to that letter. Any writers who publicly sympathized with Biermann after the 1976 uproar were subject to government retribution and to surveillance and chicanery by the Stasi. As an open supporter of Biermann and one of the most influential writers in the GDR, Wolf was particularly subject to Stasi persecution. Thus her 1979 narrative *Was bleibt* was a reflection both of troubled times in the GDR and of Wolf's own problems with the Stasi.[5]

However, Wolf had not published her 1979 book in 1979 or 1980. Rather, she had waited a decade and then revised the novella in November 1989, during the month of the demonstration on the Alexanderplatz and the opening of the Berlin Wall. It was the ten-year delay between the book's creation and its publication that provoked the harsh criticism when *Was bleibt* finally appeared in the summer of 1990, during the strange twilight period of GDR history between the March, 1990 East German election victory of the conservative coalition Alliance for Germany and Germany's reunification at midnight on October 3, 1990. Wolf's (mainly West German) critics accused her of cowardice for not having published the novella immediately after she wrote it. Had *Was bleibt* appeared in 1979 or 1980, the critics argued, it would have been a devastating indictment of an authoritarian regime and might possibly have helped to ignite a protest movement against that regime. Ten years later, however, the book had lost all possibility of direct intervention in political events, since the East German regime had already collapsed. To publish *Was bleibt* in 1990 was not just pointless, Wolf's critics argued, it was also mendacious, because it implied claim to a heroic nonconformism that the author did not, in fact, represent. The main character of the novella was portrayed as a victim of the Stasi and, by implication, of the East German regime, when in fact Wolf had been the GDR's most celebrated literary personality, argued the critics. By its very existence *Was bleibt* seemed to suggest that Wolf had been a sharp critic of the East German regime, when in reality she had been one of its major literary supporters, herself an avowed Communist and erstwhile member of the Central Committee of the Socialist Unity Party (SED). Ulrich Greiner, writing for *Die Zeit*, was the most extreme in his attack on Wolf. He argued that far from being an opponent of the East German regime Wolf had in fact embodied and epitomized that regime. "There is no point in pretending we don't know who's speaking and what he is speaking about," wrote Greiner. "It is Christa Wolf, it is the SED-state." In Greiner's vision, Wolf and the East German Communist regime were one and the same entity. Wolf was a "Staatsdichterin," a poet of the state.[6]

The accusations against Wolf were twofold. On the one hand she was accused of cowardice for having waited to publish her book until the regime it criticized no longer existed – for beating a dead horse, as it were. On the other hand the writer stood accused of actually having supported East Germany's regime; of having herself been a Communist; of having chosen to remain within the German Democratic Republic and work for the reform rather than the abandonment of the Communist system. Like so many of the East German revolutionaries of 1989, Wolf had insisted on her status as a "Hierbleiber," a person who remained in rather than departed from the GDR. If the title of Wolf's novella could be understood as a rhetorical question, part of the answer to that question was that Christa Wolf herself had remained in the GDR. The novella's title was also a play on Friedrich Hölderlin's famous statement: "Was bleibet aber, stiften die Dichter" – "But poets establish what remains." As such the title of Wolf's novella seemed to suggest that if nothing else, literature itself remained of lasting worth in a world of constant change. Hence the title *Was bleibt* was both a question and a statement. It could be interpreted to mean both "What remains?" and "That which remains:" And the novella was also partly its own answer: *Was bleibt* remained.

In a sense the first accusation against Wolf was already implied by the second accusation, because the writer's failure to publish *Was bleibt* in 1979 occurred precisely because she had chosen to remain and publish her work in the GDR. A 1979 publication of *Was bleibt* would have been impossible inside the GDR; Wolf would have had to go to a West German publisher and allow the book to be published in the West. Such a publication in the West might possibly have resulted in Wolf's forced departure from the GDR. There was one major example of an East German writer who had chosen a course of action similar to the one Wolf's critics evidently preferred for her: Stefan Heym, who lived in East Germany but published his books exclusively in West Germany because of their subversive, anti-regime content. For all other writers who had chosen to criticize the East German regime so directly, the result was a move from East to West Germany and the abandonment of any hope of reform from within.

And yet even if Wolf had chosen to publish her book in West Germany and not been forced to leave the GDR, it is unclear how such a West German publication might have affected literary debate inside East Germany. One of the reasons for Wolf's effectiveness as a medium for debate and reflection in the GDR was that her books were available to ordinary East German citizens in book stores and libraries – although publication runs rarely satisfied pent-up reader demand, and Wolf's books invariably sold out. An exclusively West German publication of *Was bleibt* in 1979 would have meant that Wolf's book was available only to those who had regular access to Western publications. Such an outcome was clearly not what the author intended. As she depicted at the end of her story, in which the autobiographical narrator comes face to face with her readers at an open public forum, the most important aspect of writing for her was precisely a dialog with her readers, i.e. specifically with the East German public. A West German publication of *Was bleibt* would have meant the end of that dialog. Hence the essence of the accusation against Christa Wolf was that she had remained in the GDR and attempted through her work to effect a dialog there rather than moving to West Germany and criticizing the GDR from abroad.

In many ways, the debate about Christa Wolf that emerged in 1990 echoed the debates that had taken place almost half a century earlier in post-Nazi Germany about the relative merits of the "outer" and the "inner" emigration during the Third Reich – i.e., to what extent writers were morally obligated to leave or remain in a dictatorship.[7] A great many East German writers had chosen or been forced to choose "outer" emigration. The debate about Christa Wolf reflected a larger split in German society between those East Germans who had moved to the West and those who had chosen to remain in the GDR. For many writers who had left the GDR, staying in that country meant conforming to an intolerable political system; for many writers who had remained in the GDR, leaving the country meant abandoning all hope for positive reform from within.

The American sociologist Albert Hirschman has characterized the dilemma between leaving and staying as one between "exit" and "voice." Hirschman suggests that ultimately the GDR was impaled upon the horns of precisely this dilemma; in the end, both those who stayed and those who fled contributed to the collapse of the GDR regime, and neither group can be credited with singular agency in effecting political change. As Hirschman notes, "in some momentous constellations . . . exit can cooperate with voice, voice can emerge from exit, and exit can reinforce voice."[8] The final years of the GDR's existence were clearly such a momentous constellation. Hirschman's presentation suggests that Wolf's critics were creating a false opposition between two propositions that in fact formed a dialectical unity.

This exit-voice dilemma was unique to East German writers. No other country in Europe had a similar problem, because no other country was split between a capitalist West and a Communist East, thus forcing writers to choose between two opposing social systems. A Polish writer who wanted to live and publish in the country where her native language was spoken had no choice but to remain in Poland, even though Poland after 1945 was a Communist state. The same holds true for writers in all other European East bloc countries except the GDR. Hence writers in those other countries were never subject to angry accusations against them simply because they had chosen to live and publish in their homeland. East German writers, however, had both the privilege and the dilemma of choice: they could live and publish in a German-speaking country in either the East or the West. For this reason any writer who chose to remain in the GDR was potentially subject to the accusation that she was pro-Communist.

One of the subtler variations of the accusation against Christa Wolf and writers like her who had chosen to remain in the GDR was that by providing a relatively harmless, unpolitical outlet for critical energy and debate they acted as a kind of pressure valve ensuring that no explosion occurred, and thus strengthened the East German regime. It was not so much that such writers were, as Ulrich Greiner had suggested, identical with the regime, as that they helped to support the regime precisely through their criticism, which provided the semblance but not the reality of open public debate. Such an accusation was less unfair to writers like Christa Wolf and also at least partially accurate, because it took into account the situation of literature in an authoritarian regime. And yet if critique was just as complicit in authoritarianism as non-critique, then genuinely complicitous GDR writers like Hermann Kant were conveniently exculpated, and the very possibility of resistance or opposition was thrown open to question. Moreover, the GDR was not the only country in the world where a critical literature helped to "soften" and humanize an authoritarian regime. And was it really fair to suggest that such humanization was morally wrong? In many ways, the critique of nonconformist GDR writers who had remained inside their country was similar to Marxist critiques of private charity as a prop for exploitative capitalism or conservative critiques of détente as a support for Communist totalitarianism: they were based on the assumption that absolute opposition and apocalyptic collapse were preferable to gradual change. And yet the GDR's demise had occurred in a relatively non-violent, controlled way, partly as a result of restrained but firm critique from within. That a violent revolution would have been preferable is at the very least open to serious doubt, and more probably historically naive, especially given the presence of Soviet troops and nuclear missiles on GDR soil.

Ultimately, the implications of the Christa Wolf controversy went beyond the specific role of literature in the GDR and writers' individual responsibility in a dictatorship. As the debate developed, it was the entirety of postwar German literature that came into question. As different as the two postwar German states were, writers in both states enjoyed a prestige unknown in some other industrial countries, and they frequently engaged in explicit or implicit political dialog and activism. Parkes has suggested that "it would in fact be hard to imagine the political life of the Federal Republic without the participation" of literary intellectuals, and that writers' engagement in politics helped postwar West Germany in "the need to confront the past, the establishment of democracy and the need to preserve peace."[9] In the West, writers were an important part of an open, democratic public sphere, whereas in the East writers took on the role of substitute for a missing democratic public sphere. However, in both postwar German states writers played a significant public political role. Thus the collapse of the GDR and the perceived failure of its literary intellectuals to effect democratic change provided an opportunity for critics inside West Germany who disliked the left-liberal political interventions of some writers.

Increasingly, such critics began to equate the role of writers in both the GDR and the FRG and, in particular, to attack any kind of political role for literature at all. Literature, in their view, should be a purely aesthetic game unencumbered by the heavy and oafish moralism of political commitment. The political role of literature in the two Germanys, critics argued, was a relic from the unhappy authoritarian past, and it should therefore be discarded as writers in both Germanys integrated themselves into a normal western democracy. The essence of true art, they argued, was its autonomy from the competing spheres of politics, morality, and economics, and a politically committed literature was inartistic and inadequate. Summing up these critiques, T. J. Reed correctly notes that in 1990 "the new doctrine was that all writing or critical judgement which has politics or principles as its motive was to be out; 'aesthetic' values were to be in."[10]

Karl Heinz Bohrer spent much of the 1980s inveighing against West German culture as ugly, provincial, and moralistic. In his view, true aesthetic modernism was characterized by complete lack of concern for morality. His literary heroes were the French decadents and the English aestheticists, as well as the one German writer whom he believed to be a pure representative of what he saw as the essentially amoral modernist tradition: Ernst Jünger. These writers, Bohrer argued, had fruitfully experimented with evil as an aesthetic phenomenon, from Charles Baudelaire's *Fleurs du mal* through Gustave Flaubert's *Salammbô* and the decadence of Joris Karl Huysmans' *A Rebours* to the surrealist experiments of André Breton, Paul Eluard, Louis Aragon and Jean Cocteau up to Antonin Artaud's theatre of cruelty. In Germany however, so influenced by the Protestant Reformation and a religious pietism that emphasized the individual's personal relationship with God, the carefree aestheticization of evil characteristic of European modernism had never been allowed to blossom, Bohrer claimed. He went on to suggest that after the Second World War and the Holocaust the taboo on pure aestheticism had become even stronger because literary figures, particularly those associated with the influential Group 47 created by Hans Werner Richter in 1947, saw their role as fundamentally moral. Bohrer wrote: "The real evil, fascism, favored this strange dialectic so much that, since 1945 the long established taboo on literary evil has almost necessarily become the German method."[11] Bohrer called all of West German literature a kind of "permanent theodicy" in which the compulsion to moralism had banished the specifically aesthetic dimension of literature. The "permanent theodicy" of West German postwar culture was, Bohrer claimed, quite evident "in the example of German postwar literature under the aegis of a moral commitment that still predominates." He argued that the most powerful strand of postwar West German literature, characterized by a desire to come to terms with the unhappy German past, necessarily failed aesthetically as a result of undue moralism. "The work of Heinrich Böll has become representative of this situation," wrote Bohrer, but in fact almost all postwar West German literature and most West German authors suffered from the same problem: "For decades they have all been writing morally and politically committed novels and stories whose function lies in a very specific form of secularized moral uplift."[12] Bohrer was clearly attacking what he saw as literature's role in establishing a moralistic, nay-saying national superego that prevented both the unhindered enjoyment of aesthetic pleasure and the establishment of a "normal" nation.

Bohrer wrote this critique of postwar West German literature years before German reunification. His argument ignored those parts of the German tradition that were impossible to describe simply as "moralist" – particularly movements and writers like Friedrich Nietzsche, but also the Dadaists, the Expressionists, the early Bertolt Brecht, and Gottfried Benn – and it also treated all of postwar German-language literature as similar, when in fact writers such as Peter Handke had long since rejected a literature of political and moral commitment and defiantly declared their adherence to an "ivory tower" literature. Nevertheless, Bohrer's argument that the main strand of postwar West German literature had addressed questions of personal and public morality in the wake of the horrors of the Third Reich was doubtlessly correct. However, in spite of Bohrer's negative assessment of this moral rigor, it was not entirely clear what was supposed to be so terrible about trying to face difficult aspects of the German past. Bohrer was correct in noting that writers in many other Western nations were not similarly preoccupied by problems of the past, but he seemed to overlook the obvious fact that Germany's past was indeed irrevocably different. Such weaknesses did much to lessen the impact of Bohrer's critique in the 1980s. In the context of German reunification, however, his critique of politically committed literature won a new significance and power that it had originally lacked.

The collapse of the GDR and the debate about Christa Wolf's political role made it possible for critics who disliked politically committed literature in the West to associate the two very different societies by comparing East German and West German writers' attempts to come to terms with the Nazi past and, on the basis of such comparisons, to condemn the entire project of a politically committed West German literature. What had originally developed as a debate specific to the circumstances of the GDR and the dilemma of exit or voice thus gradually widened into a debate about all of postwar German culture, particularly in *West* Germany. The most influential proponent of such a rejection of West German literature was the critic Frank Schirrmacher of the conservative *Frankfurter Allgemeine Zeitung*. Profoundly influenced by Bohrer's 1980s critiques of West German culture, Schirrmacher declared that the literature of the Federal Republic had long since frozen into an empty moralism that exactly corresponded to the moralistic antifascism of East German writers like Christa Wolf. He suggested that West German literature was a kind of "social-psychological organ," the "instrument and mirror of the collective consciousness," indeed a "production site of West German identity," or, elsewhere, "one of the production centers of Federal Republican consciousness." Not only this, but just as people like Christa Wolf had helped to create a false legitimacy for the German Democratic Republic by producing good literature in an evil state, so too the literature of the Federal

Republic had helped to legitimate postwar society in West Germany: "It was not just the literature of the GDR that was supposed to legitimate a society and give it new traditions; the literature of the Federal Republic also felt this calling and carried it out conscientiously."

What went unsaid in this critique was that, presumably, the literature of the Federal Republic had helped to legitimate a relatively benevolent postwar West German democracy, whereas the literature of the GDR had helped to legitimate the SED dictatorship. Even if one accepted Schirrmacher's unforgiving view of the role of writers in the GDR, such acceptance did not necessarily imply a corresponding rejection of the role of writers in West German society. There is surely a difference between legitimation of an open, democratic society and legitimation of a dictatorship. Schirrmacher's parallel between West and East German writers logically implied an unacceptable parallel between West and East German society. In spite of this flaw, Schirrmacher insisted that the collapse of the GDR and the reunification of Germany meant a fundamental break in German history and the end of the moralistic Federal Republic and its politically committed literature. "The literature of the FRG became forty-three years old. Just like the literature of the GDR, it now faces its death," he declared grandly in an article timed to appear during the 1990 Frankfurt Book Fair.[13] It was probably not a coincidence that the article appeared on the last day of the existence of the GDR, a day that ended with German reunification: the timing seemed to underline the finality of Schirrmacher's pronouncement, and to proclaim that the newly unified Germany would have a new and different literature.

If young critics like Gustav René Hocke had, after the Second World War and the Hitler dictatorship, argued against an aestheticized literary "calligraphy" which they held partially responsible for the German disaster, and in favor of a politically committed realist literature which they hoped would help to usher in a more democratic Germany, critics like Schirrmacher and Bohrer were now arguing for a turn-around in which the emphasis would be on aestheticized "calligraphy" rather than politicized content. Schirrmacher's argument was echoed by Greiner, who transformed Max Weber's political distinction between an *ethics* of responsibility (Verantwortungsethik) and an *ethics* of conviction (Gesinnungsethik) to criticize an *aesthetics* of conviction (Gesinnungsästhetik). Weber

had argued that a pure ethics of conviction risked a failure to come
to terms with the real world, while an unadulterated ethics of
responsibility risked degenerating into Machiavellian power politics.[14] Ignoring Weber's criticisms of an ethics of responsibility
devoid of moral conviction as well as Weber's pragmatic emphasis
on coming to terms with the real world by creating a difficult
synthesis between conviction on the one hand and a sense of
responsibility on the other, Greiner bizarrely criticized an aesthetics
of conviction precisely for having too much concern with the real
world and not enough concern for the purely aesthetic. Art, Greiner
believed, should be above politics. How such a non-political literature might promote responsibility was a secret that Greiner left
unexplained. Meanwhile Bohrer, who had initiated the aestheticist
rejection of politically committed West German literature during the
1980s, used the pages of his journal *Merkur* to declare that with
German reunification Germany had entered the postmodern
Western world in which aesthetics is the primary category of human
existence.[15] Bohrer's almost monomaniacal claim for the importance
of aesthetics implied, of course, that even aestheticism had political
undertones: how, after all, could politics remain unconcerned with
the primary category of human existence? Bohrer did not seem to
notice, or seek to explain, this apparent contradiction.

The critique of politically engaged left-liberal authors articulated
in 1990 was by no means new. Bohrer himself had first developed his
aestheticist arguments over the course of the 1980s, and in the late
1970s Helmut Schelsky's attack on politically engaged writers in *Die
Arbeit tun die anderen* [The Others Do the Work] (1977) had touched on
substantially similar issues, criticizing supposedly power-hungry but
lazy left-wing intellectuals.[16] Schelsky, in turn, had been preceded by
the conservative philosopher Arnold Gehlen, who, in *Moral und
Hypermoral: Eine pluralistische Ethik* [Morality and Hypermorality: A
Pluralist Ethics] (1969), had already polemicized against an ethics of
conviction, specifying that the sociological bearers of the oppressive
national conscience, far from being a disadvantaged group, were in
fact the "privileged classes" of "the writers and the editors, the
theologicians, philosophers, and sociologists, i.e. ideologized groups"
who did not have to bear direct political responsibility for their
actions.[17] Significantly, Gehlen claimed that these ideologically
dominant groups were infected by a feminist "womens' thinking,
oriented toward the protection of life, peace, prosperity, and

security" within the womb of the family, not toward the manly virtues of military service, justice, and the state. Gehlen argued that because these literary intellectuals "control the mass media, their long-term influence cannot be overestimated"; and "German intellectuals believe themselves to be a ruling class."[18] Parkes's critique of Schelsky probably applies equally to Gehlen, Bohrer, and others who criticize politically engaged literary intellectuals in Germany: "he is only opposed to those intellectuals who do not share his conservative views."[19] This may be one reason why Bohrer was apparently unable to recognize the contradictory nature of his call for a triumph of pure aestheticism. What was new about the situation in 1990 were not the attacks on left-liberal literary intellectuals themselves but rather the collapse of the GDR and the perception that this collapse significantly weakened the position of left-liberal writers in both Germanys.

The debate about the function of literature that emerged with criticisms of Wolf's *Was bleibt* strongly paralleled an earlier German debate, the so-called *Historikerstreit* of the 1980s.[20] Whereas the 1990 *Literaturstreit* (literature debate) dealt primarily with the relationship between literature and politics, the 1986 *Historikerstreit* had addressed the relationship between politics and history. Both debates thus revolved around politics; and, additionally, both addressed the role of the historical past in the creation of the political present. As Claudia Mayer-Iswandy has suggested, the *Literaturstreit* was "structurally a replay of the Historikerstreit."[21] However neither Mayer-Iswandy nor any of the other commentators who have noted the similarity between the two debates has specified the precise nature of the similarity, partly because they have failed to see in the *Historikerstreit* anything but a right-wing power grab.[22] Because of the striking parallels between the two debates, I will briefly review the central argument of the *Historikerstreit* somewhat more thoroughly than other scholars have before returning to the similar arguments of the *Literaturstreit*.

Although, as H. J. Hahn claims, a right-wing critique of Enlightenment values certainly played a role in the *Historikerstreit*, this critique was by no means the central element in the debate, and it was certainly not, as Hahn implies, the connecting link between the *Historikerstreit* and the *Literaturstreit*.[23] At the center of the 1986 debate had been Ernst Nolte's claim that the memory of Germany's "Third Reich," and in particular the memory of the Holocaust, was being used for moral and political purposes by a younger generation "in the age-old battle with 'their fathers.' "[24] Quite aside from any of the other controversial political and historical claims in the *Historikerstreit*, Nolte's primary concern was the uncanny presence of the German past, which he referred to in the very title of one of his major articles as "the past that does not want to pass away" ("Vergangenheit, die nicht vergehen will"). Nolte posited a normal process of historical sedimentation and increasing abstraction which allowed for a relatively unemotional, scientific accounting for and explanation of past events. As the past passes beyond the life horizons of current generations into the realm of forgetting, it ceases to have existential political or personal meaning and comes instead into the realm of impartial, disinterested scholarship. The implication was that forgetting is just as important as memory, and that in West Germany the natural process of forgetting had somehow, unnaturally, been impeded. Instead of passing into an oblivion that would allow for impartial scholarly inquiry, Nolte argued, Germany's National Socialist past was ever more *present*, ever more part of political debate:

The National Socialist past is . . . evidently not subject to this attrition, to this weakening; on the contrary, it seems to be getting stronger and more alive all the time . . . , as a past which has in fact established itself as a present, and which hangs over the present like a sword of judgment.[25]

Nolte's complaint was a distant echo of a prediction that had been made almost forty years earlier by Alfred Döblin, who, in surveying what he called "the literary situation" of immediate postwar Germany, had predicted that as the Nazi past receded ever further into chronological distance, its profound spiritual and moral implications for the future would become ever more "present" in German literature and culture. Other peoples and nations would long remember the Nazi dictatorship, Döblin wrote,

But it will etch itself into the consciousness of the Germans even more strongly, and with increasing strength. Because things of this sort need time and distance. Only slowly will the Germans come to grasp what happened there, what they became caught up in, and what was capable of coming into being in their midst: shuddering in horror, they will use the word "demonic" to describe themselves, and they will not come to closure on this.[26]

Nolte's 1986 complaints about the ongoing presence of the German past suggest that Döblin's 1947 prediction had come true with a vengeance. Nolte's central argument favored a disinterested approach to history: what is sometimes referred to as a "historicization of history," in which what is past is acknowledged as no longer having a significant impact on or meaning for the present – a kind of normalization of Germany's relationship to its own past.[27]

What Christa Wolf's antagonists in the 1990 *Literaturstreit* were arguing for was substantially similar: a normalization of literary and aesthetic standards and an escape from the burden of coming to terms with the difficult German past in literature. Schirrmacher, Bohrer, and Greiner wanted the nineteenth-century aestheticists' *l'art pour l'art*, while Nolte had wanted a kind of *l'histoire pour l'histoire*.[28] An increasingly normal Germany needed a normal history and a normal literature. And "normal" meant, specifically, an end to the supposedly unhealthy obsessions with the German past that had contributed so powerfully to the politicization and liberalization of German literature – and of German historiography – during the postwar period. If the German "zero hour" of 1945 had marked the road toward a politically engaged and active literature, then the new "zero hour" of 1989/1990, as envisioned by critics like Bohrer, Schirrmacher and Greiner, was to mark an erasure of that postwar political engagement and a return to "normal" aestheticist quiescence.

What is particularly noteworthy about this literary debate is the unquestioned emphasis of both sides on the power of literature to shape a society. If academic critics like Jochen Vogt praised West German literature for its role in helping to create a democratic polity,[29] other critics like Schirrmacher mocked West German literature as a factory for the production of West German consciousness. But even in attacking the supposed German specificity of a politically committed literature, Schirrmacher betrayed his own very German point of view by according to literature a role and function that even the most imperious American critic would hardly have dared to claim for literature in the United States. Schirrmacher's description of writers as "one of the production centers of Federal Republican consciousness" was not significantly different, semantically, from Stalin's description of writers as "engineers of the human soul." That the conservative champion of aestheticism could share a central assumption with the Communist dictator shows that both were, at different times and in different circumstances, working with a framework in which literature was accorded central importance in human consciousness. If even their harshest critics saw German writers in this way, then it was no wonder that writers and their critics continued to appear regularly in the nation's newspapers, magazines, and television shows, as well as in books and literary journals. The literary debate surrounding German reunification provided powerful evidence that in spite of the Federal Republic's increasing Westernization and postmodernism, literature still played a profound role in German national consciousness in both Germanys, even for the critics now attacking that role in the hope of achieving a literary "normalization" in the future reunified Germany. Andreas Huyssen has suggested that the attack on Christa Wolf may be an ironic "testimony to the strength of the ties between aesthetic and political discourses in Germany."[30] The irony is that the very critics who complained about the strength of the ties between the literary and the political in postwar Germany were nevertheless forced to accept, indeed presuppose the continuing existence of those strong ties. Indeed, one could argue that literary critics like Bohrer and Schirrmacher faced a structural problem: since their own prestige as critics depended on a continuing acceptance of literature as a privileged discourse in Germany, they depended symbiotically on the very writers they criticized – and vice versa. This dilemma suggested that any relocation of literature in post-1989 German national consciousness would be highly problematic, if not impossible. The path toward "normalization" was fraught with contradictions.

The literary debates connected with German reunification had moved from a specific criticism of Christa Wolf to a generalized criticism of GDR writers and on to a broad-based attack on postwar culture and politically committed literature in West Germany – what Emmerich has called a battle "for the power of cultural definition" in the new Germany.[31] Meanwhile, however, Wolf's focus on her relationship to and problems with the Stasi suggested that, at least in East Germany, the idea of an autonomous art had been completely illusory. Indeed, the debate about Christa Wolf presaged a major battle soon to emerge about literature and the Stasi in the GDR.

CHAPTER 4

Literature and the Stasi

THE ONLY ONES WHO AREN'T WITH THE STASI ARE THE ONES
WHO ARE WITH IT.

Rainer Schedlinski[1]

AUTHORS AS STASI

Even before German reunification officially occurred on October 3,
1990, debates about the role of literature in the German Democratic
Republic began to center around the problem of the national
Ministry for State Security (Staatssicherheit or "Stasi" for short) and
its influence on East German literature. As early as 1990, Leipzig
writer Erich Loest, who had emigrated to the FRG in 1981 and had
managed to acquire some of his own Stasi files via friends in citizens'
committees, decided to publish them in book form as *Der Zorn des
Schafes* [The Rage of the Sheep] to demonstrate the extent of
personal spying and betrayal in the GDR under the old regime.[2]
Reiner Kunze, a writer who had left the GDR in 1977, also published
a book based on his Stasi files, revealing in *Deckname "Lyrik"*
[Codename "Lyric"] that Ibrahim Böhme, one of the founders of
the East German SPD, had spied and informed on him for the
Stasi.[3] In *Was bleibt*, Christa Wolf reflected not only on her own
persecution by the Stasi but also on the vast influence the Stasi had
on East German society through spying, informing, betraying, and
threatening. Large numbers of East Germans worked for the Stasi as
either official agents or so-called "Informelle Mitarbeiter" (informal
collaborators) or IMs. In one of her story's many internal mono-
logues, Wolf's autobiographical narrator reflects on the fate of those
fellow citizens whose job it was to spy on their friends and neighbors:

A steadily growing swarm of people who had to resign themselves to
working in the shadows. The word "shadow" got lodged in my mind; I

wrote it down on a scrap of paper. The occupation of large sections of the population is relegated to the shadows. I saw crowds of people sinking into a deep shadow. Their lot did not seem enviable to me.[4]

If huge numbers of people were working in positions that could not even be talked about, then society itself was somehow split in two. For every open, official act or agency there was a hidden, secret act or agency whose job it was to keep the first, more public act or agency under control. And behind the first agency and the second agency, perhaps there was a third and a fourth and a fifth agency, each agency watching the other agency in a crazy-mirror world of shadows reflected and refracted infinitely. In the paranoid words of the poet and Stasi informer Sascha Anderson, a major figure in the avant-garde literary scene that had developed in East Berlin during the 1980s,

> every satellite has a killer satellite
> every satellite has a killer satellite
> every satellite has a killer satellite
>
> every day has a night
> every tank has a bazooka
>
> every first program has a second program
> every second program has a third program
> every third program has a fourth program
> every fourth program has a fifth program[5]

Although these lines were published as part of Anderson's first major volume in 1982, appropriately entitled *Jeder Satellit hat einen Killersatelliten* [Every Satellite Has a Killer Satellite], they painted a picture of infinite regression that exactly fit the Stasi world. Rainer Schedlinski, another poet subsequently revealed to be a Stasi informer, had also painted the picture of an unending labyrinth of betrayal in the mid-1980s, long before his Stasi activities became known:

> . . . where is the way
> out of the labyrinth here everything
> is every agent a double
> agent and almost everything re
> versed like an untouch
> able phantom . . .[6]

Unbekown to their colleagues and many admirers, both Anderson and Schedlinski had long since been working for the Stasi under pseudonyms like "David Menzer," "Fritz Müller," "Peters," and "Gerhard", as moles in the avant-garde literary scene. In the fall of 1991, Wolf Biermann accused Anderson of having worked for the Stasi against his fellow poets and writers throughout the 1980s.[7] Biermann's accusation, which subsequently proved to be true, caused a lengthy controversy – a second *Literaturstreit* – in the newly reunified Germany about the influence of the Stasi over East German literature. Soon a number of other significant East German writers were "outed," ultimately including Schedlinski; the playwright Heiner Müller, who cynically acknowledged that he had started a nonconspiratorial[8] dialog with the Stasi in the 1980s because the Stasi, in his opinion, was the only agency with which one could seriously discuss the present and future situation of the GDR; Christa Wolf herself, revealed to have engaged in nonconspiratorial dialog with Stasi agents for three years during the late 1950s and early 1960s when she was just getting started as a literary figure; and Monika Maron, who, from 1976 to 1978, had agreed to report to the Stasi on the activities of West German citizens with whom she came in contact.[9]

One of the outcomes of the Stasi debate was the passage of a liberal freedom of information law in Germany concerning Stasi documents. As of January 1, 1992, the law granted citizens general access to their personal Stasi files. Henceforth, in principle, anyone was allowed to look at her Stasi file, and at the beginning of January 1992 a great many people did so. Along with Stasi headquarters in East Berlin's Normannenstraße, Stasi records and offices now became part of a Stasi archive informally named after its chief, the East German Protestant pastor and former oppositionist Joachim Gauck; the "Gauck-Behörde" (Gauck Agency) became, in 1992, a kind of literary salon in which former dissident writers met and chatted while looking over files which resembled badly-written modernist novels in which they themselves were the main characters. Klaus Schlesinger described his own almost comical encounter with his files thus:

Fortunately I did not remain alone for long in the reading room. My former wife Bettina Wegner, with whom I share the operative file "Writer," soon joined me. Then came the Heyms, Inge and Stefan, and in the last week even Kurt Bartsch.[10]

Everyone who was anyone had their own lengthy Stasi file. As one joke ran, the only thing worse than finding out that the Stasi had spent years spying on you was finding out that it had not.

East German writers were not the only national figures affected by the Stasi controversy. The names of important German politicians – including Manfred Stolpe, Lothar de Maizière, Ibrahim Böhme, and Wolfgang Schnur – were swept into the debate as prominently as the names of German writers. In the midst of these revelations about its power, the Stasi became a synechdoche for the tyranny of the GDR itself. The identification of the part with the whole sometimes led to gross exaggerations, as when the normally accurate American journalist Jane Kramer wrote: "With three hundred thousand informers, the Stasi was not so much a mirror of East Germany; to a large extent, it *was* East Germany," as if a one to fifty-three ratio in any way justified such an exaggeration.[11] The grand master of paranoid exaggeration about the Stasi and its power was the pundit Henryk M. Broder, who, also in 1992, made the preposterous claim that the collapse of the GDR had been the Stasi's greatest success rather than its greatest failure. Broder insisted that the Stasi was all-knowing and all-powerful, and that the revolution which brought their own power to an end was the most Machiavellian trick of the GDR's former leaders.

Why should the Stasi, possessing all information about past and future happenings in the country, equipped with the most modern technology and an army of highly paid assistants, have failed? The opposite was the case; with the so-called revolution the Stasi finished up its work; the "peaceful revolution" was its magnum opus. The Stasi saved the best for last.[12]

A less daring logician might have concluded that maybe the Stasi had not been all-knowing and all-powerful after all. In a critique of East German intellectuals' approach to reunification, Broder was later to coin a phrase that aptly described his own approach here: "intellectual bungee jumping."[13] That Broder's thought processes were shared by others, however, was demonstrated in a definitive declaration by none less a personage than the Greek god Hermes at the end of Kerstin Jentzsch's popular 1994 novel *Seit die Götter ratlos sind* [Since the Gods Were Clueless]: "In order not to be surprised by the people, the inner ring of the secret service staged the revolution itself."[14]

In these versions of events, the Stasi seems to have taken on the same kind of role in controlling and supervising the meaning of the GDR past that Michel Foucault had once assigned to the author in literary theory:

How can one reduce the great peril, the great danger with which fiction threatens our world? The answer is: One can reduce it with the author. The author allows a limitation of the cancerous and dangerous proliferation of significations . . .[15]

If the GDR was viewed as a text, then the Stasi was the author of that text and guaranteed not only the text's readability but also the limitation of its meaning. The Stasi allowed one simple, straightforward assignation of blame for the past. Questions of individual and collective guilt vanished before the overwhelming and evil divinity of the Stasi. Via the help of this divinity, coming to terms with the past in the GDR could be reduced to coming to terms with the Stasi, and all other more complex aspects of power and complicity could be ignored. For the sixteen million GDR citizens who were not Stasi spies, the Stasi debate became, above all, profoundly comfortable. If the Stasi was to blame for everything, then individual citizens were to blame for nothing. After the Second World War Germans had used the conveniently dead figure of Hitler as a repository for historical responsibility, thus absolving themselves from individual guilt; after the collapse of the GDR, the Stasi seemed to be serving a similar role.

In addition to the various documentations of their Stasi files that German authors continued to put together throughout the first half of the 1990s, a number of literary works explicitly made the Stasi a primary topic. As already mentioned, Christa Wolf's *Was bleibt* dealt extensively with the Stasi. As early as 1968 Wolf Biermann had composed a song entitled "The Ballad of the Stasi" making fun of the secret police and its spying on him:

> I feel myself in pity bound
> to the poor deserving Stasi hounds
> who in snow and pouring rain
> must carefully observe my pain
> who built in a microphone
> to hear from me my every tone
> songs, farts, curses, plots
> in the kitchen and on the pot
> – brothers from the Stasi bureau
> you alone know all my sorrow[16]

One of the most popular plays of 1991 was West German playwright Klaus Pohl's melodramatic *Karate-Billi kehrt zurück* [Karate Billy Returns], in which the title figure, a former East

German Olympic athlete unfairly confined to a mental institution, returns to his home town and gradually discovers that everyone in the town, including his own sister, had been spying on him.[17] Far from being an accurate picture of Stasi crimes, Pohl's play was representative of a widespread tendency on the part of West Germans to equate the secret police with the entire GDR. After German reunification, Uwe Saeger's novel *Die Nacht danach und der Morgen* [The Night After and the Morning] (1991) was one of the first important literary works to contain a great many Stasi elements.[18] In his 1993 book *Das Verhör* [The Interrogation], Andreas Sinakowski explored his own experiences as a young gay man and aspiring author lured into the Stasi.[19] And in *"ICH"* ["I"], an ambitious and difficult novel in the high modernist tradition that represented a pinnacle of literary coming to terms with the Stasi past, Wolfgang Hilbig, one of the greatest and least known authors on the German scene, created an entire Stasi world that nightmarishly captured the ghoulish ironies of life as an aspiring author and Stasi agent during the last years of the GDR.[20] In her 1994 novella *Tanz am Kanal* [Dancing on the Canal] Kerstin Hensel depicted a young woman writer's complicity with and rebellion against the Stasi.[21] Brigitte Burmeister's novel *Unter dem Namen Norma* [Under the Name of Norma], also published in 1994, contained as one of its central themes the West German failure to see in the former GDR and its citizens anything other than the Stasi.[22] In this sense, Burmeister's novel was an adequate response to the uninformed exaggerations of writers like Pohl, Broder, and Kramer. Grass's *Ein weites Feld* also dealt with the Stasi problematic: its main character Theo Wuttke is constantly followed by his own personal, ageless Stasi spy Hoftaller. In Fritz Rudolf Fries's *Die Nonnen von Bratislava* [The Nuns of Bratislava] the writer Mateo Alemán functions as a similarly timeless writer-secret agent. Klaus Uhltzscht, the hero of Thomas Brussig's comic novel *Helden wie wir* [*Heroes Like Us*] (1995), not only works for the Stasi himself but comes from a family of Stasi spies. And in Kerstin Jentzsch's *Seit die Götter ratlos sind*, the main character is a woman named Lisa Meerbusch whose presumptive uncle and biological father lives and dies as a Stasi agent. As Lisa declares, agreeing with the main character of Burmeister's novel, for the West "Ossi [East German] is tantamount to saying Stasi, spy."[23] As this listing shows, post-reunification German literature dealt extensively with the Stasi theme, and, not surprisingly, East German authors tended to view the subject less hysterically than West German authors.

In 1991 Jürgen Fuchs wrote an extensive report on the Stasi's attempt to infiltrate oppositional literary circles in the GDR and persecute dissident writers entitled "Landschaften der Lüge" [Land-scapes of Lies].[24] Fuchs further fanned the flames of controversy when, in a much-discussed newspaper article, he described the Stasi's literary crimes as a "spiritual Auschwitz" (Auschwitz in den Seelen), thus leading to much fruitless debate about whether it was appropriate to compare the crimes of Auschwitz with the crimes of the Stasi.[25] With such melodramatic exaggerations in 1991, it was no wonder that by late 1992, when the GDR's most respected living authors, Wolf and Müller, were revealed to have complied with the Stasi in different ways, the revelations almost came as an anticlimax. As an exercise in evil, it was hard for either Wolf or Müller to live up to Fuchs's exaggerations about a "spiritual Auschwitz." For this reason, the two prominent authors probably benefited from the ferocity of the previous discussion.[26]

THE STASI AS AUTHOR

The many debates of the early 1990s about the Stasi and its function in the GDR tended to narrow down the range of possible meaning, to curtail more complex investigations of the GDR past. But such debates seemed to serve the opposite function in the realm of literature. They made everything more complicated. Although the Stasi's influence in the Protestant church, in factories, in the peace movement, in the women's movement, in the gay movement – indeed, everywhere in society – was strongly debated and highly controversial, it is nevertheless true that the Stasi's role in literary life remained singularly problematic. Why was this the case? Why did the conjunction of the Stasi and literature seem to produce negative resonances and vibrations that were felt nowhere else with the same vehemence?

One possible approach to answering this question is to look at the nature of literature, secrecy, and communication in GDR society. As Heiner Müller suggested after his own ties with the Stasi were revealed, the Stasi was the only authoritative institution with which one could engage in a dialog about conditions inside the GDR. Since the GDR lacked an open public sphere the need for dialog and debate was stifled or driven underground. This was of course, also one of the primary reasons for the importance of literature in the GDR: via literature it was possible for authors and readers to engage in discussion on complex social issues that were excluded from the uniform monolith of the public sphere. Hence Christa Wolf's *Kassandra* and Franz Fühmann's *Saiäns-Fiktschen* [Science Fiction] were scoured by readers for references to the current political situation and could even be read as allegories of life in the GDR or in a divided city, country, or world; and public readings by figures like Wolf, Hein, and Volker Braun became eminently political as well as literary events.

Wolf's *Was bleibt* reaches its climax with precisely such a public reading by the story's narrator, in which, through honest dialog between the narrator and her readers, "the real questions had [now] surfaced – the ones which give us life and can mean death if taken away from us."[27] Wolf characterizes GDR society as one of blocked dialog in which it is virtually impossible to talk about the truly important matters that affect people's lives. As Wolf sees it, human beings have a natural need for mutual understanding and discussion, and when that need is not satisfied, both human beings and the societies they create shrivel up and die. For Wolf, literature functions as a kind of alternative public sphere. It was not for nothing that Wolf's novel *Kassandra* took as its subject the Trojan prophetess doomed to speak the truth but to be ignored by the powers in charge of her city. Cassandra is the mouthpiece or medium of the god Apollo, but her messages are never received; in the end, all Cassandra can communicate is her own doom. She becomes the substance of her own message.

If literature functioned as a substitute for an open public sphere in the GDR, then so too, ironically, did the Stasi. Many IMs saw the Stasi not simply as a powerful and inhuman organization established for the sole purpose of controlling every aspect of life in the GDR; rather, they saw the Stasi above all as a medium of communication – a semiotic institution specialized in the reading of particular kinds of signs. If leaders like Honecker and Mielke were ignorant about the real situation inside the country, then the Stasi was able to see that which was dark and dangerous in socialist society. If newspapers like the Communist Party organ *Neues Deutschland* presented an unrelentingly optimistic picture of new production records and economic strengths, the Stasi concerned itself with failures and problems.

Schedlinski, the former Stasi IM who had spied on his friends and colleagues at the same time that he enjoyed a reputation as a daring young avant-garde poet, wrote in his own self-defense shortly after his Stasi activities became known:

A society which increasingly has no language to deal with a considerable part of its own reality must, in addition to its official channels of knowledge, also have at its disposal a secret channel of knowledge; and this was one of the functions of the Stasi. One could therefore understand the Stasi as a kind of social subconscious . . . Just as there was a second, criminal, shadow economy in addition to an official state economy, so too there was needed a second, secret public sphere – specifically the opposition and the Stasi, which both took on everything for which there was no public language.[28]

For Schedlinski, the Stasi was a medium of communication in a society where other media had broken down. Schedlinski specifically compared this "second" medium of communication to the "second" or black market economy controlled and organized in the GDR by Alexander Schalck-Golodkowski. Just as the official economy needed the shadow economy to get by, so too the official public sphere needed the shadow public sphere represented, according to Schedlinski, on the one hand by the opposition and on the other hand by the Stasi. Schedlinski did not seem to notice that "secret public sphere" was a contradiction in terms.

Like literature itself, then, the Stasi was a medium. If literature was open and public and could more adequately be described as an alternative public sphere, the Stasi was secret and private. What the two institutions shared as media, however, was the desire to understand the reality of life in GDR society, and by understanding it to affect it: the Stasi through coercion, literature through public discussion. In *Was bleibt*, Wolf describes one figure, the mysterious Stasi spy Jürgen M. who was also once an aspiring writer, as a colleague and competitor of those who make their living writing, particularly the narrator herself: Someone "who . . . want[s] to beat me at my own original game."[29] Jürgen M. truly is a colleague and rival of the writer herself, even if, unlike the two struggling young writers Wolf's narrator deals with in the course of her story, he approaches the narrator from a position of power. Jürgen M. comes to the narrator not for encouragement and advice, like the two younger writers, but in order to research his own writing project, which sets itself up in opposition to that of the narrator. As the narrator reflects, the Stasi longs to create a truer and more accurate picture of what is and what will remain than the narrator herself. Her friend-turned-enemy burns with the desire to prove his own literary prowess to himself and to the narrator:

to prove to me that not only a writer could find out everything there was to know about a person – he could do it as well, in his own way. He as well could make himself the lord and master of his objects like any run-of-the-mill author. Yet since his objects are made of flesh and blood and do not exist only on paper, like my own, *he* is the master, the real lord.[30]

The Stasi claims to know reality and the writer better than the writer herself. Whereas the narrator's method is interior dialog, remorseless introspection, an opening up to responses from the present and past, the Stasi believes in inspection of external details and external monologue. It views writing as a method of control which will make it the lord and master of its flesh and blood characters, rather than a partner in a conversation with them. The Stasi is the ultimate naturalist. In the naturalist equation art = reality − x, it seeks to reduce x to 0 and, via its absolute control of "art," to control reality absolutely. For the Stasi, writing is, quite literally, power, in the sense suggested by Jacques Derrida when he wrote that "access to the written sign assures the sacred power . . . of knowing the general structure of the universe," adding that "all clergies, exercising political power or not, were constituted at the same time as writing and by the disposition of graphic power," and that indeed "the very sense of power . . . was always linked with the disposition of writing."[31]

Saeger's novel *Die Nacht danach und der Morgen* also revolves around a kind of writing contest between the Stasi and the novel's narrator. There are at least four different stories entitled *Die Nacht danach und der Morgen* in this novel: 1) the novel itself; 2) a short story written by the narrator in the 1970s; 3) a film scenario also written by the narrator in the 1970s; and 4) a short story sent to the narrator eight days after the opening of the Berlin Wall by a young man evidently working for the Stasi under the code name "Mike Glockengiesser" and purporting to be the son of the narrator's former army buddy. "Mike Glockengiesser" writes in a letter to the narrator, "Your text provokes me to set my own experiences against it, my own *Die Nacht danach und der Morgen*."[32] The young Stasi agent's artistic ambitions become evident when he asks the narrator: "Could it be that I have a bit of the artist in me?"[33] Ultimately his letter and story turn out to be nothing but a trap for the narrator in which the Stasi solicits his services by making him think he is helping an aspiring younger writer. Toward the end of the novel Glockengiesser sends a cassette tape to the narrator in which he asserts that his and the Stasi's plan to win the author's services failed only because of the collapse of the Wall. In his drunken outburst, the agent compares the work of a writer to that of the secret police. In contrast to Wolf's Jürgen M., however, Glockengiesser suggests that an ordinary author has even more power over his characters than a Stasi agent:

> When the end came, it was really beginning to be fun for me, because I noticed that I could get my hands on people this way, too, that I could press more out of them than . . . On paper people always tell you exactly what you want to hear. Have you ever noticed that, Uwe? They may lie to each other, but never to us. Not to us. Us! Couldn't we have been a promising team? You, the well-known author in his best years extending his collegial help to a hopeful young author – to me, don't you see? – to guide him on his way? And, Uwe, if it hadn't been for this autumn, you would have taken the bait![34]

If, for many of its apologists, the Stasi functioned as a kind of medium, however, then that medium, in Marshall McLuhan's words, was also itself a message. McLuhan's point was that in post-Gutenberg society, characterized by the electronic simultaneity of sounds and images rather than by the linear ordering of print, it was not so much coherent messages that were communicated as forms of communication themselves. Television does not so much convey discrete messages to its viewers as it communicates itself. If in the premodern world of Wolf's *Kassandra* the Trojan prophetess ultimately became identical with her own message and was therefore killed, in the postmodern world, too, there is no message beyond the messenger.[35]

From the time of Biermann's expulsion from the GDR in 1976 until the end of the GDR, a younger generation of writers born in the 1950s and 1960s began to emerge in the centers of major cities like Leipzig, Dresden, and Berlin. This younger generation, which figured prominently in the accusations of Stasi complicity directed at German writers during the early 1990s, made the concreteness of language as a medium part of its program; when several members of the generation were revealed to be Stasi informers, their hermetic poetic program became subject to the criticism that it was essentially the creation of a "dreamless tightrope walker on the Stasi harness," as Biermann put it in his criticism of Anderson.[36] The Stasi scandal hence threatened to implicate an entire literary generation, in much the same way that the attack on the deconstructionist critic Paul de Man in the late 1980s had implicated not just one deceased academic but poststructuralism itself as a literary-critical movement.[37]

Whereas the older generation of writers, from Wolf and Volker Braun to Biermann, had made their work explicitly political, the younger generation of writers emerging during the last decade and a half of the GDR's existence tended toward a different literary-political tactic: the refusal of meaning itself and thus of explicit political messages. This seeming depoliticization lent a certain weight to Biermann's accusations of complicity with an authoritarian regime. The younger generation, represented by figures like Bert Papenfuß-Gorek, Jan Faktor, Lutz Rathenow, Durs Grünbein, Kurt Drawert, and Uwe Kolbe, as well as by the Stasi informers Schedlinski and Anderson, went out of its way to celebrate precisely the medium of language as language. Influenced by the then fashionable French semiotic and poststructuralist thinking, this generation tended to believe, with Jacques Derrida, that there was nothing outside of or beyond the text. Language may be a code, but when one deciphers that code one is left not with an important message but with the code itself. For this generation, language was not fundamentally about communication between people about the world; rather, language was entirely self-reflexive. As the Leipzig poet Kurt Drawert wrote: "Set free from all pseudomeanings, language fell back upon its pure material value, it was divided and deinstrumentalized via a subjective combination of its parts."[38] In language that recalled Kant's definition of enlightenment as the escape from self-imposed powerlessness, Elke Erb wrote that the younger poets had freed themselves from slavish fealty to the idea that language has to convey meaning. She referred to this liberation enthusiastically as "liberation from the tyranny of a superordinate meaning."[39] Erb wrote these words in her introduction to a crucial 1985 anthology of the younger GDR writers which she edited together with the ubiquitous Stasi spy Anderson; the volume had the appropriate title *Berührung ist nur eine Randerscheinung* [Touching is Only a Marginal Phenomenon], as if to suggest that the younger poets of the GDR were using their solipsistic theories of language to shield themselves from both the harm and the promise of interaction with a dangerous outside world.

Far from viewing their work as complicitous with GDR power structures, most of the writers in this younger generation viewed their work as nonconformist, even oppositional. In their view, the transgression of normal linguistic rules was connected to the transgression of social and political authority. Uwe Kolbe, one of the most promising young poets in the GDR during the 1980s, declared: "The text asserts a transgression of boundaries into a land beyond meaning."[40] That "land beyond meaning" was a land freed from the constraints of the authoritarian GDR. Like many other poets of his generation, Kolbe believed that the only real resistance to political authority was the refusal to engage in political language at all, since political language always already existed on the terrain created and ruled by forces of domination and repression. The only way to escape the real-life GDR was to enter into Kolbe's "land beyond meaning." In its insistence on a refusal of politics, the younger generation came close to the belief of aestheticist West German critics like Greiner and Schirrmacher that literature should be above politics, even if the neo-avant-garde East Germans used a different critical vocabulary. However, the implication of this antipolitical younger generation in the political quagmire of the Stasi suggested that even the most determined efforts to locate literature in a space beyond political meaning were doomed to fail.

The work of these authors was a kind of self-imposed emigration into a land of the spirit and the word, and, in spite of the radical differences between the socialist Stasi and the Nazi Gestapo, it recalled once again some aspects of the "inner emigration" under the Nazis – from the attempt to find refuge in an idealistic view of language to subsequent debates with more overtly political "outer" emigrants. If authors of the older generation like Biermann and Wolf had negated and criticized political domination, Kolbe refused to recognize domination at all. Referring to the work of Biermann and other older authors as "grammars we have run through," Kolbe suggested that such "grammars . . . are probably not independent grammars, because, by simply contradicting the metalanguage, they merely represent the negative image of the metalanguage."[41] In a poem entitled "Gespräch ohne Ende" [Conversation Without End], which simulates a dialog between a writer and his reader, Kolbe defended his literary practice by having the writer declare:

Belief I do not replace
with further belief
place foot before foot stop
praising the identical
praise the miracles the places
without names the signs without meaning. . .[42]

Drawert described the younger generation's program in even more explicit terms, praising its refusal

to reproduce the structures of power aesthetically. . . The program of this scene was nondiscursivity as a reflex against a one-dimensional thought landscape, including all words and meanings occupied by an ideological monopoly.[43]

The younger generation's poetic justifications for its refusal to engage in politics were not entirely convincing and betrayed their despair of ever achieving genuine social change. In a thoughtful retrospective on the poetics of his generation, the Berlin poet Jan Faktor suggested that he and his colleagues

were . . . desperately afraid of writing texts that would nail something down unambiguously and clearly. Of course we had appropriate explanations for this: that reality is so complex and full of riddles that as an artist one cannot write about it like a primitive pundit . . .[44]

The semiotic approach to language taken by the younger generation of GDR poets lent itself well to language games, codes, secrecy, and arcane knowledge – the very stuff of spying and conspiracy. In a sense this generation constituted an avant-garde trying to create an alternative linguistic reality as a response to the failure of political reality inside the country. In its search for codes that would short-circuit the linguistic control of the Communist state, this generation resorted to many of the forms of concrete, automatic, and nonsense poetry that had been explored by previous avant-gardes elsewhere from the early twentieth century on. Like many historical avant-gardes, the new avant-garde in the GDR met in small groups, usually in private apartments. By the early 1980s, the avant-garde scene was centered primarily in East Berlin's Prenzlauer Berg district, an old and dilapidated workers' neighborhood.[45] The Prenzlauer Berg poets read their work to each other in group readings and published it in samizdat journals with telling names like *Ariadnefabrik* (Ariadne Factory) that revealed the labyrinthine nature of their conception of literature. Even as they rebelled against the older generation of explicitly political writers, this generation was itself following older avant-garde traditions which set the poet and writer apart from and above society, making him privy to secret language and codes that went beyond ordinary, mundane realism. Wolfgang Hilbig referred ironically to these older traditions when, in the opening pages of his novel "*ICH*," he made fun of the Prenzlauer Berg poetry readings by comparing them to the satirical rendering of early twentieth-century avant-garde poetry readings in Thomas Mann's short story "Beim Propheten" ["The Prophet"]. This comparison suggested that even though the younger generation had sought to distance itself from an older generation represented above all by Wolf, it was nevertheless still influenced by the older generation's conception of writers as seers and prophets.

Long before writers and their connection to spying became a major issue, McLuhan had written that

The poet, the artist, the sleuth – whoever sharpens our perception tends to be antisocial; rarely "well-adjusted," he cannot go along with currents and trends. A strange bond often exists among antisocial types in their power to see environments as they really are.[46]

McLuhan's reference to poets and artists along with sleuths puts them all together in a single "antisocial" category blessed – or cursed – with particularly clear-eyed perception of social reality. For McLuhan, these figures are a kind of "opposition" to existing environments. In contrast to this view of writers as oppositional, Derrida suggests that systems of writing are also systems of power, which is, for him, always the power of signification.

The apparent contradiction between a view of writers as opposition and writers as part of a dominant power structure captures not only much of the debate about writers inside the GDR but also many of the contradictions of the Stasi problem itself: the Stasi as a kind of alternative or "second" public sphere versus the Stasi as a system of control. However, this kind of opposition can perhaps be partially resolved if one views the Stasi as part of Freud's collective superego. The image of the Stasi as a collective agency assigned the task of watching over East German citizens "like a garrison in a conquered city" (Freud) is particularly apt, given that the Stasi was originally founded as the "shield and sword of the party" to defend East German socialism against a German population only recently adherent to Nazi ideology and politics. In this way the opposition between the Stasi as an agent of control and the Stasi as an agent of opposition is resolved: it is both a controlling and an oppositional agency, and both the control and the opposition are needed because of Germans' political behavior during the Third Reich.

However, while this Freudian image may help to explain the function of the Stasi in East German society, it does not entirely explain the role of younger-generation writers in the GDR, whose flight from political meaning, framed as an opposition to the older generation's political engagement, is precisely a flight away from political morality and commitment. If Schirrmacher's and Greiner's attacks on politically engaged West German literature can be understood also as attacks on the role of literature in the postwar collective superego, so too the younger generation in the GDR is seeking to free itself from a political and linguistic authoritarianism conceived in specifically patriarchal terms. The language used by younger-generation GDR literary theorists suggests a rejection of the collective superego. Hence the insider–outsider contradiction partially resolved in the case of the Stasi is not resolved in the case of the younger-generation authors. Indeed, these authors were perhaps the most ironic example of the insider–outsider contradiction in GDR society. On the one hand, they viewed themselves as genuine outsiders in opposition to existing power structures; but on the other hand they were heavily infiltrated by the Stasi, and their abstruse poetic theories helped to take the edge off any attempt to combine literature with anti-establishment politics. Their attempt to escape to a no-place beyond politics led – nowhere.

These contradictions are related to a glaring contradiction in the understanding of language promulgated by the GDR avant-garde scene. Bathrick has identified this contradiction as revolving around the fact that, in spite of their rejection of "the linguistic innocence of the older generation," the younger generation's "own self-stylizations reveal them asserting nolens volens the viability of a self-conscious, autonomous, subject-centered, indeed Archimedean locus outside of the dominant discourse and within which to develop an 'authentic' language."[47] This contradiction could perhaps be described even more pointedly by focusing on the problem of complicity with the Stasi. On the one hand Schedlinski, Müller, and others defended their Stasi contacts as part of an alternative public sphere in which informed communication about real social problems actually occurred. On the other hand, however, Schedlinski and others in the Prenzlauer Berg scene denied or sought to destroy the ability of language to communicate at all. "how words have escaped from me," wrote Schedlinski, "language mutating like ruins." "there lies / a silence above the silence & / so that everyone knows it / we have finally broken speech."[48] Such lines directly contradict the belief in the Stasi, or in hermetic poetry, as an alternative public sphere.

The most dramatic account of an attack on language by the younger generation came from Drawert, in whose novel *Spiegelland* [Land of Mirrors]there is a chapter entitled "Der Augenblick der Beschädigung der Stimme" (The Moment of Damage to the Voice), in which the main character, a young boy, makes the conscious decision to unlearn language step-by-step, begins speaking nonsense, and finally grows completely silent:

I was the child who suddenly grew silent, who could already speak so well and who unlearned speech again, the child did not speak, the child was ordered to repeat words, very slowly, syllable by syllable, but the child did not speak, not even very slowly and syllable by syllable.[49]

In Drawert's story, the refusal of the unnamed child to speak is simultaneously the refusal of language as a Derridean method of control. This is the only revolutionary option left open to the child in a situation of absolute powerlessness. Language in Drawert's story is associated with mendacious power, particularly the power of the boy's Communist father and Nazi grandfather. The only way to escape this nexus of power-language is to escape language itself, for the entry into language is an entry into the phallologocentric power of the father.

Yet there is a problem with the refusal of language as a form of rebellion. As Drawert's novel demonstrates, such a refusal ultimately leads to isolation, loneliness, and further impotence. It is the act of the helpless child, not of the mature, constructive adult. In Drawert's novel, the son ultimately learns to master language maturely not as a slave of his father and grandfather but as their opponent. At this point, with language now used as a weapon against them, both the father and the grandfather who had previously commanded the silent child to speak now urge the loquacious man to be silent: "but, demanded father, I should not speak or even write about this, at least not as long as grandfather was still alive."[50] Language, once the handmaiden of paternal power, has now become its most potent enemy and an agent of filial liberation.

Language, in Drawert's view, is still power, and to use it is to be complicitous with power. But not to use it is even worse, since it means submission to power. Taking the Derridean notion of the trace – the idea that "language is . . . open to the wholly other, to its own beyond"[51] – and using this liberating view of language to refute those – presumably in his own younger generation – who simply refuse language, Drawert suggests that power uses the tool of language only at its own risk, for it can never completely control signs: "One can never destroy signs that are already in the world."[52] As a result of his use of language, the son is now in a position of power, i.e. speech, while the father is in a position of powerlessness, i.e. silence: "he is so speechless that he has repeated the entire speechlessness of society itself," so that "even when he felt the need to carry on a conversation, it always escaped from him."[53] At the end of *Spiegelland*, the silent boy has become the talkative man, and the father in control of language has become the father without language. It is the father who inhabits a land of meaninglessness, while the son has relocated himself to a land of meaning, including specifically political signification. It would not be an exaggeration to say that the novel ends with the linguistic castration of the narrator's father. In this text, Drawert shows that he has moved beyond the simplistic celebration of linguistic impermeability associated with the Prenzlauer Berg generation and toward a more complex under-standing of language as both complicitous with and resistant to authoritarian power.

Many of the texts of the Prenzlauer Berg poets are incomprehen-sible according to normal rules of grammar. They make use of language games and nonsense and sometimes flirt with their close-ness to the language of codes and of spying. Even in his first volume of poetry, Anderson was already writing lines like: "one can . . . deconsecrate the dreams of the father be asked to a conspirat/orial meeting be summoned be in/terrogated say a & b."[54] In spite of their apparent meaninglessness, such sentences flirt with revelation. Their resistance to meaning goes only skin deep. As an enigmatic code, Prenzlauer Berg poetry sometimes reveals more than it appears to. In this example, what at first apears to be incomprehen-sible reveals itself to be a surprisingly realistic reference to Ander-son's own mundane activities as a Stasi spy. As Bathrick has suggested, "even a language of silence . . . must define itself against the distorted discursive system that has necessitated it." The

Prenzlauer Berg generation's attempt to escape from the language of power was thus fundamentally paradoxical, revealing what Bathrick calls a "dangerous naiveté on the part of those who wanted to resist the state by claiming to ignore it."[55]

Many post-reunification texts dealing with the Stasi are focused on the creation of a new language, an anti-language that will avoid the dual trap of silence and total control. Such texts criticize a language based on rigid dichotomies and differentiations; some also make reference to Martin Luther's reiteration of the biblical command that language confine itself to simple yes's and no's as an example of the binary language they oppose. In Wolf's *Was bleibt*, for instance, the narrator reflects on

Dr. Martin Luther trying to fool me into believing that we could only refuse or accept, could only be friends or foes. Thy word shall be yea, yea and nay, nay. Anything beyond that is evil.[56]

And in *Spiegelland* Drawert's narrator reflects on a time when "I was supposed to sit in the very last row of seats in the classroom, so that I had to say yes or no loudly, always only yes or no."[57] Schedlinski even went so far as to give his first volume of poetry the title *die rationen des ja und des nein* [the rations of yes and of no].

Wolf's *Was bleibt* centers around the search for a new language beyond the binary extremes of domination and self-effacement: "One day I will . . . talk . . . in that other language which, as of yet, is in my ear but not on my tongue." But the narrator also asks herself skeptically, "Would I ever find my language?" And at the end of the story she is still searching for her new language: "One day I will be able to speak easily and freely, I thought. It is still too soon."[58] If the path toward slavery had been primarily linguistic, then the path toward liberation would also be linguistic.

DISINTEGRATION OF THE SELF

The brutal clarity of Martin Luther's dualistic language, which fails to recognize anything between or beyond the words "yes" and "no," runs counter to another form of language characterized by vagueness, imprecision, and incomprehensibility. If the first form of language is associated with a celebration of the "I" who takes it upon himself to speak, the second form of language is associated with loss of identity and ego. Anderson's poems may appear incomprehensible and coded, but his reports to the Stasi are clear and precise: the same person commanded at least two different modes of communication.

From the individuals who serve it, the Stasi demands the loss of identity. Stasi IMs take on special pseudonyms and are no longer referred to by their real civilian names. Their Stasi baptism begins a process that gradually erodes their previous personalities, so that even in their most precise reports it is no longer clear who is speaking when "I" speaks. Because the Stasi as a function of the collective and individual superego has acquired absolute domination, the individual – and collective – ego over which it seeks to exercise control disintegrates. In Wolf's *Kassandra* the praetorian guard Eumelos, who functions as the Trojan equivalent of a secret police chief, is referred to specifically as a "no one" who has no self.[59] And in *Was bleibt* the narrator describes a mode of speaking which knows no outside world because it does not know itself:

A history of bad conscience would have to be included in reflections on the boundaries of the sayable, I thought; with what words does one describe the speechlessness of those who have no conscience, how does language deal with that which is not there, that which will tolerate no adjectives or nouns clinging to it, for it is without character and certainly lacks a subject in the same way that a subject without a conscience lacks itself.[60]

The tension between "bad conscience" and "no conscience" in this passage suggests that it is precisely the domination of an outside instance (the Stasi) that has replaced the individual governance of the ego and thus led to the disintegration of the self and, in turn to, "no conscience," meaning both no remorse and no consciousness of self.

The reflection that the inability to speak is also the inability to assert one's own subjectivity is repeated in Drawert's *Spiegelland*, where gradually learning to assert one's own language also means learning to assert oneself. Anderson's poetry is full of uncertainty about the status of the self. One of his poems begins with the statement, "we will see / who i am," and ends with, "i myself wanted to find the formula / of my dying . . . i expect nothing / do you know the things forget us / faster than we think / and i do not know who it was."[61] In this poem it is things, not people which do the forgetting, and at the end of a poem that begins by promising to find out "who i am" comes the impersonal statement "i do not know who it was" – individual identity has been forgotten even as a question. In another poem Anderson again uses the impersonal "es" ("it" or "there") to designate a small part of himself that somehow remains: "there remains a remnant of me."[62] With respect to his own seeming lack of self-knowledge, Anderson once declared:

i am not schizophrenic, but i am the one who has schizophrenia as a tool at his disposal. i.e., i do not need the two worlds in which i exist and express myself, and i can always allow one to die. for the moment i am less interested in what the point of this is than in the possibility. i have at my disposal the tools of schizophrenia without being affected myself . . . the invention of this psychobomb, the conscious splitting to let the one die in order to do everything with the other.[63]

Such a statement outlines the function of the superego as being to destroy the ego in order to achieve a supposed absolute control. The monomaniacal superego believes that it can do without the ego, using "this psychobomb" to further its domination. This splitting of the personality comes at least partly from the act of speaking or writing. The voice that says "I" and that to which it refers in saying "I" are not necessarily identical. Anderson speaks of living in two worlds, letting one self die so that he can do "everything" with the other. In this vision there are at least three and possibly four different "I"'s: the "I" that dies, the "I" that lives, the "I" that can do anything with the second "I," and the "I" that speaks about all the other "I"'s. But the "I" that dies is none other than the governing mechanism of the psyche, the ego, and hence the dominance of any other "I" is illusionary and self-destructive.

Saeger's *Die Nacht danach und der Morgen* revolves around precisely such imprecision in which "I" is speaking. At a crucial point in the text the seemingly autobiographical narrator receives a supposedly autobiographical text also entitled "Die Nacht danach und der Morgen" from the mysterious "Mike Glockengiesser." In explaining the creation of this questionable text, Glockengiesser writes:

The notes I made became ever more improbable to me, as if I were writing about a stranger, or as if I had become a stranger to the person about whom I was writing. Is it possible that by writing about oneself . . . one somehow accelerates the process of one's ego development in a destructive way?[64]

Here the process of writing is itself a process of objectification and then loss of the self. The "I" about whom the author writes becomes simply a character in his own story, like all the other characters over whom he rules with such an iron hand. Here the writer becomes a function of the collective superego, hastening the destruction of the individual ego.

Anderson expresses this paradox in a short poem:

> when i speak about green
> green dies
> when i speak about red
> the neon letters over
> the train station die
> when i speak about myself
> you die
> colon[65]

Although the structure of this poem leads Anderson's readers to expect "i die" as the penultimate line, by the end of the poem "i" is already gone, not even present at its own demise.

Thomas Brussig's Rabelaisian comedy *Helden wie wir* also deals with a young Stasi agent whose personality is so shrunken that he is unable to connect his own deeds with any kind of "I":

I was certain that I only had to do what I was told, and that beyond that I had no power whatsoever. *I* was waiting, and nothing that I would do during this time was intended or wanted by me. For that reason I did not hurt anybody. *I was not the person* who committed break-ins, who kidnapped, who persecuted, who made other people insecure, who created fear. *I* was just waiting.[66]

Brussig's hero represses the knowledge of his own guilt by repressing the knowledge of his own self: "Was I really working for the Stasi? And if I was, was there such a thing as 'I'? Is there life after a double life?"[67] Not surprisingly, in *Helden wie wir* the power of the Stasi is associated with the power of the father, making clear the unity between the collective and the individual superego that unite to destroy "I." In this sense, Brussig's hero is correct when he claims "I did not hurt anybody." Since "I" was the first victim of the Stasi-superego, it was not capable of being present at subsequent crimes.

The most brilliant attempt to come to terms with the Stasi problematic in the years following German reunification was Hilbig's appropriately entitled "*ICH*," which deals with the career of a Stasi spy and aspiring writer much like Anderson or Schedlinski. The entire novel centers around the loss of the narrator's ego, which is already rendered uncertain by the quotation marks surrounding it in the novel's title. Thus the novel begins in the first person but then moves into the third person as the identity of the narrator becomes more and more confused. The narrator's loss of identity can be traced to an act of writing: specifically, to the narrator's signature on a piece of paper that declares his willingness to work for the Stasi. Because the signature becomes a formal forfeiture of identity, the Stasi insists on it. With this Faustian contract, the narrator has sold his soul to the Stasi, simultaneously signing a certificate of baptism for an entirely new creation: the narrator's second self under the appropriately cheesy French-sounding pseudonym "Cambert." All Stasi informants lose their civilian identity and receive a new name. With this baptism, the old self dies; readers of "*ICH*" never learn the narrator's real civilian name, but only his real initials, "M. W." Cambert dates his vita nuova, and the beginning of the depressive tiredness which plagues him throughout the novel, from the signing of his name on a piece of paper: "It was not much, it was only the absent trace of a signature on a piece of paper that lay in half-darkness."[68] The tiredness that comes from this apparently simple act of signing his own name onto a piece of paper is characterized as literally "stronger than I am," so much so that it ultimately destroys the narrator's "I"; his fatigue allows the narrator no rest, and from the moment of the signature he literally lives in an underworld that he seeks out in the cellars and secret passageways that connect East Berlin's vast buildings underground. Cambert is no longer a human being. He has become his own shadow.

Cambert's signature is both figuratively and literally a kind of baptism, for the document that the Stasi coerces him to sign also falsely declares that he is the father of a child by a woman with whom he has never had sexual intercourse. Cambert, himself fatherless, signs a document falsely declaring himself to be the father of a child who is also fatherless, and who subsequently disappears without a trace, just as Cambert's earlier life now disappears entirely behind his activities as a Stasi spy. Whenever he tries to remember his earlier self it is "as if I were to think about things that came before my birth."[69] Cambert, now speaking of himself in the third person, describes the erasure of his own history and thus of his selfhood in the following words:

Before . . . that was a time that was completely unreal, that had slipped away from him like the intangible ghost of feverish imaginings and self-deceptions. Piece by piece it had disappeared from his consciousness, it was a non-time.

Cambert now sees his former life as a kind of fiction and his current shadow-life as reality:

Back then he had in fact *simulated* this bit of life – for himself! – he no longer knew how it had been possible for him, it was a life in which every order . . . that governed it had come from his own person: but he had probably never been a *person* in this game! Now the situation was reversed: he received all orders from outside, and he was a person . . . the proof of this was that orders were given to him which clearly revealed that they had been tailored to specific characteristics of his lifestyle.[70]

Cambert's ego is now dissolved: he receives his personhood not from his self but from orders that are given to him from the realm of the Stasi as father-substitute and thus collective and individual superego. It is only through these orders that Cambert is able to experience himself as a person. Cambert has been born again, and the Stasi provides for him the father he never had: "A child has to have a father! they had told him."[71] And yet Cambert's second life is not a birth into the light of day. Rather, it takes the form of a return to a second womb, the womb of Cambert's nocturnal and diurnal ramblings through the darkness in the tunnels under Berlin.

Cambert's job for the Stasi is to spy on the quasi-oppositional literary scene in Prenzlauer Berg, and at the same time to try to establish himself as a respected writer within that scene. One of the things that attracts him to the Stasi in the first place is that the Stasi seems to take his literary ambitions seriously. Not only does the Stasi want reports and documentation from him, it also encourages him to write and publish. Both of Cambert's two commanding officers, who play Mephistopheles to his Faust, are highly literate, well-read men: major (or captain or first lieutenant; the rank varies) Feuerbach (or Kesselstein or Wasserstein; the name varies) is rumored to have studied philosophy and is particularly fond of postmodern American literature, especially Thomas Pynchon with his paranoid master-pieces and disintegrating characters; while "the boss," Cambert's first superior in the little town of A., is himself a kind of philosopher and connoisseur ("he was one of the rare bosses who had read Brecht"[72]) and evidently the first figure of authority to praise him for his abilities as a writer and literary figure. Led by this small-town boss, the Stasi offers to support Cambert as a writer if he will agree to write reports for them. For the first time in his life Cambert has the possibility of earning his living as a writer. Not only that, but the isolated, fatherless boy now knows grown men in positions of authority who take a serious interest in his ideas about literature. Suddenly Cambert finds himself acquiring a reputation as a writer: "It was perhaps enough that since recently there were people in the city who *recognized* him as a writer. Indeed, they strengthened him in his role as a writer."[73] If what Faust had wanted was a woman, what Cambert wants is to be a writer; and the Stasi, as the greatest collector and decoder of documents in the GDR, has the power to offer him exactly what he wants. Fantasizing on how he might introduce himself to a West German editor, Cambert reflects:

I was identical to the poet M. W., who had appeared with a total of seventeen poems in journals and anthologies, more than half of them in so-called unofficial journals; the echo of the press that had concerned itself with such subjects put him in line with the new, younger authors who were now counted as part of the unofficial literature of his country.[74]

Encouraged by his Stasi mentors, Cambert moves to Berlin, where he begins to live the Bohemian life of a member of the avant-garde literary scene. Cambert himself is never at the center of the scene; he is always on the margins, a loner. Gradually he begins to make a name for himself with the publication of a few poems in unofficial avant-garde journals. But increasingly his creative impulses are directed toward his job as a Stasi spy rather than as a writer in his own right. He spends hours, days, and weeks working on his reports to the Stasi, but less and less time on his own literary production. The only problem is that the Stasi does not appreciate the literary nature of Cambert's reports. It wants hard facts. "Leave the commentary, categorization, and context to us, that's what we have our experts for," says his boss Feuerbach.[75] Despairing of his own authorship, Cambert asks, "When . . . did I stop being the author of my own texts?"[76] Cambert briefly considers moving to the West in order to serve as a Stasi agent there, but in the end he decides to remain in the GDR, because, as he sees it, "Literature in western society did not, of course, have a necessary use value."[77] It is only in the East that literature is taken seriously. In the West the market economy has made literature superfluous.

Increasingly, Cambert's activities become irrelevant and absurd. As a writer, he fails: "He could no longer bear to look at his own texts, they were second-rate."[78] If Cambert views his entire pre-Stasi life as a simulation, however, he is wrong. It is his life as a Stasi spy that is unreal. Cambert even simulates being a spy: he creates

reports that are sometimes just as fictitious as any of his poems or
stories. And he inserts bits of his real Stasi reports into his supposedly
unreal writing. The line between reality and fiction no longer exists.
Cambert reflects that the Stasi is just like any other author, "because
ultimately we do nothing but . . . write down . . . and archive forms
of consciousness."[79] He becomes so obsessed with details and
memory that his mind is no longer able to structure reality coher-
ently. The world becomes a mass of unconnected bits of information,
a web in which Cambert is caught like any other piece of information. And the spider which is supposed to be in control, the Stasi,
is in fact, just like Cambert, losing its grip on reality. The superego's
attempt at total domination has proved not only futile but self-
defeating. As it turns out, Cambert's reports on the oppositional
writer code-named "Reader" are simply reports on another Stasi
spy, since Reader himself is working for the Stasi. The Stasi is
creating its own oppositional reality and then spying on it. The Stasi
has become an author not only in the sense that it is creating books
and poems but in the sense that it has built up a fictitious, simulated
world and can no longer distinguish between that world and reality.
Literature has importance in the Stasi world because the Stasi's
world *is* literature. Meanwhile the decline of the GDR, the growth of
the real opposition, political demonstrations, and emigration to West
Germany continue unchecked. The Stasi and its literary artifices are
losing their importance. The supposedly all-powerful and all-
knowing agency of the East German collective superego has become
a postmodernist paranoid fantasy, an endless mirror game of signs
signifying nothing. It has become its only message. As Cambert
reflects on the Stasi's writing style with its endless series of genitive
constructions,

At its core it was a form of speech that destroyed realism . . . like an
unintentionally surrealist method that produced a psychotic automatism.
Maybe the real surrealists could only dream about it . . . from them comes
the famous picture of the cube inside the cube in which once again another
cube is hidden, and then again another, and so on. – The Machine of the
Genitive takes this picture seriously, I thought. With this mirage it subverts
reality. . . it is, thus, the simulation of an infinite consequence.[80]

Ultimately the Stasi is fooled by its own fiction. Believing that it can
control its flesh-and-blood characters more completely than any
author of mere books, it finally loses the authority, and authorship,

that it aspires to. Its characters get out of control or disappear, and the Stasi itself begins to go haywire and disintegrate.

In the little town of A., where Cambert ultimately winds up again in order to escape the revolution that has already broken out in Berlin, his new "boss" insanely believes that everything is under control when, in fact, everything is already lost. "We have time," he insists, a refrain echoed throughout the book and throughout GDR society in the belief that history, whose outcome is already known, is on "our" side. "They were throwing their time out the window heartily with both hands," notes the narrator of Wolf's *Was bleibt*, referring to the Stasi, which believes itself, like any other author, in absolute control of time, convinced that if nothing else *it* will remain.[81] The agent Jürgen M. snarls at her that time is at a standstill: "We are in the Middle Ages. Nothing has changed except for appearances. And nothing is going to change."[82] The image of a frozen history corresponds to a neurotic collective and individual psyche.

With its insane belief that it can stop time in its path and achieve an end of history, Wolf's and Hilbig's Stasi is asserting precisely that chronological stasis which Goethe's Faust had believed to be impossible, and which had been the subject of his bet with Mephistopheles:

> Then may the solemn death-bell sound,
> Then from thy service thou art free,
> The index then may cease its round.
> And time be never more for me![83]

The Stasi believes that it has indeed brought time to a standstill, and that it has thus beaten history at its own game, just as Goethe's Mephistopheles had wanted to beat God at his own eternal game by winning Faust's soul. But just as Mephistopheles is wrong and ultimately thwarted by the unforeseen salvation of Faust, so too the Stasi is wrong in believing that history has come to an end and that it has achieved permanent control of human souls. The Stasi's vision of writing as a dam constructed against the demands of history proves to be just as impotent as Cambert himself. This unproductive and megalomaniac vision of writing, of history, and of politics, is doomed. Writing cannot be set up as a force outside of history without committing itself to meaninglessness and insanity. The place of writing is within, not outside of history, just as the place of the superego is within a healthy and productive ego, not as the ego's destroyer.

Hilbig's implied condemnation of the solipsistic view of writing espoused by both the Stasi and the Prenzlauer Berg generation recalls a much earlier critique by Heinrich Böll, the only postwar West German writer to win the Nobel Prize for literature, and, as we may recall, the primary representative of a politically engaged West German literature singled out by Bohrer in his 1980s attacks on postwar German writing. Böll had also argued against the aesthetic solipsism of a literature unconcerned with human reality in a 1952 reflection entitled "In Praise of Rubble Literature" ("Bekenntnis zur Trümmerliteratur"), in which he called such aesthetic solipsism the work of the "blindman's-buff writer" ("Blindekuh-Schriftsteller") who, instead of reflecting human reality in his work, tries to create with his work a new reality, locating literature outside of real time and real space. "The blindman's-buff writer sees into himself, he builds a world to suit himself," Böll wrote, arguing that the most egregious example of such writing was Adolf Hitler with his book *Mein Kampf*.[84] In suggesting this, Böll was clearly connecting pure aestheticism in its German incarnation with National Socialism. Likewise, Hilbig's critique of literary solipsism suggested that such megalomania was intimately connected with the insanity of the Stasi.

Both Böll in 1952 and Hilbig in 1994 are criticizing a conception of literature which they view as being similarly hostile to what the chorus of invisible spirits in *Faust* calls "the beautiful world": the place of the writer, both seem to be saying, is inside the real space of the nation, as participants in an ongoing dialog.

Unlike Goethe's *Faust*, however, Cambert is not saved. Instead, he recognizes, like Marlowe's *Faust*, the inevitability of his own damnation. But the concrete reality of the world, against which Cambert and the Stasi (and Goethe's Mephistopheles) had rebelled, still remains and has triumphed. After years of working for the Stasi, Cambert has a far different, more Ozymandian angle on what will remain than his megalomaniac "boss:"

The only thing that we could learn and comprehend, that we could discover and shed light on, above and below and in the middle of Berlin, was the recognition that we had to end, – but not the cosmopolitan Moloch Berlin . . . that we must disappear like a pile of dust, and that sooner or later the stones of Berlin now covered over with earth would be able to give no witness to our era. – This is what I had discovered in years of activity.[85]

Cambert's discovery at the end of the GDR is strikingly similar to the discovery of another, more self-assured author, the West German Peter Schneider, a decade earlier:

All in all, I'm one of the more durable things here. But the city outside, with its fire walls, garden walls, border walls – those walls will still be standing when no one is left to move beyond them.[86]

Although such sentences overestimate the durability of the physical, they are nevertheless a useful warning not to exaggerate the power of literature or authors, those viewers and claspers of the "wavering shapes" about which Goethe had written in his dedication to *Faust*. In spite of the poet's "yearning long unfelt, each impulse swaying," which "to yon calm spirit-realm uplifts my soul," the poet and even his creations are fleeting, as Goethe knew.[87] Hilbig and Schneider are suggesting that neither writers nor literature should place themselves outside of or in opposition to the real process of history. All authors, even the most powerful, ultimately disappear. What remains is their work, to the extent that it is real, and the world itself, and perhaps a few readers, who must face the task of interpretation, of piecing together their world and its remaining texts, alone. Neither Böll nor Hilbig is denying the importance of literature. On the contrary, their work clearly demonstrates the ability of realist literature to confront and help shape political reality by entering into a dialog with readers. But that dialog must occur within the real time of history and the real space of the nation, and as such it must always reflect the inevitable fact of its own impermanence.

CHAPTER 5

The rebirth of tragedy?

WEST GERMANY AS ISLAND OF THE BLESSED

The unexpected advent of German reunification caused a paradoxical crisis in German self-understanding. This crisis dealt with the question as to where Germany stood in relation to other world powers, particularly the West. Prior to 1945, Germany had a positive concept of a German *Sonderweg*; it defined itself as offering a middle path between the West (France, Britain, the United States) and the East (primarily Russia). The two German states that emerged out of the wreckage of the Third Reich tended to reverse that exalted definition of German alterity by seeking identity as part of Western Europe on the one hand or the Russian sphere of influence on the other.

During the *Historikerstreit*, Jürgen Habermas had argued that West Germany's most splendid achievement was its anchoring in the community of democratic Western values.[1] Habermas even went so far as to suggest that, because they had learned from their country's horrible past, West German young people were in the process of developing a "postnational" identity, moving beyond the concept of the nation, with all of its negative connotations of nationalism, xenophobia, and war. Far from basing their collective identity on old-fashioned, discredited ideas such as "Volk" and "Blut," many young West Germans found their collective identity in the concept of a civil society and in a devotion to Western democratic values and the rule of law which Habermas, borrowing a term from Dolf Sternberger, referred to as "constitutional patriotism."[2]

Many – and not only on the left-liberal side of the political spectrum, to which Habermas himself belonged – agreed with the sociologist in his positive assessment of the accomplishments of the Federal Republic. It is telling that in spite of the vehemence and frequent vitriol with which the *Historikerstreit* was conducted in Germany, none of the antagonists questioned West Germany's anchoring in the West. As young right-wing journalist Ansgar Graw subsequently pointed out in a polemical critique, "both Habermas and [his conservative opponent] Stürmer agreed in their vehement rejection of a reunified German nation-state and in a euphoric affirmation of 'the West.'"[3]

Even an intellectual like Arnulf Baring, professor of history at the Freie Universität in Berlin and significantly more conservative than Habermas, seemed nevertheless to agree with the concept of a "postnational identity" for West Germany. As Baring suggested in a book published shortly after German reunification, West Germans after 1945 had avoided their previous problems with national identity by evading the question of national identity altogether:

During those forty years a word like "national existence" was never spoken out loud. This word was gone. The Reich was gone, the responsibility was gone, and we were happy about that; because we had proven ourselves to be relatively untalented in trying to define our place in the world on our own. We West Germans observed Konrad Adenauer's commutation of Germany into a Rhinish state with great relief. Our attempts to understand our own history were accompanied by the belief that this history had become essentially irrelevant.[4]

Where there is no nation, there can be no problems with nationalism. Germans escaped the problems of their national past by ceasing to think of themselves as Germans.

In the face of surveys indicating consistently that young West Germans felt closer to youth in France, Italy, and England than to their peers in East Germany, some pollsters decried what they felt was insufficient national self-identification in a "wounded nation."[5] Habermas and his allies, on the other hand, saw the weakening of traditional national identity in the postwar Federal Republic as normal and desirable. While some older writers like Walser spoke nostalgically about Germany's lost Eastern territories, most young people and other writers and intellectuals did not speak about such a loss. If there was a "wound called Germany," in Walser's words, they did not feel it, and they certainly did not want, as Walser did, to "keep [it] open."

The advent of German reunification rapidly changed what had been a relatively stable environment, making many West Germans fear for the future of the comfortable, humane, democratic state they had achieved. Prior to German reunification in October 1990, there had been a general hope that the history of the new, enlarged Federal Republic would more or less repeat the history of the older, smaller Federal Republic. If the year 1945 had been experienced, at least in retrospect, as a radical break from previous German history, and particularly from the *Sonderweg*, the years 1989 and 1990 were experienced, rather, as a continuation of an already positive development. On both sides of the former Iron Curtain, the feeling was that the five East German states and East Berlin would be integrated into the already existing framework of the FRG without causing any significant changes in that framework. Far from being the sum of both its parts, the reunified Germany would be the old Federal Republic, expanded by 108 thousand square kilometers. As Jurek Becker suggested, "it is quite obvious that a unified Germany will be a West German Germany."[6]

In the spring of 1990 German intellectuals engaged in a heated debate about the constitutional process of reunification itself. This debate was to prove symptomatic of German concerns with continuity and discontinuity after 1989. The central question in the debate was whether reunification should proceed via the writing of a new constitution to replace the two existing constitutions in West and East Germany, or whether, instead, East Germany should accept the existing West German Basic Law. Behind the complex mechanics and legalisms of the constitutional debate was a crucial issue: the extent to which reunification would occur in continuity with previous West German history or as a break from it. In the end, those preferring a simple accession of East Germany to the Basic Law won out: German reunification was to occur not as an end to the history of the Federal Republic but as its logical continuation. Practically, reunification represented a radical discontinuity for East Germans; but psychologically many Germans believed that East Germany was simply transforming itself into an already successful model. Hence the Christian Democratic Party's strong success with its 1990 slogan "No Experiments!" – itself a repeat of a famous 1957 election theme. The constitutional debate showed the strength of German desires for continuity with the Federal Republic. A constitution intended in 1949 as merely provisional had by 1989 become a hallowed document which Germans feared to change.

It was not only in the constitutional debate that partisans of continuity with the Federal Republic won out in the wake of the

GDR's collapse. At a great many levels the concept of West German continuity triumphed over the concept of discontinuity during the year of German reunification, throwing into question the idea of 1989 as a new "zero hour." Indeed, many of the debates of 1990 can be understood only in the context of the larger concern about continuity. An example of the triumph of West German continuity over discontinuity in 1990 was the decision to integrate all of the reunified Germany into the territory and command structure of the North Atlantic Treaty Organization rather than neutralize part or all of the country. Reunification was to ensure the political, legal, economic, and military continuity of the new Germany with the structures that had developed in West Germany over the course of the previous forty years. Helmut Kohl, the Basic Law, the Deutsche Mark, faster automobiles, and NATO were all to come to East Germany, courtesy of its Western counterpart; nothing was to go in the other direction. Even the debates over the location of the German capital that emerged in 1990 and 1991 became a touchstone for the degree of acceptance of West German continuity or discontinuity. The Rhineland town of Bonn came to stand for a cosy Western continuity, while the overpoliticized East German Berlin represented at least a modicum of discontinuity.[7] It is significant that even many years after reunification had occurred and the move from Bonn to Berlin was clearly a settled matter the proposed move nevertheless remained highly controversial. Indeed, what is most remarkable about the Bonn-Berlin debate is that it happened at all, after forty years of cold war testaments to the status of Berlin as the once and future German capital, after the drama of the 1948–49 Berlin airlifts, the powerful symbol and reality of the Wall, and the many visits by American and other world leaders.

Meanwhile the realization that German reunification would ultimately affect the Federal Republic as well as the GDR caused the emergence of a new nostalgia for the postwar West German state. "I am a little sad to think that the boring, tiny, unloved, practical Federal Republic of Germany, in which I grew up, will no longer exist in the future," wrote Patrick Süskind.[8] The extent to which life in the pre-reunification Federal Republic became idealized after 1989 can be seen in Arnulf Baring's 1991 suggestion that prior to 1989 the Federal Republic had been a kind of "Insel der Seligen" ("Island of the Blessed") in which previous political conflicts were virtually eliminated: "In hindsight the old Federal Republic . . .

appears as an idyllic phase in our history."[9] Several years later, Baring's words were echoed by Michael Mertes and Hubertus von Morr, intellectuals in Helmut Kohl's chancellery, in the form of a parodic fairy tale. For them, the Federal Republic had been a serene paradise:

Once upon a time there was a tiny island in the middle of the ocean of time, the ocean of blood and tears called Western Europe. On this island lived the tribe of the Germans. The Germans believed themselves to be something very special . . . Because the Germans were thorough people and left nothing to chance, they decided at their party and church conventions that war had been done away with, and that the ocean surrounding them consisted not of blood and tears but of ecologically correct fresh water.[10]

Nostalgia for the Federal Republic, even in such ironic tones, was a measure of just how praiseworthy and precious its achievements were considered to be. At the moment of its demise, many in the West discovered, perhaps for the first time, that they loved their country.

THE CONSERVATIVE TRADITION

Not everyone in Germany had loved the Federal Republic, however, and nostalgia was not the only German reaction to the events of 1989/1990. As we have seen, the proponents of a "third path" in the GDR in the autumn of 1989 did not wish for simple continuity with the FRG. Authors like Stefan Heym, Christa Wolf, and Christoph Hein dreamed of a socialism with a human face: the preservation of collective ownership of the means of production but the introduction of basic political freedoms and democratic principles. For this reason opposition to German reunification, at least if it meant continuity with the Federal Republic of Germany, has generally been considered "leftist," even pro-GDR, while support for a German reunification implying West German continuity has appeared "conservative" or even right-wing. Such simplistic categories, however, overlook the extent of the intellectual transformation of 1989 and in particular the complete bankruptcy of German socialism and the rising prestige of the German right.

There were other reasons for opposing continuity with West Germany than support for East Germany or the Soviet Union, and those reasons have largely been overlooked in discussions on

German reunification. Such reasons go to the heart of German national identity and the German intellectual and cultural tradition. In 1990 Stefan Ulbrich, at one time a functionary in the radical-right Viking Youth, wrote, "We will yet come to feel that reunification was a defeat for the real national project."[11] That it was possible not only for left-wingers and socialists but also for conservatives and right-wingers to oppose German reunification may seem unlikely and surprising, but only because the forty years of the existence of the Federal Republic witnessed a remarkable decline or at least silencing of more traditional conservative German anti-Western voices.

In the wake of the European revolutions of 1989, it became fashionable to suggest that socialism was dead and that there was therefore no longer any serious opposition to capitalism, or to the Western model. Such a viewpoint was shortsighted both historically and as a prognostication for the present and future. In fact, of course, there has always been and continues to be significant opposition to capitalism, especially to its Western-American model; indeed, in the absence of any outside opposition to itself, capitalism seems to generate its own internal opposition. Moreover, not all opposition to capitalism is or ever has been socialist; a significant part of the opposition to capitalism is and has always been conservative in nature. It is particularly difficult for Americans to understand such opposition, because the North American continent never experienced the feudalism out of which such conservative opposition frequently grows; only the so-called "Old South" with its anti-capitalist values preserved such a memory, and that memory has largely been eradicated with the rise of the enthusiastically capitalist "New South." Moreover, forty years of the cold war's rigid dualism caused a virtual erasure of memory about the true historical meaning of the word "conservatism," since they taught Westerners to think of capitalism as in some unexplained way "conservative" and opposition to capitalism as "leftist."

History suggests, however, that opposition to capitalism is as often or even more often "rightist" than it is "leftist." Capitalism is after all, even in Marx's admiring view, a revolutionary force that dissolves old structures of community and value, tending to reduce all these complexities to purely monetary calculations: capitalism is the rule of capital, not of princes, philosopher-kings, priests, or warriors. From thinkers like Coleridge in England, Novalis in Germany, and

Dostoyevsky in Russia there has always been political, romantic, conservative, and/or clerical opposition to capitalism. Capitalism, in other words, has traditionally been opposed by those older ("conservative") forces which it displaced, not only by the newer ("revolutionary") forces which believed they would displace it. To this day the Roman Catholic Church, one of the few major world institutions with a history that significantly predates the rise of capitalism, continues to speak out against the naked rule of money at the same time that it inveighs against homosexuality and abortion. In doing so, it is preserving a long tradition of Christian anticapitalism most contemporary Christians have forgotten.

Fritz Stern has referred to the conservative anticapitalist tradition in Germany as the "politics of cultural despair." In his pioneering study of 1961, Stern focused on such significant late nineteenth and early twentieth-century right-wing figures as Paul de Lagarde, Julius Langbehn, and Arthur Moeller van den Bruck. But the romantic anticapitalist tradition includes many other important writers, philosophers, and cultural figures – Arthur Schopenhauer, Richard Wagner, Friedrich Nietzsche, Thomas Mann, Ferdinand Tönnies, Oswald Spengler, Martin Heidegger; the list is long and distinguished. Because the National Socialists often invoked this pessimistic anticapitalist tradition, it tended to be taboo in Germany after 1945, and especially after the cultural revolution of 1968. Nevertheless, the tradition has continued to exist. From time to time this conservative anticapitalism has become conjoined with more "leftist" or Marxist critiques – as in the work of the early György Lukács, Walter Benjamin, or the Frankfurt School. As these examples show, such rare conjunctions of the left and the right have sometimes produced penetrating critiques of modern industrial society.

After having been forced out of Germany during the Third Reich, Theodor Adorno returned to his homeland several years after the end of the Second World War. Trying to explain why he chose to return to Germany, Adorno suggested that Germany's very economic and social backwardness vis-à-vis the United States provided an autonomous sphere for culture and thought sheltered from the demands of the market economy – paradoxically progressive precisely because of its backwardness:

Here in Germany . . . economic backwardness – and it is uncertain how long such backwardness will be tolerated – is a hiding place for all those progressive aspects that do not see the whole of truth in the currently valid social rules. Once the spirit is brought up to speed, as so many wish, once it is made to order for the customer who is ruled by business, . . . then the spirit will be just as finished and done for as under the cudgels of the fascists.

As Adorno clearly showed here and elsewhere, he viewed the "culture industry" of the USA as almost as dangerous for the creative, philosophical spirit as fascist Germany. Insisting that "qualitatively modern intentions live from backwardness in the process of economic utilization,"[12] Adorno concluded that Germany, as an economically and politically backward country, still guaranteed a kind of freedom of the spirit unavailable to him elsewhere:

In a political phase which to a large extent relegates Germany as a nation to a function of world politics – with all the dangers of a reawakening nationalism that this brings with it – this may be the chance of the German spirit.[13]

One cannot imagine the materialist Marx, who admired capitalism as having "created more massive and more colossal productive forces than have all preceding generations together,"[14] celebrating the supposed qualities of the German spirit so enthusiastically. In Adorno's partiality for the backwaters of economic development one clearly sees the traces of a non-Marxist, idealist anticapitalism. In a book entitled *The German Ideology*, Marx and Engels had written that German philosophy "descends from heaven to earth," ignoring material, economic reality; and that they, in reverse, "ascend from earth to heaven," basing their theory on the bedrock of concrete relations of production in a society.[15] Adorno and many other Western Marxists reversed the process yet again, thus combining Marxism with the more conservative German philosophical traditions that Marx and Engels had gone out of their way to criticize. This reversal has in turn made possible what Eva Geulen has called "the German New Right's surprisingly enthusiastic reception of the Frankfurt School in general and Adorno in particular."[16]

Germany's late national political and economic development and its relative political, economic, and social backwardness led to a society of simultaneity in which the most advanced forms of capitalism warred against the most antiquated social, religious, and economic structures. This "late, fast, and thorough" modernization led to a particularly poignant and strong form of romantic anti-capitalism that culminated in the so-called "Conservative Revolution" of the 1920s, in which conservative cultural figures inveighed against the dual dangers of materialist capitalism and parliamentarianism on the one hand and materialist Communism on the other. Many of the conservative revolutionaries, and particularly the so-called National Bolsheviks spearheaded by Ernst Niekisch, argued for an alliance between Germany and Russia against the capitalist, materialist West. Although National Socialism presented itself as precisely a "third path" between these two evils, it betrayed the idealists of the "Conservative Revolution" and failed to live up to the anticapitalist expectations it had awakened, even within its own ranks – particularly in the SA. Much recent research on the National Socialists has focussed on their role as modernizers of the German economy, not as reactionary misfits intent on turning back the economic clock.[17] In fact, National Socialism in practice was primarily anti-Bolshevik, not anticapitalist; Hitler was intent on destroying the Soviet Union, not on working with it.[18] For this reason most of the conservative revolutionaries of Weimar Germany felt betrayed by Hitler and either refused to join or ultimately broke with Hitler's National Socialist German Workers' Party, which was a socialist workers' party in name only, not in practice. Conservative, romantic anticapitalism has been on the decline in Germany since 1933, not just since 1945. One of the unexpected outcomes of German reunification in 1990 is that it has spurred a revival of precisely this old, buried tradition.

WEST GERMANY AS ISLAND OF THE ZOMBIES

Conservative critiques of the reunification process are based above all on critiques, indeed rejections of the Federal Republic as it existed prior to 1989. Such critiques bear a remarkable resemblance to the "Ideas of 1914," the Germanic anticapitalist ideology with which Imperial Germany had gone into battle with the western capitalist powers France and England at the outset of the First World War. The critiques of the Federal Republic center on a number of common themes: 1) the Federal Republic's increasing Americanization and/or Westernization; 2) the dangers of a materialism which treats only economic issues as being of primary importance and leaves cultural values marginalized; 3) the death of authentic national or regional cultures; 4) the ecological devastation caused by modern industrial production; 5) the aesthetic ugliness of the capitalist/American way of life; 6) the lack of national autonomy, especially a position of fealty toward the United States; 7) personal rootlessness, alienation, and loss of values; 8) interpersonal coldness and violence; 9) criminality; and 10) the concept of the forty years of West German history as a period of artificial frozenness without natural development or change.

One of the most important figures in such a critique of the Federal Republic has been the film director Hans Jürgen Syberberg, author of the much-debated philosophico-filmic diatribe *Hitler, Ein Film aus Deutschland* [*Hitler, A Film from Germany*] (1977). In that film, Syberberg had presented Hitler as the ultimate tool in capitalist world domination, not as its enemy. In 1990 Syberberg published a controversial book entitled *Vom Unglück und Glück der Kunst in Deutschland nach dem letzten Kriege* [On the Misfortune and Fortune of Art in Germany after the Last War], in which he argued that postwar West Germany had betrayed its own national cultural identity. Hence, Syberberg argued, real German culture continued to exist only in the eastern part of Germany, where it had been protected by the Wall from the ravages of western materialism. Combining the critique of American military occupation of West Germany with that of American cultural values, Syberberg, who had himself fled from the GDR to the Federal Republic as a teenager, wrote, "The plastic world has invaded us,"[19] suggesting that the only possibility for the salvation of German culture came from the not yet decadent East:

Everything will depend upon how much strength the eastern part of Europe will have to resist the western dangers, to hold out against the many temptations at the core – if the East frees itself from its deadly ossifications. Already many western attacks have been broken by the originality of the eastern spirit. The western danger of tendencies toward self-annihilation is deceptively strong, but in spite of many self-blockades in the East and lack of freedom in the political system, once these obstacles have been removed the reunification of eastern and western Europe may be one last chance. Because after the erasure of Prussia, western temptation and eastern strengths – not yet wasted depths of spirit and feeling – stand in opposition to one another. Perhaps the East will awaken to new dedication toward an intelligent symbiosis . . . The wealth of Eastern Europe is not what was created through socialist achievements; rather, it is what remained, what Marxism left out due to refusal and incapacity.[20]

Syberberg's theses were an interesting twist on the popular 1990 theme of "What remains," for they suggested, in absolute contradiction to smug West German certainties, that "what remained" was to be found primarily in the East, not in the West. It was in East Germany that the true Germany had always existed, in hiding, like the medieval Holy Roman Emperor Friedrich Barbarossa of folk legend in his subterranean cavern at the Kyffhäuser mountain in central Germany. Syberberg hoped for a reunification that would proceed as a kind of awakening of that Barbarossa, of the true Germany that would eradicate the alienated, Americanized Germany of the Federal Republic.[21] If the political strategists of the FRG under Konrad Adenauer had viewed their state as a German core ("Kerndeutschland") that would preserve the idea and reality of Germany pending a future reunification with the East, then rightwing anticapitalists like Syberberg had an opposite vision of a cultural core that existed in East Germany and would ultimately reinvigorate the West via traditional German cultural values.

Syberberg's 1990 critique of West Germany was by no means new. In the context of his *Hitler* film, the director had already painted the picture of a "brutal," "materialist" West Germany that had abandoned the most significant aspects of its cultural tradition. The primary achievement of the German intellect had been the critique of sterile western rationalism, the director believed, and in his view that achievement had now been squandered:

In the course of assiduous lessons in rationalism and materialism, they [West Germans] repressed one of their most important traditions, the accursed main strand of their nature, pinning it all on the Nazis without a demurrer, putting the curse of Fascism upon the long history of irrationalism and what relates to it. Hence everything that is mysticism, *Sturm und Drang*, large portions of classicism, the Romantic period, Nietzsche, Wagner, and Expressionism, and their music and parts of the best things they had, were surrendered, relocated, repressed.[22]

In the *Hitler* film Syberberg had underscored this pessimistic view with a powerful soundtrack heavily dominated by music from Richard Wagner's operas. Already in the 1970s the director had come to the conclusion that one of the worst effects of National Socialism had been the making taboo of what was best in the German cultural tradition. He believed that this taboo had led to a spiritual amputation far worse than Germany's geographic shrinkage. What was new in Syberberg's 1990 reflections – besides a number of passages of overt anti-Semitism which led to a minor literary scandal – was the coupling of a romantic anticapitalism anchored in a hatred of West German postwar culture with an explicit acknowledgment that a positive German alterity had, in spite of forty years of Communist dictatorship, been preserved not in the West but in the East.

Syberberg's concept of a repressed tradition was echoed by an unlikely source: Karl Heinz Bohrer, who in the 1980s had developed the concept of postwar German cultural life as a kind of "permanent theodicy" in which evil and the irrational had to be repressed and ignored. According to Bohrer, German postwar intellectual life could recognize only that which was good, rational, and positive; it was incapable of dealing culturally with the problem of evil. Echoing Voltaire's parodic critique of Leibniz's "best of all possible worlds" in *Candide*, Bohrer suggested that for West German intellectuals the problem of evil had ceased to exist. This led to the destruction of entire zones of the imagination:

Historical, political, and social experiences made zones of the imagination taboo for German literary consciousness, or, more precisely: could not even begin to open up such zones. This was certainly a therapeutic necessity, but just as surely it was also a loss of imaginative power.[23]

The critic had painted a picture of West Germany not as Arnulf Baring's "island of the blessed" but as a land of zombies without any aesthetic or political sense and with an absolute fear of conflict and responsibility.

As already noted, Bohrer's ideas were to have great influence in the literary debates following German reunification, and they could also be felt in the concepts of the new German conservatives. It is important to note, however, that Syberberg and Bohrer differed on one crucial point. While both mourned the loss in Germany of the irrationalist tradition, Syberberg identified that tradition as specifically German, whereas Bohrer tended to identify it with non-German cultural figures such as Flaubert, Wilde, and Baudelaire. What that difference meant in practice was that Bohrer appeared as an intellectual Westerner, Syberberg as a supporter of the irrationalist Germanic *Mitteleuropa*.

Syberberg's and Bohrer's thoughts on what they saw as the crippling in Germany of an important intellectual tradition were echoed by many others on the right. Such arguments frequently picked up on the simultaneous debate in the United States about left-wing "political correctness" and suggested that openness to the conservative German tradition was also a question of defending intellectual freedom against left-liberal philistines who wished to destroy the best fruits of German culture. Arguing that it was German thinkers like Nietzsche, Heidegger, and Spengler who were seen as particularly important representatives of the German tradition abroad, Jan Ross suggested that "even embarrassing and dubious aspects of the German tradition" could be fruitful, and that it would be "grotesque" to ban such intellectual products from the country of their origin when they enjoyed such prestige elsewhere.[24]

By the early 1990s more and more young right-wingers began to challenge what they saw as West Germany's traditional intellectual domination by the pro-western liberal left. During the 1960s and 1970s citizens of the Federal Republic had witnessed a political transformation away from the conservative anti-Communist politics of Adenauer and toward Social Democratic-Liberal government, along with an emerging *Ostpolitik* of détente. At the same time West German state and society underwent widespread democratic, grass-roots transformations in which revolutionary and reformist youth sought to change what they saw as ossified, even postfascist structures in Federal Republican society. In contrast to this cultural ferment of the 1960s and 1970s, the 1980s had been years of protracted struggle in which the conservative Christian Democratic Union (CDU) under Kohl regained power and proclaimed a "geistig-moralische Wende" (spiritual-moral transformation) and a return to basic Christian values. However, just as the Social Democratic Party under Willy Brandt and Helmut Schmidt had been plagued by its critics on the left, so too the CDU under Kohl had its critics on the right. The 1980s saw the growth not just of the Greens on the ecological left of the political spectrum, but also of the *Republikaner*, the *Deutsche Volks-Union*, and a plethora of legal and illegal smaller groups and subgroups on the radical right, many of whom criticized Kohl and the Christian Democrats for failure to carry out the conservative national spiritual-cultural transformation that had been promised a decade before.

As early as 1987, in a controversial book entitled *Der Geist steht rechts* [The Intellect Stands on the Right], the left-leaning political scientist Claus Leggewie had warned that the liberalizing trend of the 1960s and 1970s was coming to an end, and that the spiritual future of Germany might well belong to the right wing, which was hoping for a change in Cold War polarities and an intellectual defeat of the left-wing cultural reformers of 1968 by the end of the 1980s. "_That_ is where we will get the themes of the 1990s," predicted Leggewie with remarkable perspicacity.[25] By the early 1990s the left-wing daily newspaper _Tageszeitung_, a product of the post-1968 demo-cratic-leftist cultural transformation, had its complement on the right in a hip young conservative weekly entitled _Junge Freiheit._ Not surprisingly, one of the fundamental tenets of the new young right-wing movement in the wake of 1989/90 was that the very concepts "right" and "left" had lost all value, and that the more significant political distinction was to be made between those who supported the materialist, pro-western German status quo and those from both the former left and the former right who opposed it. For these groups, the East German revolution, yet another "Wende" (trans-formation), offered the promise of a genuine national revolution, along with the hope of picking up thousands of new supporters among the ranks of disillusioned former leftists for whom Commun-ism was no longer an option.

Young historian Karlheinz Weißmann, one of the most important theoreticians for the New Right, wrote a much-read book entitled _Rückruf in die Geschichte_ [Return to History], which demanded Germa-ny's return to "history" after forty years of what Weißmann saw as Federal Republican stagnation. Meanwhile, Weißmann and other conservatives put out a volume of essays entitled _Westbindung_ [Western Ties], in which they called into question the Federal Republic's anchoring in the West. Weißmann suggested that the New Right was a reaction to the destruction of the bipolar world of Yalta and to disillusionment with what, in analogy to the First World War's "Ideas of 1789 and 1914" – i.e. the liberalism of the French revolution and the German conservative revolution of World War One – he called the "Ideas of 1968." As he put it, the intellectual world of the Federal Republic was "just as completely doomed . . . as the inventory of its antifascist reorientation."[26] In this picture, the New Left Ideas of 1968 had been beaten from the intellectual field by the New Right Ideas of 1989. The German spirit stood to the Right, and the collapse of the GDR followed by German reunifica-tion demonstrated to the right-wingers, now styling themselves the "generation of 1989," the necessity for a reorientation of national values. "1989 has become the decisive date for a new generation whose political thought is governed by the decline of socialism and the renaissance of the national," declared the journalist Rainer Zitelmann, one of the primary thinkers of the New Right.[27] In an effort to inaugurate a reactionary numerology, the New Right journalist Frank Hauke wrote, "If one turns the number 68 upside down, 89 appears. To break through the philosophical taboos of the 68ers, to turn the reality that they have created upside down, on its head – for all these reasons the number 89 has cachet."[28]

The attack on 1968 and what that year stood for – the German student movement and left-liberal social transformation – connected the young conservatives not only with older conservatives but also with other members of the younger generation not necessarily associated with right-wing ideology. Following 1989 one of the standard critiques of German culture was that it was dominated by middle-aged left-wing idealists of the 1968 generation who refused to make way for their younger peers, much in the way that, in the United States, baby boomers were seen by members of the so-called "Generation X" as standing in their way. Considering himself a spokesman for this German "Generation X," Zitelmann suggested that "The 'Zeitgeist' is determined by those classes and groups in which the ideology of 1968 predominates," who thereby thwart and exlude those born too late to have been part of the 1968 movement.[29] Using a term from Antonio Gramsci, Zitelmann argued that 1968 had created a "cultural hegemony of the left."[30] Syberberg also made use of Gramscian terminology when he declared, with reference to the generation of 1968, that "This generation, which stepped onto the scene with high moral aspirations, now sits upon the thrones of power and controls the great institutions as the morally good people, . . . invincible in their moral hegemony."[31] This sentence makes it clear that the domination of the 1968 generation is perceived as a function of the antifascist collective superego, which thwarts the rebirth of a healthy nation.

At the core of the critique of the so-called "68ers" were two fundamental problems, one economic and one ideological. Economically, the critique reflected high levels of unemployment – frequently in excess of ten percent, even by overly euphemistic official statistics – in Germany throughout the 1990s. Such unemployment made it extremely difficult for young Germans, whether intellectuals or not, to find adequate employment at acceptable levels of remuneration. This economic problem caused envy and hatred of the previous, more economically successful generation. Ideologically, 1968 seemed to many of those born too late to have experienced it as the last genuinely exciting and important historical event: a time when people still believed in ideals and hoped for change in the political system, when it was still possible to shock the bourgeoisie and its moral structures. For many members of the younger generation, such possibilities now seemed irretrievably lost: all ideals were gone, all ideologies lost, the dream of a better world an illusion. What remained was the search for a decent job, material gratification, and acknowledged or unacknowledged despair about a life without hope and without dreams. To add insult to injury, the younger generation also saw itself criticized for materialism and apathy. Speaking to members of the younger generation, the Green politician Joschka Fischer, a member of the generation of 1968, is said to have declared "Your generation bores me. You are boring and lazy."[32] Fischer's bureau chief, himself a member of the younger generation, responded tartly with an attack on the myth of 1968: "The 68 mythos is nothing but a puddle on whose surface street battles, sexual liberation, the horniness of the commune, and further accomplishments of that time shimmer weakly from the bottom. Why, for all the world, should we be splashing around in this puddle?"[33] As Karen Leeder writes, "The young see themselves as caught in structures which were set up before they were born, and a future which owns little perspective for change. They are a generation born into a finished, resolved society, where there are no struggles to be fought or experiences left to be had."[34] The journalist Jochen Buchsteiner seemed to agree: "The great visions are fulfilled, there's probably nothing more. One can be happy if what we have remains alive and is improved here and there."[35]

One of the most telling examples of the younger generation's frustration was film and theater director Christoph Schlingensief's 1996 production *Rocky Dutschke, '68* at the Volksbühne in East Berlin. A chaotic performance-art happening, *Rocky Dutschke* sought both to recreate the experiences of 1968 for a younger generation and to make fun of them. Promotional material for the show included the following statement attributed to Heiner Müller: "There are no more utopias, there is no point to anything any more, there is no more meaning, only this vacuum, this empty space is there. One doesn't know where one is going in this empty space, one doesn't know how to move, which direction makes sense. Therefore one plays. Out of this the play is created."[36] For the younger generation represented by Schlingensief (born in 1960), the vacuum was all they knew: they had never experienced Müller's socialist utopia or the sense of purpose and meaning that accompanied it. On stage during the production, Schlingensief decried the dominance of 1968 as both a generation and an ideology and stated that as a thirty-five-year-old he would also like to experience something significant. The slogan for the entire production, hung on a large banner outside the Volksbühne, was telling: "Mehr Emotionen!" (More Emotions!), as if the younger generation were bewailing its own lack of affect. Another important aspect of the production were two mock readings of names of Jewish victims of the Holocaust. These readings suggested that it was time to leave the German past behind, and that in a postmodern age of meaninglessness even the worst crimes of the twentieth century had lost all power to compel respect for their victims. *Rocky Dutschke* played to sell-out crowds during May and June of 1996. In its attack on 1968 and its evident frustration with the commemoration of crimes committed long before the birth of its maker, *Rocky Dutschke* demonstrated eloquently that the concerns of the New Right were shared by other members of the younger generation, even by self-critical left-wingers seeking to explode liberal pieties. That the left-wing Schlingensief, albeit in a different form, shared motifs with the staider conservative thinkers Weißmann and Zitelmann clearly shows that Germany in the 1990s was experiencing a critical discourse on the 1968 cultural revolution and a desire for escape from the pangs of the national "conscience" that transcended ideological boundaries.

Ulrich Woelk's 1993 novel *Rückspiel* [Playback] had as its central theme this same frustration and ambivalence. Its main character and first-person narrator is the interior decorator Johannes Stirner, born around 1960, whose entire life is dominated by the memory not so much of Nazi crimes committed by members of his father's and grandfather's generation many decades before his birth as of his older, baby-boom brother's 1968 attempt to come to terms with that patriarchal Nazi past. If Stirner's older brother designs his own life as a moral response to the crimes of his father's generation, Stirner himself designs his life as a hostile response to that father–older-brother conflict. The primary orientation is not toward the father, but toward the older brother. As Stirner notes, it annoys him that his older brother "acts as if his generation had acquired exclusive rights to the revolution back then."[37] For Germany's Generation X, the brother's baby-boom generation has already won everything: the moral and political victory over the father's generation, represented in the novel by a conservative teacher named Kampe; good jobs with economic power; and access to beautiful women. In the course of this novel we learn that Stirner has lost his job, his self-respect, and his girlfriend. It is his brother's friend Johnny, a quintessential representative of the 68ers, who has taken the girlfriend. Stirner's Oedipal conflict is in fact a sibling rivalry: it is his brother, not his father, who always already has access to phallic power and, because of his attack on the generation of German Nazis, to a clear conscience. Stirner describes his brother-conflict by declaring that, while he had always previously seen his brother as a "role model," "as someone who knows what's what,"

In the last few years that has all changed. In the end he could do whatever he wanted, and for me it was all nothing more than a big lie. Maybe this was the real reason for my trip to Berlin: not that I wanted to do him one last favor by bringing forward proof that Kampe was a fascist; rather, perhaps my real motivation was to prove precisely the opposite: that Kampe was not a fascist, thereby causing the last pillar of his understanding of the world to come crashing down.[38]

The battle against the dominant 1968er brother, in other words, is fought out over the bodies of the father's and grandfather's generations, the latter represented by Kampe; this is a battle for both the collective and the individual superego. If the older brother's battle cry is a coming to terms with the Nazi past, the younger brother's battle cry is that the older brother's attempts at such a coming to terms were from the very beginning hypocritical. And yet all such efforts on Stirner's part are both metaphorically and literally impotent, because Stirner is almost as neurotic as Hilbig's Cambert. When Stirner tries to force his former girlfriend to have sexual intercourse with him, he finds that he is incapable of doing so,

because one cannot *desire* to rape, one can only rape, and I saw myself as ridiculous . . ., because I was now at the end of my tether, I could have opened up my pants, and she would have seen what she knew anyway, that she had no need to defend herself.[39]

Stirner is incapable of controlling either historical or sexual power. For him, all power is in the hands of his brother's baby-boom generation. Woelk's novel is a critical study of both the left-wing pieties of 1968 and the attempts of a German Generation X to deconstruct those pieties. Far cleverer than Schlingensief's theatre, it nevertheless also demonstrates the discursive power of the 1990s critique of 1968.

With respect to German history and the problem of *Vergangenheits-bewältigung* (coming to terms with the past), the New Right picked up where the *Historikerstreit* had left off several years earlier. In that debate, Nolte had argued that the Holocaust was by no means unique but rather part of a general modern trend to genocide, and that West Germans were unduly concerned with "coming to terms" with the Nazi past. It was therefore time to let that past finally pass away and proceed instead with the problems of the present. An undue concern with German guilt for crimes committed so long ago weakened the nation and tended to perpetuate the self-destructive power of the collective superego. As Ludolf Herrmann had already declared in 1983, "We have . . . come to terms with Hitler. What we have not come to terms with is the coming-to-terms with Hitler." Hermann went on: "The transformation that we need consists not in once again chewing the cud of 1933 or 1945, but rather in overcoming the belated disobedience to Hitler. We have become alienated from ourselves historically, and we must now attempt to overcome this alienation."[40] So too, after 1989, the New Right argued that it was time for Germans to put the "metaphysics of guilt" (Karlheinz Weißmann) behind them. As historian Karl Richter suggested, "The therapeutic approach to the past is at an end. The future has other tasks in store than the prayer wheel of singular German war-guilt. In the face of the dance on the Wall, Auschwitz has become insignificant for the . . . soul of the strength-ening nation."[41] Syberberg suggested that postwar West German art had been dominated by a dishonest obsession with Nazi crimes. He characterized such art as a neo-Papist "indulgence-art" (Ablaß-Kunst) because, as he believed, it sought an all-too-easy monetary escape from the past. The future of German art, he believed, would leave coming-to-terms-with-the-past behind.[42] In order to become a "normal" nation, Germany needed to escape from the demands of an all-too-powerful national conscience.

Like Stefan Ulbrich, some of these conservatives opposed reunifi-cation because they feared it would mean the triumph rather than the end of the FRG and its cosmopolitan westernization. In February 1990 Gerd Bergfleth, an important right-wing thinker and translator of Georges Bataille, published what he called a "German Manifesto" in the rightist journal *Staatsbriefe* asserting that the "true" Germany was the people's movement in the GDR, which was, he believed, directed against the liberalism and "European-Atlantic nihilism" that supposedly dominated the Federal Republic. West Germany, Bergfleth argued, still had to be freed from its domination by foreign, unhealthy influences and slavery to America, just as East Germany had freed itself from the brutal Russians. Political journalist Marcus Bauer, former organizer of the "Working Group for Young Republicans," a youth organization of the radical Right, opposed a western-dominated German reunification and frequently contributed to subcultural right-wing periodicals such as *Europa Vorn*, *Junge Freiheit*, and *wir selbst*. Bauer echoed Syberberg's idea that East Germany was the true core of German cultural integrity, suggesting:

A German–German confederation . . . with neutral status, within which the GDR would continue to exist as an independent commonwealth reforming itself but not giving itself up. Supported by the economic potential of the Federal Republic, the GDR, as the culturally more intact and socially more creative part of our land would become the genuine core of a future, united Germany. Such a development would have done more justice to the term "reunification."[43]

Roland Bubik, editor of a book that claimed to represent the dreams of young German conservatives, wrote about the East Germans: "In questions of getting along together it is they who will most likely be able to provide role models, not we in the West. In the year 1989 I had the hope that in the wake of reunification our culture would indeed be able to receive new strength from the middle [i.e. East Germany]."[44] Heimo Schwilk, another major figure in the German New Right, suggested similarly: "The Germans from the former GDR are . . . the 'more genuine' Germans, because, in their experience of deprivation and authoritarian state oppression, they have better preserved German virtues such as communitarian spirit, solidarity, inwardness, and knowledge of tradition."[45]

In many ways the right-wing criticisms of West German cultural barrenness echoed not only the tradition of the conservative revolution and the "Ideas of 1914" but also the rhetoric of West German ecological fundamentalists during the 1980s. In his attack on pop culture, for instance, Karl Richter sounded virtually indistinguishable from the cultural eco-fundamentalists of a decade earlier:

The psychic control of industrial society occurs not via books or the symphony hall. Rather, it occurs via subtle background bombardment during one's morning drive to work, it occurs via the permanent wall of sound in the supermarket, at the barbershop, in the pub. Tuning out is impossible, and the mechanisms of reception are largely unconscious.[46]

Richter continued,

Whether the executive organs of alien power are occupation troops or television and radio institutions makes little difference in the long run. What is decisive is the fact of creeping loss of identity via the painting over of traditional, culturally determined structures of consciousness and life with a layer of amorphous, supra- and antinational civilisation-trash. This process is now in effect globally, and it is insignificant whether the processes of cultural erosion occur among Thai mountain tribes or in solitary villages in upper Bavaria.[47]

Such an argumentation is, of course, perversely multiculturalist in its approach, since it is directed against a unifying, dominant culture – in this case American popular culture. Such a right-wing multiculturalism may seem paradoxical but is entirely intentional. Stefan Ulbrich suggests that in the battle against Americanization "multiculturalism [seems to be] the only perspective for the future which allows one to experience modern industrial society not as egalitarian monotony but rather as a colorful togetherness."[48] Syberberg has also spoken in favor of an anti-American multiculturalism. He writes that

What is concentrating itself here in the realm of the media is a transatlantic battle in which Africa, Asia, or even the America of its original inhabitants, as well as other continents, now have no more voice and no more weapons. Even the Japanese are only providing the apparatus now, while the meaning and the programs come from America . . . Words like occupation come to mind, and comparisons to hamburgers. This is a battle for images and sounds, for words, for what we desire, what we live for, what we eat, how we dress, what we . . . love . . .[49]

Eva Geulen has accurately identified the psychological impulse behind this right-wing multiculturalism by suggesting that in the German New Right "the older imperialist '*Sendungsbewußtsein*' is inverted into the consciousness of a threatened minority."[50] This multiculturalism denies the claims of liberal individualism and treats cultures as given organic structures to which human beings must conform. It denies the claims of the universal and asserts the claims of the particular. Richter's thoughts fuse contemporary multiculturalism with German cultural critique to produce a eulogy for dying memories, and for lost organic communities. In Richter's case, the potential racism of such an insistence on the preservation of cultural essences is not far below the surface: Richter also inveighs against racial mixing and stops just short of a call for asserting the purity of German blood.[51]

For many Germans in both the East and the West, the old Federal Republic is associated with American cultural domination. The main character in Jentzsch's novel *Seit die Götter ratlos sind* suggests that West Germans are simply imitators: "They act perfectly, the Wessis. Their perfection is a second-rate copy of the American way of life."[52] Because of the close association between the Federal Republic and the United States, anti-Americanism and an opposition to the "old" Federal Republic go hand in hand. The anti-Americanism of the German right hooked into a tradition of anti-Americanism as anti-imperialism that went back to the anti-missile movement of the early 1980s, which some right- as well as left-wingers had seen as a genuine opportunity to assert German independence. In their relationship to the National Socialist past, the young right-wing anti-Westerners of the post-1989 period took up the historical debates about a German *Sonderweg* that had occurred in the early 1980s. Whereas left-liberal historians tended to oppose the *Sonderweg* and support the integration of Germany into the West, the young right-wingers supported the *Sonderweg* because of their resistance to what they saw as the cultural hegemony of the West. As Richter suggested, "The 'German *Sonderweg*,' a permanent mote in the eye of the standard bearers of the Atlantic community of values, ought really to be seen as a sign of quality of what is German in the world, not as a stigma."[53] Here again the young conservatives were seeking to go back beyond the "zero hour" of 1945 and connect the reunified Germany to a new pride in national identity and therefore difference from the West. If Kohl's goal for German reunification had been the final and irrevocable normalization of the Federal Republic, the elimination of anything that would substantially differentiate it from other western countries, the Chancellor's conservative opponents in the flourishing young right-wing milieu insisted on German alterity as a precious value against the materialist and decadent West.

THE SONG OF THE GOAT

One of the most important contributions to the ongoing conservative reorientation in the wake of German reunification was an essay published by Botho Strauß in February 1993 entitled "Anschwellender Bocksgesang" [Goat Song, Swelling Up]. Strauß's plays, books, and essays had frequently depicted the empty sterility of West German life. In *Schlußchor* [Final Chorus] (1991), whose title was probably a reference to the final chorus of Beethoven's Ninth Symphony, played during the festivities of German reunification, Strauß had portrayed a self-absorbed West Germany completely unprepared to deal with the arrival of the national in the form of a St. John the Baptist-like crier who repeatedly shouted the word "Germany!" into the quotidian boredom of postindustrial Western life. In the final passage of the play, one of the characters symbolically defeathers and devours a German eagle.[54] In the play *Das Gleichgewicht* [Equilibrium] (1993), Strauß painted the picture of a Germany beginning to lose its equilibrium in the face of deep emotional currents. *Das Gleichgewicht* is the story of the relationships between a materialist German businessman who declares that "the world will be liberal in its entirety, or it will not exist at all any more!", a fundamentalist son who calls West German materialism a "spiritual bully, a liberal moloch that has transformed our life into a stinking trash heap,"[55] and the businessman's mysterious wife who declares that beneath the façade of placid materialism deeper mythic forces are seething:

Somewhere there behind all the silly words, behind our tortuous nervousness there must still be hidden a bit of the tragic life, for which we do not possess the right expression. Do you understand? We make faces, we hurry by each other, and yet we sense it: just there behind us something large and powerful is moving . . .[56]

Strauß's 1993 essay seemed to sum up much of the post-reunification ferment in German intellectual life. At the same time, as Sigrid Berka has suggested, it made explicit much of what had always been "hermetically, allegorically, or metaphorically present" in Strauß's work, partially transforming a "hidden message into a journalistic, i.e. polemical," clarity.[57] The "song of the goat" was a literal translation of the Greek word *tragöidia*, which means "goat-song." In giving his essay this title, Strauß rather vaguely alluded to

Nietzsche's *Birth of Tragedy*, in which the figure of the goat-man or satyr, "the offspring of a longing for the primitive and the natural" as well as "the archetype of man, the embodiment of his highest and most intense emotions," is the choral singer whose song gives birth to tragedy itself.[58] Nietzsche's essay of 1872 had been an invocation of the power of art, particularly tragedy, in the face of a sterile Socratic rationalism which Nietzsche believed to have run its course. Strauß's essay was also an invocation of the power of tragedy which lurked behind the shallow accomplishments of West German consumerism. If Nietzsche had argued that the root of human life was suffering, and that in its Greek origins tragedy had been a sacred musical-religious ritual which enabled human beings to endure an otherwise unbearable existence, Strauß declared that the materialist West had reached its limits and was facing catastrophe without the hope of cultural traditions that would help it survive:

The rumbling of which we are now aware, the negative sensibility of the enemy reactions, which immediately become orgies of hatred, are seismic indicators, anticipations of an even greater affliction which is making itself known through those people who will have to feel its worst aspects.[59]

The young right-wing hooligans in East and West Germany beating up foreigners, the disabled, and homosexuals, Strauß argued, were in fact the unfortunate messengers of even greater tragedies and catastrophes to come. The increasing volatility of German public life, he suggested, came from the feeling that an entire way of life had reached its unnatural limit, and that it was impossible to continue with the smug, wasteful materialism of the West German past. Strauß referred to the general feeling of fear as "the terror of premonition" (der Terror des Vorgefühls).[60] Like Syberberg, Strauß mourned the loss of what he saw as the most valuable part of Germany's cultural heritage: its irrationalism as a critique of economic utilitarianism. An economic philosophy which saw money as the sole standard of value offered no protection in a time of declining standards of living, whereas spiritual values remained unaffected by economic shrinkage. But Germany's cultural heritage was dead, Strauß mourned, and those who had helped kill it – German liberals and pro-westerners – were the ones who would need it most in the coming crises:

It is too bad, simply too bad that tradition has been spoiled. Yes, it is turning rotten in front of the gates like a shipment of valuable foodstuffs which the population will have to do without because of some silly tariff conflicts. Tradition is dying in front of the barriers of an arrogant overestimation of contemporaneity, it is dying in the face of the ignorance of those educational and training institutes that have been constipated for one or two generations, eyries of the darkest enlightenment, which find themselves in an eternally ambivalent battle of temptation and rejection against the ghosts of the repetition of history: "Resist the beginnings!" . . . Oh! Make a useful beginning yourselves![61]

Once again, Strauß's description of the West German antifascist consensus as enforced by "eyries of the darkest enlightenment" recalls Freud's description of the individual and collective superego as an agency set up for the "weakening and disarming" of the (individual or collective) ego, determined "to watch over it, like a garrison in a conquered city." Strauß's frustration is a function of his belief that such a punitive stance is not only unfruitful but suicidal. In the face of a growing cultural sterility that was partially the function of an overwhelming national guilt, Strauß suggested, tragedy was inevitable, even if one knew nothing of the form it would ultimately take:

We know nothing of the nature of the future tragedy. We hear only the noise of the mysteries becoming louder, the song of the goat in the depths of our actions. The songs of sacrifice that are swelling up at the core of what we have done (im Innern des Angerichteten).[62]

For Nietzsche, tragedy had been an art form that helped people cope with inevitable suffering. For Strauß, tragedy was the suffering itself, and there seemed no hope for a healing art. Nietzsche's essay on tragedy's origins had also been a lament on what he saw as tragedy's death, the dying out of all that was natural, honest, and real in human culture – culminating in the cry that nature itself was gone: "Great Pan is dead!" – a lament that antedated and fore-shadowed the philosopher's widely misunderstood and more famous lament that God Himself was dead.[63] Strauß's essay, on the contrary, was a reminder that in spite of appearances, magical, irrational forces were at work in society and nature that would bring about the end of western sterility. Nietzsche's essay had been a call for the rebirth of tragedy as a saving art form; Strauß's essay was a call for the rebirth of tragedy as beautiful catastrophe, as a purifying Armageddon, of the sort that some ecological fundamentalists had dreamed of in the early 1980s.[64] Like so many other cultural conservatives, Strauß had been strongly influenced by German ecological philosophy of those years: "It was the ecologists who first declared that things cannot continue in this way."[65] And like other cultural conservatives, Strauß declared that there was no such thing as a "third path" between socialism and capitalism, since both socialism and capitalism were different manifestations of economic materialism. On the contrary, there were only two paths, according to Strauß: acceptance of the materialist, economist status quo or forceful opposition to it.

Alain de Benoist, the leader of the French Nouvelle Droite, whose influence was strongly felt among young right-wingers in Germany, had also declared, in spite of his sympathy with the proponents of a "third path," that such a path did not exist:

If one admits that liberalism and Marxism are heirs to the same ideological matrix, specifically the philosophy of the Enlightenment . . ., one can assert with equal validity that there are in fact only two "paths." The collapse of the Soviet system can only strengthen this way of looking at things. Our problem, in fact, is to put forward an *alternative* to the dominant ideology (the axiom of special interests, the terrorism of consumption, political spectacle, etc.).[66]

Echoing de Benoist, Strauß also suggested that there was only one significant conflict in modern German society: between (decadent) materialism and (healthy) idealism. All other conflicts and forces were merely paper tigers:

Today irreconcilability exists only between the realm that is seeking to achieve political-social hegemony over spirit, morality, science, and belief; and, on the other hand, the vigorous resistance to such claims of hegemony. In a certain sense there is a political correlate to the battle against and the denial of the claims to omnipotence of the political. A spiritual reserve which, in the name of the wisdom of the peoples, in the name of Shakespeare, in the name of diminishing the value of worldliness, in the name of improving the human power to suffer, is battling against the political relativizations of existence.[67]

In suggesting such an opposition, Strauß was aligning himself with a long German tradition of dichotomies: culture vs. civilization, art vs. money, spirit vs. politics, personality vs. masses, community vs. society, quality vs. quantity, in which the first term in the dichotomy always represents the "healthy" wisdom of Germanic tradition and the second the decadent rationalism of Western materialism.

Increasingly it became clear that with reunification it was not just the old German Democratic Republic that had disappeared. With it had disappeared an entire framework of international, intellectual, and political antagonisms and structures which had previously served to provide the Federal Republic with a political and military focus. The "change from the Federal Republic into Germany," as Dan Diner called it, had meant more than simply the expansion of the old Federal Republic. It had meant a qualitative change in social and political culture. Diner suggested that the change affected "fundamental concepts of political language and semantics, is transforming institutions and, apparently, undermining the party system."[68] Not only that, but the Federal Republic's Western identity was seriously being called into question by conservative intellectuals for the first time since the end of the Second World War. Arnulf Baring wrote that sixteen million East Germans were perfectly capable of pulling sixty million West Germans substantially to the East, and Mathias Wedel wrote that East Germans were changing the face of the Federal Republic: "The Eastification (Ossifizierung) of the Federal Republic has begun."[69] Elisabeth Noelle-Neumann suggested in the fall of 1994 that "in a spiritual sense the West Germans are becoming more like the East Germans."[70] There was growing fear that West Germany's commitment to western values had been nothing but an epiphenomenon of the larger East–West struggle, destined to disappear with the struggle itself. That German conservatives and left-liberals could be found on all sides of these issues contributed to the ideological confusion. Conservatives both supported and opposed Germany's westernization, just as they supported and opposed the *Sonderweg*. While most conservatives favored a reaffirmation of the German nation, they were profoundly ambivalent about if not downright hostile to those representatives of German *Kultur* whom they viewed as overly critical of the nation. Hence it was unclear exactly what their concept of a future German *Kulturnation* entailed; and, moreover, because of some conservatives' critique of reunification itself it was not entirely clear where they wished to locate the nation: in the East, in the West, in a revitalized whole, or in a sacrosanct sphere of *Kultur*. Did German "conservatism" mean an upholding of the German past, and of history, or did it, instead, mean that the past should "pass away" (Nolte)? German conservatives were almost as divided on all of these questions as German liberals. With the growing internationalization of the world economy, further progress on European integration, and "normalization" of Germany itself, this debate promised to be one of the most significant aspects of post-reunification German culture and politics. Reunification had opened a path to an almost forgotten cultural past; but it had done so in a way that made the connections between the German past and the German present as problematic, and as paradoxical, as ever.

CHAPTER 6

The defense of childhood and the guilt of the fathers

The surprise bestseller of 1991 was *Die Verteidigung der Kindheit* [The Defense of Childhood], by Martin Walser. The novel tells the life story of a lawyer named Alfred Dorn, a man unusual not because of particular talent, beauty, or intelligence, but because he does very little in the course of over five decades. Born on September 9, 1929 in Dresden, Dorn has a domineering mother, Martha, whom he dearly loves and a somewhat licentious father, the dentist Gustav Dorn, whom he dislikes. Because Gustav frequently has affairs with other women, Frau Dorn ultimately divorces him. She has a strong tendency to use her son as a weapon in her war with Gustav. At the age of fifteen, Alfred Dorn experiences the February 13, 1945 destruction of his home town and with it of much of his life. He survives, but the shock of the disaster in Dresden becomes yet another contributing factor to a neurosis that slowly eats away at him. Dorn becomes obsessed with the past and incapable of living in the present. Like the Stasi in Hilbig's *Ich*, Dorn would like to be able to stop time in its tracks. The passage of time is unbearable to him, because it inevitably brings with it destruction; and Dorn ultimately devotes his life to the impossible "defense of childhood" in the novel's title. His great trauma is a failure to preserve the past after Dresden's destruction:

This fear of decay could break out at any moment, the terror awakened by the passage of time. The thirteenth of February 1945. That was always the day at which he landed. He frequently descended into a weeping that made him seem to himself like a little child. Why, in the summer of 1945, had he not searched and dug longer in the charred ruins of the house? Maybe the pictures, the albums could have been saved. There had been nothing more essential than digging in the ruins of the house at Borsbergstraße 28d. And he had failed to do it.[1]

Because of his feelings of guilt as a result of Dresden's destruction,

Dorn becomes the one-man curator of his own personal museum; like the Stasi, he is a collector. He saves photographs, objects, and pieces of writing; he devotes his life to searching for any flotsam and jetsam that may have survived the destruction of Dresden. Dorn writes to friends and acquaintances asking for objects and memories, because: "Without his past he was nothing." Dorn's mother becomes "the storehouse of his past"; and when she, inevitably, dies, he is devastated: "The death of his mother made his past into an inaccessible continent."[2] Left alone by the only woman he has ever loved, the middle-aged lawyer turns one room of his house into the site of what he calls his "Mother Cult." The result of this neurotic obsession with the past and with memory is that, just like Hilbig's Stasi, Dorn ultimately forgets the present and the future. He remains forever a psychological child; he never has a close personal friend, he never has a lover, he never marries, he never has children. His chief self-identification is as a child. Toward the end of his uneventful life he begins to try to act on some vague homosexual inclinations, but by this time it is too late; Dorn has lost the ability to connect with real life. When, in his mid-fifties, he takes an overdose of pills, Dorn's relatives and acquaintances find a wealth of material about the past, but they cannot find anything about the future. Alfred Dorn

had died without making a will. This passionately careful man, who had written to persons who were hardly or barely related to him that they should not neglect to write down on a piece of paper that old photographs which might be located in their possession should be given to Alfred Dorn after their death, this untiring promotor of orderly testate procedures, had died without determining what should happen with the photographs, accounts, postcards, letters, receipts, newspaper clippings, and notes.[3]

Die Verteidigung der Kindheit is above all a psychological novel. It deals almost entirely with Alfred Dorn's mind. The third-person narrator remains objective and cool, with a modicum of sympathy for Dorn, but also with irony. Throughout, the narrator achieves a kind of distanciation from his main character that makes it impossible for readers completely to identify with Dorn. As Parkes has suggested, the novel's "major aesthetic achievement . . . is the balance between identification with and distance from the main character."[4] In some ways Walser's novel reads like an exhaustive psychological case study. Precisely because the narrator does not resort to bathos, the novel becomes a powerful experience in which readers learn to know a man who is himself incapable of intimacy with other human beings, and who is also quite incapable of observing his own problems objectively.

In the context of reunification, *Die Verteidigung der Kindheit* struck a powerful chord with German readers. Its main character is both East and West German: he is born and spends his early years in Dresden and subsequently Leipzig, but in the first half of the 1950s he moves to West Berlin and then, in the 1960s, to Hesse. Heike Doane has suggested that Dorn is "a character who registers with seismographic sensitivity not only the losses that shaped his life but also a sense of being that is part of the German identity," and that his experience is typical of "the collective consciousness of a whole generation" of Germans.[5] Because of the time and place of his birth, Dorn represents the last generation of Germans that had still experienced Germany as a unity prior to 1945 but also the first generation to finish its education in the newly formed German states in East and West after 1945: the generation born between 1925 and 1935, who, at the time that *Die Verteidigung der Kindheit* was published, were in their late 50s and 60s – in other words the older generation in both East and West Germany, whose representatives included, among others, the former Chancellor Helmut Kohl (born in 1930) and a great many other major political figures, as well as most of the country's leading writers, including Günter Grass (1927), Siegfried Lenz (1926), Christa Wolf (1929), Hans Magnus Enzensberger (1929), Heiner Müller (1929), Rolf Hochhuth (1931), and Walser himself (1927). This generation is sometimes referred to in Germany as the "Flakhelfer-Generation" (anti-aircraft generation) because of their work in defending Germany against the Allied Armies in 1944 and 1945, made famous in such postwar novels as Walter Kolbenhoff's *Von unserem Fleisch und Blut* [From Our Flesh and Blood] (1946) and films like Bernhard Wicki's *Die Brücke* [The Bridge] (1958). The center of this generation's experience is therefore the utter destruction of their country, followed by the remarkable postwar rebuilding summed up in the concept *Wirtschaftswunder* (economic miracle). Also a significant part of their moral world is the realization that as children they or members of their generation, as well as their mature fathers and mothers, had supported a dictatorship that resulted in a catastrophe for Germany and Europe and the deaths of fifty million people in the Second World War. That this generation could not, because of its age, bear direct responsibility for any of these crimes is expressed in Kohl's frequent 1980s references to a "Gnade der späten Geburt" ("grace of late birth"). But that this generation was nevertheless deeply affected by the events of its childhood is testified to in many other political speeches, in films, and above all in literature.

In one of his most famous poems, Enzensberger expresses the feelings of his generation thus:

> What am I doing here,
> in this country
> to which my elders brought me
> intending no harm?
> Native but comfortless
> absently I am here,
> settled in cosy squalor
> in this nice, contented hole.[6]

Enzensberger describes a sense of hurt for which the older generation of parents and uncles is assigned responsibility: it is the "elders" who have "brought" the poem's "I" to "this country" and hence to participation in German guilt. Many of the greatest works of postwar German literature deal directly or indirectly with the experiences of this generation, from Grass's *Die Blechtrommel* through Uwe Johnson's *Jahrestage* [Anniversaries] to Walser's *Die Verteidigung der Kindheit* itself. Frequently such works have as their main figure a child, such as Grass's Oskar Matzerath, who experiences the actions of his parents as a profound trauma and becomes deformed and grotesque as a result. Walser's 1991 bestseller precisely fits this pattern. Its literary success was a testament to the continuing influence of Walser's generation at the same time that it clearly showed the dangers of dwelling in the past. It is quite probable that in the character of Alfred Dorn, many older West and East Germans recognized part of themselves as they had been half a century earlier: wounded children facing the destruction of their lives, their families, and their fatherland and desperately trying to recreate a past that, in spite of all their efforts, is irrevocably gone.

And yet Alfred Dorn's failure to grow up even after half a century of life could also be taken as a metaphor for German culture more generally. In the wake of the East German revolution, Grass's Oskar Matzerath was taken as precisely such a metaphor. In Syberberg's controversial polemic *Vom Unglück und Glück der Kunst in Deutschland nach dem letzten Kriege*, the director railed bitterly against a West

German cultural scene which, he believed, allowed no possibility for growth, "no other branch . . . and precisely no development."[7] Syberberg used the figure of Oskar Matzerath as a metaphor for postwar West German culture generally. With reference to what he saw as the West German "preference for the small, the low, for crippling, for the sick, for filth,"[8] Syberberg declared: "The fact that the central figure of the best known postwar novel in Germany is a dwarf illustrates my observations."[9] Several months later, Schirrmacher used the same metaphor to invoke the vision of a stunted West German cultural history: "Oskar Matzerath, the hero of *Die Blechtrommel*, is the representative of [West German] consciousness . . . from a certain point on it refused to grow, it has become old, but it still likes to play the child."[10] The critic suggested that all of West German literature was characterized by such a standstill, what he called the "frozenness, the timeless ageing of the Federal Republic,"[11] and that this strange state of affairs represented the life experience of a single generation, specifically Grass's and Walser's generation of "Flakhelfer."

The concept of 1945 as a "zero hour" had implied, for the younger generation of the immediate postwar years, a complete break with the crimes of its forebears and hence both a kind of moral absolution and a moral revolution. Younger writers insisted on their desire for a clean slate that would break with the older generation and indeed the entire German cultural tradition. "Our hatred, the hatred of the younger generation, has the justification of unconditional necessity," declared Alfred Andersch, during the Nuremberg Trials in 1946.[12] Two years later he wrote:

Because of the dictates of a completely unprecedented situation, the younger generation stands before a tabula rasa, before the necessity of achieving, through an original act of creation, a renewal of German spiritual life.[13]

The claims of Andersch and others suggest that from the beginning postwar Germany was haunted by unusually strong intergenerational conflict. A subsequent "generation gap" occurred in the cultural revolution of the late 1960s, in which German youth, like their American counterparts, demonstrated against imperialism and war, only with the added complication that for Germany's youthful revolutionaries of the 1960s and 1970s, the generation of their parents also represented the generation of Nazis and supposedly "apolitical" conformists to Nazism who had made the German catastrophe possible. This "generation gap" ultimately resulted in an epidemic of terrorism in West Germany in the mid- to late 1970s in which members of the "guilty" older generation were actually assassinated by Red Army terrorists seeking a violent *Vergangenheitsbewältigung.* This period also resulted in a spate of books by younger German authors writing about the difficult situation of children in dealing with Nazi parents (usually fathers) – so-called *Väterliteratur* or "father literature." Examples of this literature include Ruth Rehmann's *Der Mann auf der Kanzel* [The Man at the Podium] (1979), Christoph Meckel's *Suchbild: Über meinen Vater* [Search Picture: About my Father] (1980), and Brigitte Schwaiger's *Lange Abwesenheit* [Long Absence] (1980).[14]

Undoubtedly the most influential and popular postwar German book on collective psychology was a 1967 study by Alexander and Margarete Mitscherlich entitled *Die Unfähigkeit zu trauern* [*The Inability to Mourn*], in which the Mitscherlichs used their experience with clinical patients to draw conclusions about West German society as a whole. The Mitscherlichs believed that because of Germany's horrific past West German society was characterized by particularly strong intergenerational problems. They wrote that the most typical kind of youthful figure in the Federal Republic is the young person who

tends to regression, and shows a need for early social and material security. Basically, he does not detach himself from his parents, not even when he has little respect for them. This fixation makes it difficult for him to form vital relations with people and things outside the world of the family.[15]

As Bohrer had written during the 1980s, "The contemporary diagnosis developed in Alexander Mitscherlich's concept of an 'inability to mourn' still characterizes, in one formulation, the state of consciousness of West German society in its majority and in its elites."[16] The typical West German, according to this diagnosis, remained fundamentally childish, incapable of growth and development, fixated on the traumas of a long-gone and unhappy youth – rather like Walser's Alfred Dorn.

Part of the shock of reunification was precisely an encounter with the collective and personal past as reflected in the distorted mirror image of the other Germany. For West Germans, East Germans represented elements of the authoritarian, impoverished past from which they had so successfully escaped; while for East Germans, West Germans represented traditional German arrogance and privilege. As early as the late 1960s the Mitscherlichs had suggested that, in addition to its obvious political significance, German division enabled the mechanisms of psychological repression and projection by allowing Germans to associate all negative images with the "other Germany." They wrote that during the cold war, West German–East German relations took on the character of a schism:

Without being aware of the part they play in the collective fantasy life of the two states, the Chairman of the Council of State there and the Federal Chancellor here have, like the successors of Alexander the Great, been conducting a truly Diadochian struggle for the legacy of Adolf Hitler – for the time being, the last pan-German ideal.[17]

The most important psychological study of the German–German situation to come out of the period of reunification were three works by the East German Hans-Joachim Maaz, born in 1943. A psychotherapist at a hospital supported by the Protestant Church in Halle, Maaz, in 1990, published a book called *Der Gefühlsstau: Ein Psychogramm der DDR* [Emotional Blockage: A Psychogram of the GDR].[18] As its title suggests, this book paints a psychological portrait of the German Democratic Republic and suggests that both the individual psychology of citizens in the GDR and the larger social psychology of the country itself is best characterized by the concept of *Gefühlsstau*, emotional blockage. This book caused a great deal of controversy. Many saw it as yet one more attack on the GDR in the hour of its death, while others noted Maaz's equally stinging attacks on the West and suggested that such attacks against an obviously superior system were at best naive, at worst an implict defense of GDR authoritarianism. Maaz followed up *Der Gefühlsstau* with two other similar attempts to connect his own psychotherapeutic theory and practice with an analysis of the psychological situation in Germany at the moment of reunification: *Das gestürzte Volk: Die unglückliche Einheit* [The Fallen Nation: The Unhappy Unity] in 1991 and *Die Entrüstung: Deutschland Deutschland Stasi Schuld und Sündenblock* [Outrage: Germany Germany Stasi Guilt and Scapegoat] in 1992. The progression of these three books followed the progression of East German sensibilities after the collapse of the SED system in the fall of 1989: first, in *Der Gefühlsstau*, a critique of the psychology of authoritarianism inside the GDR itself; second, in *Das gestürzte Volk*, a critique of the process of reunification, with its attendant disappointments; and finally, in *Die Entrüstung*, a critique of what Maaz saw as a hypocritical coming to terms with the GDR past.

Strongly influenced by the work of the Mitscherlichs, Maaz also centered his concept of German collective consciousness around the problem of Hitler and the Third Reich and relations between parents and their children. However as a 1990s psychotherapist also informed by ecological concerns, Maaz couched his theories about German collective psychology in a far more sweeping pessimism about the chances for industrial society as a whole. The psychotherapist from Halle saw modern consumer societies as an unsustainable attack on the basic structures of life on earth. Moreover, he believed that a powerful repression of this bleak prognosis was at work in contemporary society. If people came to recognize the harmfulness of their way of life, Maaz reasoned, they would be forced to make painful changes, as well as to recognize their own complicity in the destructive system they continued to support. This repression of guilt created, he believed, a vicious cycle: the greater the guilt, the greater the denial, the more unstoppable and inevitable the destruction. In *Die Entrüstung* Maaz wrote:

The self-inflicted global destruction of the human species . . . has for the first time in our history become possible and, one suspects, even very probable. Because even the western concept of society, the pretty utopia of life in constantly expanding prosperity and progress, is false and has long since inaugurated its own decline.[19]

Moreover, Maaz suggested, the so-called "victory" of the West in the cold war had blinded Westerners to the dangers of their own system:

It is, perhaps, a great misfortune that the West is not even capable of thinking differently any more and would now like to imagine a massive economic miracle in the East. In doing this the West is becoming the victim of a grandiose overestimation of the supposedly blessed powers and effects of the market,[20]

in spite of the fact that "this 'social market economy' reached its limits long ago."[21]

Alison Lewis has rather unfairly suggested that Maaz's critique of capitalism is "a product of envy, motivated by the destructive and even spiteful desire to spoil the object of desire once it is in danger of being enjoyed by others."[22] Unfortunately, Lewis provides no textual support for the claim that western consumerism is indeed an "object of desire" for Maaz other than Maaz's own professions of hostility toward consumerism, which she reads as proof of repressed envy. Operative in her analysis of Maaz seems to be the – unarticulated – belief that any critique of consumerism must necessarily be the result of spite. Such a reading is, I believe, tautological, because it assumes from the beginning what it ultimately pretends to prove. Rather than treat Maaz's arguments on their own terms, Lewis resorts to unfounded speculation about Maaz's intentions in making the arguments. It is, of course, possible that Maaz is not immune to the very envy of West German capitalism that he ascribes to his fellow East Germans. But this fact alone, even if true, would neither refute nor in any way affect the psychotherapist's critique of capitalism.

Maaz's bleak diagnosis of the seemingly so triumphant capitalist system should be familiar not only to those who followed the proponents of a "third path" in the East German revolution of 1989, but also to historians of German ecological philosophy and politics during the 1980s, as well as to those who follow radical American ecological groups such as *Earth First!* But Maaz added a psychological twist to his negative diagnosis of the world's ecological catastrophe. According to Maaz, humankind's destruction of the world was an outward projection of the inner destruction of their own souls. Human beings wrought havoc on the world only because they had already wrought havoc within themselves. Sickness loves company, and sick human beings need a sick environment, because a healthy environment would remind human beings too painfully of their own lack of health:

The wasting of natural resources, the exploitation of nature, the awful pollution and destruction of the natural environment, the attempt to rule over nature, are nothing but the symptoms of the alienation of human beings and the outward expression of their *in*vironmental pollution (Innenweltverschmutzung). Thus the irrational becomes comprehensible in the lethal ecological crisis that we ourselves have produced: the real ecological problem lies *inside* humankind today. We are alienated from our own nature, and above all we are blocked in our emotionality.[23]

Maaz's analysis of the world ecological crisis and its psychic origins formed the context for his specifically national understanding of Germany and German history, particularly the National Socialist past and German division and reunification. Maaz viewed each of these three main stages in recent German history as different responses to the same fundamental problem: what Alexander and

Margarete Mitscherlich had already referred to as Narcissist wounds, attacks on German feelings of self-worth which, as the Mitscherlichs had suggested, lead inexorably to a possibly unbearable melancholy unless they are denied and repressed. Therefore, the Mitscherlichs had insisted, what follows such attacks is "an all-out rejection of guilt."[24] As Maaz noted with respect to German history of the twentieth century,

The people of Germany suffered disastrous collective mortifications after the First World War: The loss of empire, the loss of the war, and the conditions of the Versailles Treaty had them longing for a new strong man who would compensate them for all these humiliations. It is not at all surprising then that they preferred to choose a psychopath to take on the role of savior. Hitler brought this evil game to its consummation. How could he have done otherwise? The consequence was another serious humiliation of the German people, the "unconditional surrender" in 1945. But Germany was already in a pathological state of emergency between 1933 and 1945. The psychological problems that were present on an immense scale were acted out primarily against the Jews and then exploded in the Second World War.[25]

Maaz painted a picture of a Germany and of German citizens obsessed with chronic doubts about their own self-worth. In the Third Reich, the feelings of inferiority and guilt were eliminated through identification with a god-like *Führer*; but after the devastating German defeat, as well as massive further guilt due to the Second World War, the Holocaust, and Germans' own cowardice and acquiescence, self-hatred and melancholy were repressed via an ingenious mechanism: the splitting of the German personality and of the German nation into Jekyll and Hyde "good" and "bad" Germanys incarnated by the geopolitical products of German division – the GDR and the FRG. Maaz suggested that the splitting of the German personality enabled German shame and anger to be projected onto an "evil" doppelgänger Germany. Germany's division was for Maaz even more a psychological than a political necessity:

From a psychological viewpoint, this partition [of Germany], from the very start, was the big chance for suppression of guilt. The joint guilt was divided between the two camps – polarization was established – and the dammed-up emotions had their distraction without any "work of mourning."[26]

For the psychotherapist from Halle, then, the cold war was not primarily a political or an economic event; it was, rather, a psychological event which for almost half a century enabled a relatively stable system of paranoia, denial, and projection.

If the division of Germany had been a psychologically necessary answer to an otherwise unbearable melancholy, then why the collapse of the Wall and of the GDR? Maaz referred to the events of autumn 1989 as an "uprising of neurosis" (Aufstand der Neurose).[27] He suggested that after forty years both postwar German states were in a "mid-life crisis,"[28] the usual time for the painful realization that one has spent one's life sacrificing for false ideas and false gods. Moreover, Maaz believed that neither system had any long-term stability, since in his view, systems of denial and repression always ultimately lead to their own self-destruction; they are, in a sense, inherently suicidal. The vicious cycle of German guilt and denial inevitably led to an explosion. Half a century after the last war, the world itself was under substantial revolutionary pressure as the political and psychological systems that had governed it for almost half a century began to crack. As the cornerstone of the divided European and world system, Germany was subjected to particularly strong pressures, and therefore the change happened first there. In essence, Maaz viewed the collapse of the Berlin Wall not as a triumph but as a defeat of the "psychic revolution": it enabled psychic energies to be projected harmlessly outward rather than painfully inward.

Without the opening of the border, we in the east would for the most part have had to carry out and be responsible for the clarification of our situation on our own. In spirited debates we would have had to make judgment on our own guilt and would, in the process, inevitably have run up against the persons and structures that had carried out our subjugation very concretely.[29]

Maaz summed up the opening of the Wall thus:

I would almost like to call the fall of the wall an act of "psychoinkesis" (Psychoinkese), because it protected all participants – the party officials and the security forces, the opposition, the West German politicians, and the population on both sides – from very unpleasant realizations.[30]

Maaz's neologism "psychoinkesis" is a play on the word "psychokin-esis," which denotes the movement of physical objects by purely mental means. Whereas a magician seems to use his mind to move objects in the outside world, Maaz is suggesting that East Germans used the collapse of the wall as an object in the outside world to protect their own damaged psyches. For East Germans, the opening of the Wall once again allowed an evasion of individual personal responsibility. It was now possible for them to throw responsibility – and, crucially, blame – for themselves and their country into the hands of West Germans. For West Germans, meanwhile, the collapse of the GDR and the fall of the Wall provided a massive feeling of self-worth; it enabled the avoidance of serious investigation into the problems of West German and world capitalism.

As Maaz saw it, the speed with which Germany moved from the collapse of the Wall to reunification in less than a year had less to do with political necessity than with a need to avoid reflection. Out of the botched process of reunification, according to Maaz, came the subsequent problems that were to plague united Germany: 1) the hatred between the East and the West; 2) the attempt to localize and limit guilt via the obsession with the Stasi; and 3) the projection of specifically German failures onto foreigners, homosexuals, and the disabled, with a consequent rise in neo-Nazi violence. As Maaz notes, "The East–West conflict bound up destructive energies; this compensatory function is exhausted." Consequently, "The emotional blockage, which last exploded with horrific destruction in the Second World War, is once again beginning to reach a critical threshold."[31] Maaz suggests, "Involuntarily, Germany has become a psychological laboratory."[32]

Finally, underlying this bleak view of the contemporary German situation was a pessimistic analysis of the German family structure, which, as Maaz saw it, was still largely authoritarian. In the psychotherapist's view, German children were raised to deny and repress their feelings. Instead of receiving unconditional love from their parents, German children were denied the fulfillment of essential emotional needs. Raised in an atmosphere of pain and repression, German children from the very first learned to project their natural feelings of anger at their parents onto safer objects. Out of these child-rearing practices came adults who were unable to deal naturally with their own emotions, and who had learned to project feelings of anger onto those perceived as weaker than themselves. In Maaz's analysis of the German family structure, it is easy to see the outline of Freud's explanation for the development of a tyrannical superego more generally.

In contrast to Lewis's critique of Maaz's attack on the West, my own criticism of Maaz's framework focuses on the psychotherapist's relentless approach to the problem of German identity and guilt. While Maaz may well be correct in viewing both the postwar division of Germany and the 1989 collapse of the Wall as mechanisms for the evasion of guilt, it is unclear why such an evasion must necessarily be viewed as self-destructive and wrong. Maaz does not ask whether the burden of German guilt might not have been so unbearable in the immediate postwar years as to make the projection mechanisms he accurately describes necessary and useful for psychic survival. Feelings of guilt, far from being entirely positive, as Maaz seems to see them, are, for Freud, at the root of individual and collective unhappiness and self-destructiveness in the modern world. Within a Freudian framework, such feelings stem precisely from the authoritarian patriarchal sphere that Maaz otherwise criticizes. The story of Alfred Dorn demonstrates precisely how an obsession with the past can lead to self-destruction. Such a story suggests that Maaz's emphasis on guilt is not as nuanced and differentiated as it should be. Moreover, whereas Maaz refers to a collective German identity in 1945, identifying the division of Germany as a means to escape the burden of guilt implied by that collective identity, he seems to assume that such a German identity had ceased to exist by 1989, and that the only surviving collective identities were "East" German and "West" German. The collapse of the GDR thus becomes, for him, a means of eliminating a specifically East German guilt and strengthening feelings of West German superiority. However, if Maaz is wrong, and there was still a larger "German" identity in 1989, then political reunification could mean that the time is now ripe for raising precisely those questions of collective guilt and responsibility which Maaz believes were wrongly evaded in the postwar years. Moreover, it is probably unfair to suggest that German reunification meant an end to East Germans' attempts to come to terms with their own past. As the many debates of the post-reunification period show, the problems of the GDR past are still very much present. Hence, although I accept much of Maaz's diagnosis, I do not accept his uniformly negative interpretation of the process of reunification.

If the collapse of the Nazi Reich had ultimately led sons and grandsons of Nazi leaders to write books about their experiences, the collapse of the GDR very soon led a number of writers to put into words their experiences with their fathers. While the description of family structures in these novels matches Maaz's definition of German patriarchy, these writers demonstrate an anger against the patriarchy that refuses to be satisfied with deflections onto weaker objects. This writing shows both the attempt to escape from the destructive power of the father and the paradoxical, problematic nature of such an attempt.

Whereas it had taken three decades for father literature to appear in the Federal Republic, father–son and father–daughter literature from writers of the former GDR began to appear almost immediately. In one typical response, the writer Gabriele Eckart, born in 1954, wrote an angry open letter to her father, a former minor party official, in which she accused him of brutal mistreatment. Eckart insisted that her father's cruelty had caused her to remain forever at the emotional level of a five-year-old: "To look at me, I am a grown-up woman; how could they know that because of your guilt I am condemned to remain a child?"[33] Eckart remembered the chief reason for her failure to grow up as an incident when she was five years old and her mother had been forced to go to the hospital. Eckart had been happily wearing braids, but as soon as he was alone with her, her father had taken a pair of scissors and cut off the braids. Eckart was to remember this incident for the rest of her life, for it showed that it was not she herself but her father who controlled her image. Hence she began to hate herself as someone created in her father's image: "Although people say that I look like mother, I know that is not true, I look like you." Because of this similarity between herself and the object of her thwarted love, Eckart writes that she "was disgusted by my own body, which exuded your sweat," but that the similarity of bodies was secondary to the similarity of thought patterns: "The structure of my thinking is equivalent to yours, but its contents are one hundred and eighty degrees opposed to your thought; what that means is that I am nothing but a kind of negative image of yourself."[34] The incident in which Eckart lost her braids becomes for her the symbol of a castration which condemns her forever to being an impotent "slit Indian" (Schlitzindianer), as her father spitefully refers to women. Eckart's father has, she believes, taken away from her all power to grow and change: "Because of this brutal intervention in my mirror image, development was arrested for me; in forty years I will probably be buried as a five-year-old."[35] For Eckart her own individual trauma has significance for the entire GDR, whose population, she claims, is also "inwardly deformed."[36]

The most demanding generational exploration to be produced immediately after German reunification was Drawert's *Spiegelland: Ein deutscher Monolog*, a remorseless attack on two generations of German authoritarians and on the entirety of GDR life. As Drawert wrote in an epilogue at the end of the book, "The object of thought was the world of the fathers, it was about this that a report was to be made, about how lost it made one and how lost it was – as a ruling order, as language, as damaged life."[37] At the center of the book is a boy who is never named, but who appears to be an earlier incarnation of the narrative voice that says "ich" in each chapter, and who also resembles Drawert himself in many ways. The boy has a father who is a Communist official and a grandfather who was a Nazi; what binds the two together is an authoritarian pedagogy characteristic of the entire country, in which, the narrator argues, all educational institutions serve the cause not of liberation but of stupefaction. "We were born and became slaves immediately."[38] Drawert's novel is an indictment of German fathers and grandfathers and an anguished plea for individual freedom; significantly, Drawert dedicated the book to his own two sons.

Another important reckoning with the generation of the fathers was Monika Maron's semi-autobiographical book *Stille Zeile Sechs* [*Silent Close No. 6*] (1991). Anna Kuhn has dubbed this book "the first East German *Tochterroman* (daughter book)," suggesting that it exemplifies "a subgenre of the Väterromane (father books) so popular in West Germany in the 1970s."[39] Born in 1941 and therefore technically not part of the postwar generation, Maron was the stepdaughter of GDR Interior Minister (1955–1963) Paul Maron. Her novel relates the story of the forty-two-year-old writer Rosalind Polkowski, whose task it is, shortly before his death in 1985, to take dictation from Herbert Beerenbaum, a former high party official at Berlin's Humboldt University.[40] Beerenbaum is working on his memoirs, but his shaky right hand makes it impossible for him to write. For Polkowski, Beerenbaum becomes the incarnation of an entire generation of Communist fathers who, in fighting against Nazi totalitarianism, ultimately paved the way for a totalitarianism of their own making. Coming from humble, working-class backgrounds, these fathers ultimately fought their way to positions of power in the GDR's major institutions; but they never escaped their origins. Polkowski's feelings toward Beerenbaum become inextricably bound up with her feelings toward her own deceased father,

also a narrow-minded Communist – in this case a school principal.
The lasting trauma of Polkowski's life is her father's failure to love
her. Wrapped up in his own ideological straitjacket and chained to
an educational career that did not suit him intellectually, the elder
Polkowski had ignored his daughter even when she tried desperately
to please him. Hence her ultimate opposition to the Communist
regime originated not in a mature recognition of its inefficiency and
authoritarianism but rather in a childish desire for attention from
her father. Since the young Polkowski could not get her father's
attention when she tried to please him, she went out of her way to
annoy him by siding with his ideological enemies. What made the
little girl's situation so difficult emotionally was that beneath her
hatred for her father – and, much later, for the father-substitute
Beerenbaum – was a deep and abiding longing for love. As the
middle-aged Polkowski reflects, hatred comes "when one has loved
and not been loved in return."[41] Also problematic for Polkowski as a
school girl was the fact that her private and public life ran together
because of her father's prominent position as principal of the very
school in which she was a student. In Maron's world the German
family is also a political problem. Polkowski believes that her father
and his generation of "victors" in World War Two have ruined her
own life and the lives of her generation. "Everything belongs to
Beerenbaum" and his cohorts, she reflects; "even I belonged to
them."[42] As Polkowski shouts at Beerenbaum during the climactic
confrontation between them that precipitates the old man's heart
attack and death,

Your own life was not enough for you, it was too mean, so you used up our
life, too. You are cannibals, slave owners with an army of torturers.[43]

As part of her work Polkowski must transcribe and type the words
that Beerenbaum dictates to her; and even though she vowed long
ago not to let her rational thoughts interfere with her employment –
not to work with her head for money, as she likes to think of it – she
cannot help but take issue with the one-sidedness of the old man's
memories. Her work with Beerenbaum forces Polkowski to relive her
unhappy childhood and once again to subordinate herself to the
dictates of the older generation which she has spent her life trying to
escape. Ultimately Polkowski can no longer tolerate this humiliation
and explodes with anger at the old man. When she goes to his
funeral it is not so much to mourn him as to make sure "that he was

truly buried and gone from this world."[44] As she throws dirt into his grave, she muses: "This is the sound I came to hear."[45] At the age of forty-two Polkowski hopes that she is finally free of Beerenbaum, of her own father, and of the generation that they represent. And yet her triumph is ambiguous: at the end of the novel Beerenbaum's son, a high-ranking officer in the Stasi, carries out his father's last wish by handing her a packet that contains the very manuscript she had spent months typing for the dead man. Even as Polkowski promises herself that she will destroy or hide the manuscript, it is clear that Beerenbaum's words, transcribed by her, still exercise a magical power. As Fritz Rudolf Fries remarked in a 1992 review of *Stille Zeile Sechs*, "Like the author herself, this generation will not be able to free itself from these papers."[46] Through the words that he has dictated to her, Beerenbaum has power over Polkowski even in death.

Maron's obsession with the harm done to a younger generation by its fathers is also clearly demonstrated in her next novel. Primarily the story of a love gone wrong, *Animal triste* (1996) also features a middle-aged woman who believes that her father is at least partially responsible for her ruined life, and who makes explicit parallels between herself and the entire generation of children born to World War Two soldiers. Life for her generation would have been much better, she suggests, if their fathers had never come home:

They should not have been allowed to come back. Back then . . . they should have left us alone with our mothers . . . Somewhere, far from their sons, they should have found a place where they could have cured their injured bodies and their branded warrior souls.[47]

Because of her disgust with her father and her rejection of her mother's subservience to paternal authority, Maron's character learns to hate her own femininity, which she associates with weakness. As Lewis has suggested, femininity in this novel "becomes inseparable from compliance with a patriarchal order and with submission and subjugation to the will of the father."[48] In words strikingly similar to Eckart's description of her own real-life experience, Maron has her first-person narrator declare: "My naked body in its unequivocal designation was disgusting to me."[49] The battle between two generations is epitomized for Maron's heroine in the story of a male classmate from her university days who commits suicide because his father, a high military official, declares that all students who fail to learn Marxist-Leninist ideology with sufficient eagerness should have their bones broken. Upon hearing this declaration, the son obediently places his neck under the wheels of an oncoming train. For the middle-aged woman remembering this incident, the son was simply carrying out a judgment already made by his own father. Her hatred of her own father makes it impossible for her ever to live happily with men. After years of marriage she leaves her husband, who never becomes a character in the novel, and she contends that her life with him was so insignificant that it is not worth telling. When, at the end of the novel, the man whom she claims to love is about to desert his own wife and move in with her, she pushes him under the wheels of an oncoming bus, as if executing upon him the same judgment that her former classmate had executed upon himself. It is clear that what the narrator thinks is a straightforward love story is also a story about revenge: on males in general, and on her lover as a representative of her father's gender. Significantly, the punishment that Maron's character chooses for herself after she has murdered her lover is the self-punishment of Oedipus, the father-killer: blindness. For Maron, female impotence is the result of castration carried out by fathers, and that castration demands murderous revenge.

In her second major work published after the collapse of the GDR, Christa Wolf also deals critically with fathers' misdeeds toward their children. Her novel *Medea* (1996) is, like *Kassandra*, the feminist retelling of an ancient Greek patriarchal myth – in this case the myth of Medea, princess of Colchis, who betrays her father and murders her brother for the love of the Greek hero Jason, only to be betrayed by him in turn. In the Greek myth, Medea takes revenge on her former husband by killing their two children and murdering his new wife, the princess of Corinth. In Wolf's feminist retelling, it is not Medea but her father Aietes, king of Colchis, who kills his son Apsyrtos as a human sacrifice in order to retain absolute power. Medea leaves Colchis not because she is infatuated with Jason, as the Greek hero vainly believes, but rather because she longs to escape the brutality of her father's rule. However, just as male power in Colchis is based on child-murder, so too in Greece: Creon, the king of Corinth, where Jason and Medea seek refuge, has ordered the murder of his own daughter Iphinoe for the same reason that Aietes had murdered his son. Arrived in her new home, Medea finds that human sacrifice is just as common in Corinth as it had been in

Colchis. When Jason deserts her for the Corinthian princess Glauke, Creon's only living daughter, his new wife commits suicide because she has learned that her father killed her older sister, and because she knows that Jason does not love her. Medea's children are killed not by their mother but by the vengeful power of the Corinthian patriarchy. Ultimately Medea finds refuge in nearby mountains with a group of outcast women who carve out a poor existence for themselves away from the centers of male tyranny. For Wolf, it is not so much castration as murder that is the problem with patriarchy. Her novel ends with an implicit answer to the question posed in *Was bleibt*: "What is left to me. To curse them. My curse upon you all."[50] Whether in Colchis in the East or in Corinth in the West – and, implicitly, whether in the former East or West bloc – patriarchy means murder.

Ingo Schramm's novel *Fitchers Blau* [Fitcher's Blue] (1996) depicts the lives of a son and daughter who have been ruined by a psychotic father named Joseph, another member of the "Flakhelfer" generation. Joseph's life experience has taught him always to take the side of the strong over the weak. In order to exercise absolute control over other human beings' lives, he becomes an army doctor. His two children by different mothers become human guinea pigs for him. He is particularly brutal toward his son Karl, who, he insists, should grow up to be a strong officer like himself. Joseph likes to pin his son to the floor and then force Karl's mother to read him, over and over again, the brutal fairy tale "Fitcher's Bird," about a sorcerer who chops his human victims into little pieces:

Behind the door . . . a large basin had been placed into the path, the basin was filled with human parts, arms and legs, feet, heads, half torsos and individual hearts, with hands, above all with hands, which were good for nothing other than to swim in the blood there with the other body parts . . .[51]

Joseph makes this experience even more painful for his tiny son by using his extensive doctor's knowledge of body parts to describe precisely the smells of the organs involved. Since the original Grimms' fairy tale has a happy ending, Joseph changes it. When, after many years of mistreatment, Karl begins to masturbate, Joseph again punishes him:

Finally Karl began to masturbate. He sought pleasure in himself, because he found no one else. His father caught him one evening in bed, when he was intending to observe his son's sleep and the outward appearance of his dreaming. He pulled the boy from his pillows. Whipped him with his belt. That could not be tolerated, that his son strove pointlessly for pleasure.[52]

And finally, when Karl refuses to follow in his father's footsteps and become an officer in the army, Joseph beats him:

Father's hands and feet had done their work, they had hardened the son, made him wooden under hits and kicks. For the fathers do what they like with their children, whom they create in order to increase their property, whom they carve to their liking in their own image, with sharp knives that are as old as obsidian.[53]

This last declaration suggests that, at least in Karl's mind, he has become a victim of his father in the same way that Fitcher's victims succumb to the sorcerer's knife. Of course Joseph is not noticeably more humane to his daughter Janni, whom he also whips mercilessly. The result is that both Karl and Janni are tormented by various neuroses and incapable of leading normal, productive lives. And both have a horror of reproduction: they refuse to bring children into a world that has proven so miserable for them.

Castration anxiety, impotence, and frustration are not always deadly serious topics in post-1989 literature about generational problems. Probably the funniest novel about the collapse of the GDR to appear after reunification was thirty-year-old Thomas Brussig's cult favorite *Helden wie wir* (1995), a 323-page fantasy about penis size. *Helden wie wir* is, as the hero tells us, "die Geschichte meines Schwanzes" (the history of my cock).[54] The novel's hero, who has the unpronounceable name Klaus Uhltzscht, is born with a penis of unusually diminutive proportions. To add insult to injury, Klaus comes from an uptight petit-bourgeois family in which anything having to do with sexuality is strictly off limits. Not surprisingly, Klaus's father works for the Stasi, and ultimately Klaus does, too. Little Klaus is tyrannized by both his mother and his father. He becomes a pathetic mama's boy, neurotically obsessed with parental approval. Klaus's relationship with his father is particularly unfortunate. As the narrator declares, he has "a father who thought so little of me that he couldn't even muster the energy to complete a scathing sentence like 'Pah, that boy will never amount to anything!' . . . nor did he ever utter my name aloud. It's a fact: I never once heard my name on his lips!"[55] The narrator sums up his relationship with his father in the following words:

[My father] had written me off as hopeless. Whatever I said, thought, felt, wanted, believed, wrote, gave, or asked for – whatever I *did* – I could hear his unspoken verdict: "Typical!" I never made a blunder, however small, without involuntarily thinking of my father, who had always known that I would perpetrate it. He could give me looks that would have withered flowers. He could, when checking into a hotel, engage the receptionist in an argument about incorrectly installed fire extinguishers that lasted longer than the sum total of his conversations with me in the entire decade of the 1970s.[56]

When this tyrannical father dies, Klaus finally gets his longed-for revenge. Alone in the hospital room where the corpse is lying, Klaus castrates the man who had symbolically castrated him:

I pulled the bedclothes down and looked at what he'd always concealed from me: his *balls* . . . I hope my father saw me take his balls in my hand and squeeze them. *Go on*, I thought, *if you're so damned omnipotent you'll sit up with a jerk, knock my hand away, and box my ears.* But he was too dead for that. I squeezed his balls for twenty seconds. He'd squeezed mine for twenty years, from the look of them . . .[57]

Klaus is of course a social and sexual failure. His first sexual intercourse results in gonorrhea; and when he attempts intercourse a second time with a woman he believes is ugly enough to accept his advances, she breaks out into uproarious laughter at the sight of his petite member. Thereafter Klaus resorts primarily to frequent masturbation, usually in semi-public spaces like apartment house stairwells. Klaus's own pathetic desire is to become a world champion in onanistic perversion. Unexpected historical significance comes to the diminutive German hero precisely because of his penis. Due to a mysterious operation that the Stasi performs on him in order to carry out a blood transfusion on the dying leader Erich Honecker, Klaus's formerly minute organ becomes, by the crucial November 1989, a massive sexual tool; and when, on November 9, at the Bornholmer Straße border crossing in Prenzlauer Berg, Klaus whips it out and waves it at the once so potent GDR border patrol, the representatives of Communist power are so awed by his masculine potential that they immediately open up the Wall. The rest is history. As the proud narrator declares, "The history of the Wall's end is the history of my willy" ("Die Geschichte des Mauerfalls ist die Geschichte meines Pinsels").[58] Thus one man's sexual anxieties and father complex become fantasies of sexual mastery and political power.

As humorous as it is, Brussig's novel tells a story that is strikingly similar to Maron's and Drawert's works. This is the story of the death of the father and the usurpation of the father's power by his offspring. The mysterious blood transfusion that Brussig's "hero" undergoes makes explicit the transfer of phallic power that is implicit in the other works. As a result of the father's death, which is desired and possibly even caused by his offspring, the offspring acquire the phallic power that had previously been monopolized by him. This individual coming of age is associated in Brussig's novel with the opening of the Wall and thus with German reunification: the now potent Klaus is able to force open the barrier created by his father's party, thus achieving both full manhood and national reunification. Man and nation have come of age. Within Maaz's framework, the fact that the offspring's aggressive energies are directed toward the father and not deflected toward others (as Klaus's energies had been previously) is relatively positive and healthy. However, within a more strictly Freudian analytic framework, the death of the father is precisely the event which perpetuates the father's rule: in death the father acquires more power than he ever had in life. The dead father becomes the God of monotheistic religions, and he takes up permanent residence inside the individual human psyche as the superego, punishing his offspring with feelings of guilt that constantly increase. Peter Schneider had, perhaps unwittingly, hinted at a similar mechanism when, in the 1980s, he had imagined a "Wall in our heads" that would remain even after the physical Wall's demise.[59] The continuing presence of Beerenbaum's manuscript for Rosalind Polkowski is an emblem of the man's continued power, now no longer as a hated outside figure but as part of herself. For Alfred Dorn, the embalmed superego takes the place of the dead mother – who had consciously sought to weaken the bond between father and son, but who had simultaneously become an even more dominant father-substitute – and ultimately destroys the son.[60] The very death of the parent – usually the father – that makes possible a succession of power also perpetuates the parent's power and leads to self-hatred and uncertainty. Walser's work paints a picture of psychic collapse that resembles both Schirrmacher's critiques of postwar West German literature and the state of late GDR society as described by Hilbig, whereas Brussig, Maron, and Drawert tell the story of the rebellion against the father and his power. In Brussig's and Drawert's novels, that rebellion leads to new power and a strengthening of the ego; in Maron's novels, however, aggression against the power of the father leads to a paralysis similar to that experienced by Walser's Dorn.

Maron's and Drawert's work is a particularly poignant example of the double guilt felt by a generation of East Germans whose fathers and grandfathers were both Nazis and Communists. All Germans in both the West and the East were of course faced with the problem of collective and generational guilt after the end of the Third Reich. While the concept of collective guilt – the belief that an entire nation or "Volk" had to accept guilt for the crimes committed in their name – was controversial and problematic, it was nevertheless a powerful discursive and psychological phenomenon. Carl Gustav Jung suggested at the end of the Second World War that whether or not the concept of collective guilt was morally justified, it was nevertheless a psychological fact: Germans *felt* guilty, regardless of the existence or nonexistence of such guilt in fact.[61] The most famous attempt to address the question of collective guilt was Karl Jaspers' *Die Schuldfrage* [*The Question of German Guilt*] (1946). While Jaspers had acknowledged that criminal guilt could be borne only by those directly responsible for crimes, he nevertheless claimed that in a larger sense the acceptance of moral guilt by those seemingly unaffected as well as by later generations was a function of political maturity:

When it [the population] knows itself to be responsible, that is the first sign of awakening political freedom. Only inasmuch as this knowledge exists and is recognized is freedom really present and not just a superficial claim made by unfree people. Those who lack inner political freedom feel the opposite. On the one hand they obey, on the other hand they feel themselves not to be responsible. To feel oneself guilty and therefore responsible – that is the beginning of the inner revolution which seeks to achieve political freedom.[62]

To those who consider themselves innocent, Jaspers replied: "We must take upon ourselves the guilt of our fathers,"[63] and he finally urges the acceptance of German identity not so much as a descriptive fact but as a prescriptive task and obligation:

Since I cannot escape from the collective feeling deep in my soul, being German is not a state of affairs but an obligation for me, for everyone.[64]

Try as he might to identify with others, with anyone but the Germans – Jews, English, Dutch – Jaspers could not escape from his Germanness. It came back to haunt him:

The fact of being German – I mean essentially living in the mother tongue – is so indelible that I feel myself in a way which cannot rationally be grasped – indeed, in a way which can be rationally refuted – to share responsibility for what Germans do and have done.[65]

To be a German is to accept responsibility. The only escape from that responsibility is the relinquishing of German identity itself. Jaspers' association of responsibility with "the guilt of our fathers" is a specific acknowledgment of generational identity. One cannot escape from one's father, because whether one likes it or not, one's father is a part of one's own identity. Hence true maturity lies not in the futile attempt to achieve a complete disconnection from one's father but, rather, in accepting one's connection with him and the burden of the guilt which this connection brings. Both Jaspers after 1945 and Maaz after 1989 argue strongly in favor of an acceptance of responsibility; but, unlike Maaz, Jaspers makes the important point that such responsibility can be accepted only by a specific subject: the German. Precisely because the crimes of the Third Reich were committed by Germans, responsibility for those crimes must be accepted by Germans. Such acceptance necessarily implies the continued existence of a national identity. However, that national identity has been rendered problematic precisely by the crimes for which Germans must accept responsibility.

With the collapse of the GDR the problem of guilt became compounded, because it included not just guilt for the Nazi regime and its crimes but also the burden of Stalinism. Germans in the GDR hence faced the task of "coming to terms with" two pasts; and some in both the East and the West feared that the more recent past would tend to cancel out the earlier crimes of Nazism and thus create a clean slate or tabula rasa of normality, at least for those unburdened by the crimes of Stalinism. However it should be noted that within a Freudian – as opposed to a Maazian – framework the lessening of pressures from a collective superego is not entirely negative: such a mechanism might allow for a growth in self-esteem and self-confidence without the need for outward-directed aggression. It is true that 1989 as a new "zero hour" could partially eclipse the earlier "zero hour" of 1945, thus paving the way for a "normalization" of German history and identity. This is why writers such as Grass used the moment of reunification to remind all Germans in East and West of the continuing relevance of Germany's Nazi past. And yet, as understandable as such arguments are, they overlook the self-destructive force of the collective superego and the need to make the ego more independent of the superego; they neglect the psychic dilemma of Alfred Dorn so movingly depicted in Walser's novel.

Bohrer succinctly addressed the problem of guilt during the reunification debate by insisting that, in principle, there are only two possible kinds of punishment for a crime: the death penalty on the one hand and, on the other, "the chronologically limited loss of liberty."[66] Since Germany did not receive the death penalty in 1945, what it received was the second, lesser punishment. However, this lesser punishment implies that the nation must be able to continue to live, and that the postwar division of Germany, in which "a truly national identity was unable to develop," must be overcome. Bohrer notes that the destruction of Germany would be an evasion of guilt: "One simply separates oneself from the physical circumstances of the father," thus avoiding responsibility for what the father did.[67] What Bohrer is suggesting is that left-liberals' attempt to escape from German national identity is also an attempt to escape from guilt. Given this framework in which identity and responsibility are intertwined, some lessening of the pressure of the superego might well be healthy, even if only because the superego cannot exist without the ego; but it is unlikely that such a lessening would lead to a forgetting of national crimes, because those crimes have now become part of German national identity itself. German conservatives cannot have national identity without national guilt; and German left-liberals cannot have national guilt without national identity. Bundestag President Philipp Jenninger expressed precisely this recognition in a controversial 1988 speech:

People will remember Auschwitz till the end of time as part of our German history. – Thus the demand to "finally put an end" to the past is pointless. Our past will not rest, and it will not pass away.[68]

The problem of guilt gained a new significance with German reunification. If in the generational equation of postwar West Germany Hitler and the Nazis had been the fathers and grandfathers from whose guilt later generations sought to escape, frequently by dissociating themselves from a specific German identity completely, the collapse of the GDR and German reunification occurred as a kind of return of the East German prodigal brother who reminded West Germans of their own previous, discarded identity. It was not coincidental that many observers in the West, fascinated by the events of 1989 and 1990, used genetic terminology to grasp what was happening. Schneider spoke of East and West Germans as long-lost twin brothers who had finally rediscovered each other, while psychoanalysts and psychologists such as Tilmann Moser and Annette Simon suggested that the metaphor of East and West Germans as twins had a deep psychological relevance. As Moser wrote, "The image most commonly used is that of the twins who have been separated for decades, with different historical chances, possibilities, and hinderances."[69] The twin metaphor met with bitter resistance from the West because it implied a familial similarity which West Germans preferred to deny. Nevertheless, German reunification seemed just as likely to prompt a renewed interest in "coming to terms with" the common German past as to provide an excuse for burying that past. In 1986 – the very year in which the *Historikerstreit* had broken out over Nolte's complaints that the German past would not "pass away" – the distinguished West German psychoanalyst Horst-Eberhard Richter suggested in his memoirs that the Nazi past was so horrible that only the grand-children of the Nazis would truly be able to carry out the task of "coming to terms" with it.[70] If Richter was right, then Nolte's observation about the increasing presence of the past acquired a theoretical justification: the past was more present half a century after the end of the war because the distance of two generations from Nazi crimes made it possible for the first time to deal with that past honestly. The double "coming to terms with the past" now necessary with respect to Nazism and Stalinism might well mean not an erasure but a heightening of historical sensitivity. However, in order to address its problematic national past, Germany had to have – a national present.

CHAPTER 7

The time and the place of the nation

Now that's a real German! Everywhere in the world you see them standing around brooding about why they can't move like other people. And most of the time they try to prove that the reason is their intelligence, and then they start to teach the rest of mankind.

Sten Nadolny, *Die Entdeckung der Langsamkeit*[1]

The Germans always come too late.

Thomas Mann, "Deutschland und die Deutschen"[2]

I

Writers were caught off guard by German reunification as much as politicians and the general public. For GDR writers, reunification meant the collapse of their state and hence of a portion of their own self-identification. Most West German writers were probably closer to Patrick Süskind in their lack of interest in the "German question" and in viewing reunification more as an unwelcome revisitation by an anachronistic national problem than as the longed-for return of national sovereignty. For them, their nation was far removed in time and space, a distant memory. Speaking for his entire generation of West Germans born in the first postwar years, Süskind wrote, "Austria, Switzerland, Venetia, Tuscany, Alsace, Provence, yes, even Crete, Andalusia, and the Outer Hebrides – and I am speaking only of Europe – were infinitely closer to us than such dubious geographical constructions as Saxony, Thuringia, Anhalt, Mecklen- or Brandenburg."[3] Jakob Arjouni describes the main character in one of his novels as having the following relationship with one of the five states of the former GDR: "Mecklenburg-Western Pommerania sounded to him like Swasiland."[4] Andreas Neumeister is similarly offhand in declaring his pre-1989 lack of interest in and knowledge of the GDR. Referring to one of the former GDR's largest cities, he writes, "Where Magdeburg is was of course completely uninteresting to me back then."[5]

Even such a West German champion of German national unity as Martin Walser acknowledged his own relative marginality by citing the Bavarian playwright Franz Xaver Kroetz for his far more representative declaration: "The GDR is as foreign to me as Mongolia."[6] As Walser acknowledged, Germans born after the end of the last war were largely free of the national nostalgia that plagued him and others born prior to its commencement: national feeling was more generational than geographical or political. "What does Timbuktu or Königsberg mean to them?" he wrote.[7] In a book entitled *Wendewut* [Reunification Fever], published in 1990, journalist-turned-diplomat-turned-novelist Günter Gaus had an autobiographical West German character admit, "The majority of people at home, in the Federal Republic, were not at all interested in the smaller of the two German states; not even its demise was really important for them, no matter what they claim now."[8] This statement is certainly true for the typically West German character Nathan in Peter von Becker's *Die andere Zeit*: "He had not read a single GDR novel or seen a GDR film in his life, he was moved by pictures and books from America and the former colonial empires, from France, England . . . Also from Budapest or Warsaw, not from Leipzig."[9]

Perhaps the most eloquent testimony to West Germany's lack of preparation for the collapse of East Germany was the fact that no contingency plans had been made by the West German government for such an eventuality. Germans everywhere had come to see the division of their country as natural and permanent. Tellingly, the most common reaction in Berlin at the opening of the Wall on November 9, 1989 was the word "Wahnsinn" (craziness). It was the return of normality which was seen as crazy; whereas the absurd situation prior to November 9, in which a wall had divided an entire city, was seen as "normal." As Ulrich Woelk writes with reference to one fictional character's complete inability to cope with the consequences of the Wall's opening, "the ninth of November was not foreseen." On that fateful evening,

Not just the border guards, everyone was running around like frogs that had just been kissed, still completely absorbed by themselves and their own metamorphosis, with the new standpoint from which they now saw the world, and everyone had his own way of confronting the inexplicable, hysterical laughter and tears, but most of them were wandering through the fog, couples holding each others' hands and constantly giving voice to their amazement like a prayer from the psalms: I don't believe it, this just can't be true.[10]

For many writers and other citizens in the East and West, the events of 1989 and 1990 seemed to occur with breathtaking speed. One of the popular word-plays during the period of reunification was to change the words from Johannes R. Becher's national anthem of the German Democratic Republic – "Deutschland, einig Vaterland" (Germany, united fatherland) – into "Deutschland, eilig Vaterland" (Germany, fatherland in a hurry). The fatherland – or at any rate those charged with the planning of its political future – seemed to be in a great rush to unify.

And yet as quickly as events were happening, there was also an uncanny delay. Particularly for West Germans, the events of 1989 and 1990 seemed peculiarly anachronistic because the concept Germany itself as a nation-state seemed anachronistic. After all, German national unification had been the task of the Iron Chancellor Otto von Bismarck over a century earlier, and when Germany was finally unified in January 1871 even that unification had been belated. In a famous book the philosopher Helmuth Plessner had referred to Germany as "die verspätete Nation" (the delayed or belated nation).[11] In 1988 the SPD politician Oskar Lafontaine declared that "the German nation [is] so very belated that in its striving for statehood it has become outdated."[12] If in 1871 Germany had already been a delayed nation compared to France, England, and the United States, all of which had achieved national unity decades and even centuries earlier, then the unifying Germany of 1990 seemed almost a phantom from the distant past: a nineteenth-century entity in a world moving rapidly toward the twenty-first century. In that twenty-first-century world, nation-states seemed to be losing their importance rapidly to multinational corporations and international organizations such as the European Union. What could the nineteenth-century concept of "Germany" possibly mean in such a twenty-first-century world, a world of what Habermas had referred to as "postnational identity?" One of the minor debates of 1989 and 1990 revolved around whether the events in Germany should be referred to as a "reunification" (Wiedervereinigung) or simply as a "unification" (Vereinigung). The vehemence with which some Germans sought to eliminate the prefix "re-" (wieder-) was a testament not only to previous West German taboos against the "German Question" but also to many Germans' discomfort with the sense of déjà-vu, of time warp. The admission that what happened in 1990 was not the first German "unification" in history seemed extraordinarily difficult for many Germans, used to a concept of 1945 as a "zero hour" that negated previous, all-too-difficult connections to history.

One of the most famous statements of 1989 had been Mikhail Gorbachev's declaration: "Those who come too late are punished by life." In its original context the statement was understood as a warning to Erich Honecker and the GDR Politburo. And yet Gorbachev's declaration is a general historical proposition that can be applied to anything, including German reunification itself. The timing of German reunification contained within it a certain historical irony of the kind Thomas Mann might have appreciated. Germany had always been the "delayed" nation, and in its reunification over a century after the first national unification it was doubly or even triply delayed. Only five years after the end of the Second World War, Theodor Adorno had already commented on this German belatedness. Discussing the world-historical significance of the Nazi attempt to achieve global domination, he wrote:

Germany has ceased to be a political subject in that sense of the nation state that set the standards for the past one and a half centuries. In a broad historical perspective, German fascism was the attempt to "get one's turn" as . . . a planetary subject, specifically as a planetary exploiter, at a time when not only the cards of the world had already been dealt, but even the concept of the nation itself had already outlived itself in view of humanity's spiritual and material forces of production. The condition of the German spirit has something to do with acknowledging this fact. In his inner being, everyone knows that it is "too late."[13]

Time has a way of playing tricks on people, and perhaps on nations as well. If Adorno's belatedly resurrected Germany of the immediate postwar years was already questionable as a national subject, the triply "delayed" Germany of the 1990s was unified as a nation at precisely the moment when the concept of the nation itself as a primary political category was coming into question as a result of economic globalization processes that seemed increasingly to render national governments impotent.[14] Was Germany once again – too late?

"The past seen from the point of view of today – can there be anything more superfluous?" Walser had asked in thinking about the concept "Germany." The writer confessed that for him "Germany" itself was "a word out of that past."[15] Süskind called the German problem "completely obsolete" and added, speaking of his generation of postwar baby-boomers:

No, the unity of the nation, the national itself, simply wasn't our topic. We believed it to be a completely out-dated idea from the nineteenth century, disproved by history itself, an idea we could easily do without. Whether the Germans lived in two, three, four, or a dozen states was completely irrelevant to us.[16]

As Walser suggested, "Germany" might have been a useful concept for European weather reports, but as a political or ideological concept it had lost all significatory power.

In a 1992 novel entitled *Abschied von den Kriegsteilnehmern* [Farewell to Those Who Participated in the War], Hanns-Josef Ortheil, like so many other Germans of the postwar generation, also suggested that the very concept of "Germany" was outdated. The main character in Ortheil's novel is a man in his late thirties, born like Ortheil himself in 1951, and trying to recover emotionally from the death of his father. "In bad moments I believed that the history of the country in which I had been born after the war was finished once and for all," reflects Ortheil's character, who admits that his "hatred of my father" is the hatred of a "living remnant of the past."[17] The father and the fatherland are connected by more than just a linguistic coincidence. There is a psychological connection as well: Germany is the land of the narrator's father, the country for which his father fought and almost died in World War Two, and for which the father heaped upon himself the moral ignominy of lack of resistance to a totalitarianism whose ultima ratio had been the Auschwitz death camp, near where the father had worked as a postal surveyor during the war. It is from this country that the narrator seeks to escape by flying to the United States and losing himself in the vast length of the Mississippi river and, ultimately, the Dominican Republic and Ernest Hemingway's Key West. In New Orleans the narrator descends into a drunken stupor whose original cause he describes thus:

I had numbed out the remembrance of everything German; I had avoided that which was German more than anything else, I had attempted not to think in this language any more . . . Any mumbo-jumbo had been all right with me, any mixing; arrogantly I had immersed myself in foreign language simply in order to avoid the German, anything but these well-known sounds which, with every word, would summon everything back up again.[18]

Ortheil's picture of a postwar generation desperately trying to escape its self-identification as German is at least partially accurate. The West Geman postwar picture of Germany as obsolete is based on two factors: on the one hand the belief that nationalism and the nation-state are indeed outdated geopolitically; and on the other hand the conscious or unconscious desire for an erasure of painful identification. Germany is dead for the younger generation both because all nations are in a larger historical sense dying and because the younger generation wants Germany to be dead so that they can no longer be a part of it and hence tainted with guilt by association. In thinking about the concept "Germany," the filmmaker Wim Wenders declares, "that is first of all something that does not exist any more . . . therefore a vacuum."[19] Claus Leggewie writes that "the more or less severe implication of our parents and grandparents in the Nazi terror and the annihilation of the Jews . . . 'implicated' *us* too, it was uncomfortable to *us* to the point of self-denial, of denying everything 'German.' "[20] Benedikt Waller, the main character in Irene Dische's novel *Ein fremdes Gefühl*, also hates being a German: "he disliked even the thought of being a German."[21] What is true of fictional characters is sometimes also true of flesh-and-blood human beings. Asked whether he loved Germany, the social scientist Jan Philipp Reemtsma once replied: "Do you think that I am a necrophiliac?"[22] When the main character in Arjouni's *Magic Hoffmann* receives a question about what he associates with the concept "German culture," his response is, quite literally, to vomit all over "table, papers, and all the people around him."[23] In von Becker's *Die andere Zeit*, the character Nathan views Germany in essentially the same way as Wenders: "Germany, that was basically nothing but a hole." For Nathan even the German word for Germany is taboo: "In discussions with foreigners the demilitarized and economized word 'Germany' rolled over his tongue easily; 'Allemagne' sounded a bit darker and more foreboding; but in his mother tongue the fatherland was as extinct as was a differentiated people."[24] In this West German world both the word "Deutschland" and a "Volk" that might constitute that taboo nation are dead. In October 1990 the journalist Andreas Kilb succinctly summed up the postwar generation's belief that Germany is dead:

Some stories never have an ending, but ours has one. German history came to a definitive end on May 8, 1945. Since then we have been the first people in the world . . . to be living in after-history, posthistory.[25]

For Kilb, the "zero hour" is a *finis Germaniae*. Here the historical view of Germany explained by a prestigious journalist in one of the country's most important fora of public opinion at the moment of its greatest postwar historical transformation comes remarkably close to that of Ortheil's fictional escape artist. Many West Germans, especially in the younger generation, desire nothing more than to escape their problematic fatherland. Hans Magnus Enzensberger cites two particularly telling popular slogans from the post-reunification period: "Never again Germany!" and "I am a foreigner."[26]

Botho Strauß captured this state of affairs aptly in scenes from his play *Schlußchor*, in which West Germans go about their tedious postmodern business interrupted from time to time by a "caller" who shouts one simple word at them: "Deutschland!" The word is incongruous: Strauß's characters are concerned with their own private problems and desires, and they are incapable of understanding the caller's word; it comes from a different world. In the postmodern, postnational world of Strauß's plays, "Deutschland" has no significance. It is the call of John the Baptist in a time long since accustomed to the death of God.

From a slightly different perspective, Monika Maron has also described the word used to designate a unified fatherland as belonging to the past. Growing up as an East German Communist, Maron had always associated the West with capitalism and exploitation and the East with progress and human freedom, but she had never been able to assign a present meaning to the word "Germany." According to Maron,

When I try to remember what I associated with the word Germany as a child, I think of the darkness of German fairy tales, the gloom of German songs, a cruel, dark Before known as the Middle Ages. The present was never called Germany. The present was socialism or capitalism, the Federal Republic or the German Democratic Republic, East or West Berlin.[27]

What is striking about all these documents is their agreement in consigning the very concept of "Germany" to the distant past. Whatever meaning it may have, the united fatherland belongs to the past perfect, not to the present tense. Germany may be many things to many people, but it is not the Here, not the Now.

The philosopher Ernst Bloch created the term "non-contemporaneity" (Ungleichzeitigkeit) to refer to a situation in which elements from different historical periods seem to coexist at the same time; and in which elements from the past contradict the present, what Bloch calls the "Now" (Jetzt). The very speed and remorselessness of economic "progress" creates for Bloch a nostalgic resistance located everywhere in values, traditions, institutions, and social groups that are threatened by that "progress." Bloch writes that "home, soil and nation are such objectively raised contradictions of the traditional to the capitalist Now, in which they have been increasingly destroyed."[28] Bloch speaks of the "non-contemporaneous" as consisting of both subjective and objective elements: subjectively it consists of cultural values that are now outdated but nevertheless still present in a left-over form; and objectively it consists of the "continuing influence of older circumstances and forms of production," such as traditional craftsmanship coexisting uneasily with mass production.[29] The concept of "non-contemporaneity" seems to contradict a strict understanding of the Western idea of progress, since it implies that "progress" – itself now a controversial term – is never sweeping and complete, and that at any given historical moment human beings are confronted with elements from many other historical periods, both from the past and from the future. And yet Bloch's concept is confirmed by both common sense and historical experience: the United States, for instance, is home to both the devout Anabaptist Amish in Pennsylvania, whose lifestyle and language date back to seventeenth-century Central Europe; to large, entirely residential suburban areas with single-family houses, more or less intact nuclear marriages, and two-car garages, a product of the 1950s; and to inner-city gay zones such as San Francisco's Castro neighborhood, in which men and women in the last few decades of the twentieth century have created a lifestyle completely new to human history. Bloch's concept of "non-contemporaneity" has the advantage that it acknowledges the messiness of human history and the uneasy coexistence of all these "times" at one and the same time. The American futurologist Alvin Toffler envisioned a somewhat similar effect at the beginning of the 1970s in the concept of "future shock."[30] As history moves forward or "progresses" with ever greater speed, human beings have trouble keeping pace; and so ever larger numbers of them are left behind, stranded in mentalities and ways of life that are both objectively and subjectively non-contemporaneous. Adorno writes, "It would be not simply inhumane but also abstract and superficial to see and judge history solely from the standpoint of the supposedly main tendency of history. The state of affairs of the total society expresses itself just as much in the non-contemporaneity of historical development . . . as in the main tendency taking place."[31] While scholars and journalists like to think in terms of clear-cut, unidirectional movements with specific outcomes, reality is usually far more complex and less satisfying. In *Civilization and its Discontents*, Freud argued that "it is rather the rule than the exception for the past to be preserved in mental life," and that for psychical entities "nothing that has once come into existence will have passed away and all the earlier phases of development continue to exist alongside the latest one."[32] As difficult as such a state of affairs may be to imagine in physical space, it is perfectly plausible, indeed inevitable, for the life of the mind. Freud's reflections apply not just to the individual psyche, but to human civilization itself. Time travel may well be impossible as a science-fiction fantasy, but it is entirely possible as a sociological phenomenon in the contemporary world: the fantasies of both technophiles and technophobes express a fundamental truth about the culture in which we live. Christa Wolf's 1996 figure Medea embodies precisely this truth; she is "the shape with the magical name, in whom the epochs meet – a painful process," and as her story is told, "the millenia melt away under heavy pressure."[33]

The concept of non-contemporaneity also applies to the situation of German politics and culture after reunification. As I have sought to demonstrate, many observers in both the East and the West had long since relegated the concept of the nation-state and of "Germany" itself to the same "rubbish-can of history" to which Leon Trotsky, in October 1917, had sought to consign his Menshevik opponents.[34] For many Germans and their neighbors, national reunification came as an unexpected and to a large extent unpleasant reminder that the past is not yet completely past and the present not yet completely present. As Bloch himself had already written in 1935, the concept "nation" is itself non-contemporaneous because it is increasingly subject to decay and destruction. The "wieder-" in the word "Wiedervereinigung" served as a linguistic reminder of history, of "once-again-ness." For West Germans, the eastern half of their now unified nation seemed caught in a time warp; it reminded them of a common past they believed long since disappeared. Conservatives tended to welcome this resurgence of the past into the present, while liberals and leftists resented and feared it. For almost all, the "five new states" were the locus of everything that was not part of the West German present, but that was nevertheless a part of national identity, however uncomfortable: the revenant, the "Wiedergänger." In this sense, East Germany was uncanny in the Freudian sense: that which is at once alien and familiar, at once dead and undead, at once hidden and obvious.

Was it true that the nation-state and, hence, Germany as a nation-state, was outdated? Even after reunification many people seemed to think so. Not only did Habermas continue to talk about a "post-conventional" or "postnational" identity, but many others inside and outside Germany also suggested that nations were passé. The American political scientist Benjamin R. Barber declared that the new free-market ideologies of globalism were "a battering ram against the walls of the nation-state."[35] Similarly the historian John Lukacs asserted that "the functioning, the authority, perhaps the very existence of the modern state that . . . emerged in Europe five hundred years ago, are weakening."[36] Even the President of the real-existing German nation-state himself, Roman Herzog, acknowledged in the late summer of 1996 that the nation-state was on the decline: "At the end of this century we are in the process of overcoming the form of the nation-state which, in its ideological excesses, once drew the continent into the abyss," he declared, adding that "the nation-state with its ideas of sovereignty has outlived itself."[37] National reunification occurred for West Germans as a return of the national which had been repressed in an era of globalism and internationalism. In Germany, the twenty-first-century world of globalization in West Germany met the nineteenth-century world of national unification in the East. For West Germans, the encounter with East Germans was an encounter with a self in conflict with what American President George Bush had referred to during the 1991 war between the United States and Iraq as the "New World Order."

The clash of two different political cultures that characterized German reunification at the political level was reflected on the literary level by a clash of two different literary cultures. For East Germans, literature had served a largely identificatory and political purpose. Both dissidents and conformists in the GDR had viewed literature as primarily political and didactic. Jurek Becker writes that "without doubt literature in the former GDR played a different role than in the West, a bigger and more important one." The reason for this different role was that literature provided an alternative public sphere; Becker refers to this as literature's "Ersatzfunktion," its "function as a substitute."[38] Hence debates about GDR literature were always also debates about GDR society and about the future of German socialism. In the West literature had also played a significant political role, but more and more critics and writers had become uncomfortable with that role; West German observers were increasingly speaking of a West German postmodernism, with literature filling the need for elegant entertainment rather than for national identification or moral and political guidance. The collapse of the GDR made it possible to identify political literature with the now discredited East German state. The attacks on the GDR's most prestigious writer, Christa Wolf, in 1990 were directed not just at Wolf herself or even at GDR literature as a whole, but rather at an entire literary-cultural world in which literature was precisely not confined to the merely aesthetic. Similar attacks were made repeatedly on Grass, who stood for a parallel view of literature, and who, in his novel *Ein weites Feld*, sought to provide a literary-cultural interpretation of German reunification that was not only aesthetic but also historical and political. For Grass's and Wolf's critics, such a historical/political role for literature was just as outdated as "Germany" itself had been outdated several years earlier.

And yet the popularity and political influence of Grass's book and many others in Germany and the rest of the Western world suggests that literature very much retains a political and identificatory power, at least for certain segments of the population, and in conjunction with a whole host of other, newer media: television, film, radio, computer networks. The fact that even in the supposedly more modern and hence less "belated" United States two of the most talked-about political movements of the 1980s and 1990s – radical ecologism and right-wing vigilantism – were largely inspired by novels – Edward Abbey's *The Monkey Wrench Gang* and Andrew Macdonald's *The Turner Diaries* respectively – clearly demonstrates that even in an "advanced" West literature still serves a profoundly political role.[39] The national and international popularity of Joe Klein's 1995 bestseller *Primary Colors*, a roman à clef about Bill Clinton's 1992 presidential campaign, once again proved the point that literature and politics are natural, and popular, bedfellows. The postmodern world is in no way a world without political – or any – literature; it is, rather, a world so full of multiple media that it has become possible even for otherwise astute observers to overlook the continuing importance of older print media. But those media continue to dominate public discussion nevertheless. It is not so much literature as the commonality implied by the word "nation" that is in question: if the "nation" is no longer a viable concept, then neither is the concept "national literature," no matter whether or not people continue to read and be influenced by books.

Perhaps the most remarkable aspect of Grass's controversial novel is that it gave voice to precisely the non-contemporaneity of events in Germany in and around reunification. Grass's main character is the public intellectual Theo Wuttke, also known as "Fonty" because of his vast knowledge of the life and works of the late nineteenth-century German novelist Theodor Fontane. In addition to being an erudite representative of GDR culture, Wuttke is also a twentieth-century reincarnation of Fontane himself, and his life directly parallels that of Fontane: both born in the city of Neuruppin, both married to a woman named Emilie, both with fathers who were economic failures but nevertheless important philosophical and personal influences on their sons, both with one daughter and three sons, both with an ambiguous relationship to political power. In a quite literal sense, for "Fonty" nothing belongs entirely to the past, "but everything is present-time, is on call."[40] In Fonty's world the past exists "in a present drunk with the future."[41] Everything in the world can recur, can come again. Fonty's universe is full of historical analogies and reflections: every significant event in the Prussian-German world of Theodor Fontane has its reflection in the GDR-German world of Theo Wuttke. The primary such reflection is the constellation between Bismarck's unification of Germany in 1871 and Kohl's reunification in 1990. Wuttke is non-contemporaneity personified: he is a man of both the twentieth and the nineteenth centuries; but it is not just Wuttke himself who inhabits this "multi-layered" world (Bloch). Rather, Wuttke becomes the epitome of the non-contemporaneous German, living in a world of historical mirrors: at once part of the present and part of the past. Germany itself is as non-contemporaneous as Grass's main character.

Fritz Rudolf Fries's *Die Nonnen von Bratislava* also plays with the concept of noncontemporaneity. Its main character is the Spanish Golden Age novelist Mateo Alemán, alias Matthäus Teutsch, now traveling through Europe by car in the year 1991. Alemán is a Spanish *converso* or Jewish convert to Christianity whose identity and person are always suspect to the Christian authorities; they use their mistrust and coercive power to secure his services. Alemán, whose real name and alias both mean "German," worked as a spy for the Holy Inquisition four hundred years earlier; he has now been reprogrammed to work for a mysterious organization – probably the Stasi – which seeks to make huge profits in the central and eastern parts of Europe currently experiencing the transformation to capitalism. Alemán's traveling companion, and the man he is ordered to spy on, is Dr. Alexander Retard, alias Rudolf Frais, described by Alemán himself as "a man who has been slowed down, who has been delayed, who has come too late."[42] A man, in other words, like Germany itself.

Many 1990s novels dealing with the theme of reunification reflect an uncertainty about and even fear of time already manifested in Hilbig's "*ICH*" and Walser's *Die Verteidigung der Kindheit*. Woelk's character Johannes Stirner views what is happening in Germany in and around the opening of the Wall as a "time machine," and he sees his excursions into East Berlin as excursions into the past: "I wanted to view the past, as it now still existed, and I did not want to wait, because tomorrow it could already be too late, the time machine was moving quickly."[43] Woelk's novel climaxes with New Year's Eve, 1989 and New Year's Day, 1990, at a moment when Stirner has lost all control over time and life. The title character in Helmut Krausser's novella "Durach," which, not coincidentally, takes place on the same New Year's Eve and New Year's Day, is also working on a time machine which he describes thus:

Under controlled conditions, I attempt to force my way into the in-between-time, which I also call the never-time, which, to put it popularly, means the unused time between two seconds, so to speak the chronometric version of no-man's-land.[44]

At the end of the novella Durach does in fact disappear into the nowhere, no-time of his "in-between-time." Matthias Zschokke's novel *Der dicke Dichter* [The Fat Poet] (1995) also takes place on the same New Year's Eve and deals with a man undergoing a mid-life crisis at precisely the moment when Germany radically changes.[45] Arjouni's character Magic Hoffmann is a modern German Rip Van Winkle who emerges from a penitentiary after four years of imprisonment only to find his fatherland reunited and the world transformed. The novel traces Magic's inability to cope with the new world he finds around him. Kerstin Jentzsch's Lisa Meerbusch escapes the changes in Germany by exiling herself to the island of Crete for most of a year. Her exile, unlike Magic Hoffmann's, is entirely voluntary. Lisa uses a metaphor that was quite common in 1990 to describe her feeling of being left behind: "Time is racing ahead like an express train. In the train stations the Ossis are standing around . . . The train does not stop, it does not even slow down in its travel! No one can jump off, it's going too fast . . ."[46] One can directly compare the fictional heroine's feelings with the standpoint of the real-life Grass in the same year: " 'The train has left the station,' we were and are being told, 'and no one can stop it.' The suckers stay behind, at a noticeable distance from the edge of the platform."[47] Irene Dische's Benedikt Waller is described as a man forgotten by time: "time practically overlooked him."[48] Waller's lonely, neurotic existence in a Berlin apartment is also a kind of exile, an inner emigration. The main character in Monika Maron's *Animal Triste* also lives locked up in her Berlin apartment and has lost all track of time. She does not even know how old she is. Even as a healthy person, her primary companion had been the skeleton of a dinosaur that died one hundred and fifty million years ago. Her only solace in life is prehistory. Wolf's Medea lives in exile, cut off from history. Hilbig's Cambert escapes from history in the underground tunnels below Berlin. Few of the major figures in post-1989 German literature seem able to master the historical world around them.

While some critics writing after 1989 suggested that in the new Germany literature specifically and culture generally had lost their identificatory political power, such a thesis did not acknowledge the non-contemporaneity of the current situation, which was characterized not just by Bush's postmodern New World Order but also by the return of the national repressed. To a large extent, and in spite of all pronouncements about the "death of literature," Germans even after 1989 saw themselves as a *Kulturnation*, even if the significance of those terms in the 1990s was no longer the same as a century or half a century earlier. As the German foreign minister Klaus Kinkel declared in January 1996, "Germany is a great economic and industrial nation. We ought to assign great importance to our also remaining a great *Kulturnation*."[49] The treaty of reunification worked out between the GDR and the Federal Republic in the summer of 1990 spelled out explicitly that culture would continue to play an important role: "The status and prestige of a united Germany in the eyes of the world are dependent not only on its political weight and economic achievement, but equally on its importance as a cultural state."[50] Even in a world where, for the American president and for the German chancellor, the primary leitmotiv of politics seemed to be Clinton's 1992 slogan "It's the economy, stupid," national culture continued to play a crucial role. Far from indicating a decline in the national importance of literature, the many literary debates in Germany after 1989 were eloquent testimony to the continuing power of literature in the national imaginary. Literature continued to play its traditional role as a way to escape worldly cares, but in doing so it also continued to create utopias and to point toward possible futures. In a world in which national identity was being called increasingly into question, it was precisely in the realm of culture that such identity might be found. This had always been the case in Germany; but the existence of fierce "culture wars" in the United States during the 1990s suggested that the term "culture" was beginning to have a similar significance in an increasingly fractured and discordant American politics. In an era in which citizens and politicians alike felt increasingly impotent in their efforts to shape the course of events in the weakening nation and the increasingly interconnected world, "culture" provided a refuge for dreams of unity, identity, and prosperity long since lost in the "real" world. The vehemence with which such "culture wars" were carried out was a testament to the despair and frustration of political life in the postmodern, postindustrial, postnational world.

One of the most influential ideas of the year 1989 was the American philosopher Francis Fukuyama's Hegelian concept of "the end of history." In an article published in the neoconservative American journal *The National Interest*, Fukuyama suggested that with the triumph of what he called "liberal" free-market capitalism over the command economies of the socialist East bloc, history in the sense of a struggle of ideas had come to an end. Henceforth, Fukuyama believed, "liberal" capitalism was the undisputed and sole ideology for the entire world. While history in the sense of wars and catastrophes continued in certain unfortunate parts of the world, the liberal West had essentially arrived at its permanent ideological destination. The future would contain essentially administrative, not ideological problems. Fukuyama wrote:

> What we may be witnessing is not just the end of the Cold War, or the passing of a particular period of postwar history, but the end of history as such: that is, the end point of mankind's ideological evolution and the universalization of Western liberal democracy as the final form of human government.[51]

It is not my purpose here to explore the philosophical or empirical underpinnings of Fukuyama's argument. What is probably more significant about the argument itself than whether it is true or false is the fact that it was made at all and received widespread credence in 1989 and 1990, even finding its way into the pages of Andreas Neumeister's novel *Ausdeutschen* [Germaning Out] (1994):

> Dr. Biller articulates the diagnosis that young idiots like us don't know how to develop visions. At almost the same time the acting chief of planning at the State Department aggressively proclaimed the end of history: democracy and the market economy are ultimately the highest goods, a continued development neither possible nor desirable. In the next few months, therefore, it is only the details themselves that will still be worked on, the copyright for the new world order is being permanently assigned. History, which has now come to an end, will be divided into little, round, digital stories.[52]

As this excerpt suggests, Fukuyama's concepts had wide currency and inspired significant disagreement in Germany precisely as German history seemed once again to be on the move. The idea of "the end of history" spoke to a pervasive sense that the end of the East bloc meant more than simply a final triumph over what Reagan, during the 1980s, had called the "evil empire." What had come to an end was socialism itself as a two-century-old challenge to the dominance of the capitalist system. Many of Europe's best and brightest intellectuals had supported the idea of socialism in the nineteenth and twentieth centuries, and particularly in Germany the concept of socialism had found strong adherents. Not only were Marx and Engels themselves German, but Germany had the oldest and strongest working-class movement in Europe. Because Hitler's National Socialism had chosen Communism as its primary ideological and military enemy, the defeat of Hitler in 1945 also immeasurably strengthened the prestige of Communism in Germany. Hence the founding of the GDR in 1949 had tapped into profound currents of hope for a better and more just human society. And even though the Communist system in the Soviet Union and the East bloc largely discredited itself throughout the twentieth century because of its cruelty and economic inefficiency, the very existence of an alternative to capitalism in such a huge part of the world gave hope to Western critics of capitalism, most of whom shied away from supporting the specific tyrannies of the East bloc. Nevertheless, those tyrannies proved that it was at least theoretically possible to conceive of a noncapitalist, nonexploitative economy. With the collapse of Communism in the East bloc the very idea of an alternative to capitalism came to seem utopian and unrealistic. If this was true, it meant that many people had sacrificed most of their lives working for a cause that ultimately proved futile. It meant that utopia itself had become a dirty word. What was the point of working for a better world if the only system that would remain triumphant was Fukuyama's "liberal" capitalism? Moreover, Marx's socialism had also implied a progressive and optimistic theory of history. In Marx's view, history marched from exploitation in the past and present to freedom in the future, and the goal and end of history was a just, fair, and happy world. For Marx, this goal was not just a dream but a scientific inevitability. Eastern Marxists believed they knew the future. The events of 1989 suggested that maybe they had been wrong. But they also suggested, uncomfortably, that anyone who claimed to know the future might be wrong: that human beings at the end of the twentieth century are just as unknowing as any of their supposedly more primitive ancestors.

It was just this problem that the East German biophysicist and novelist John Erpenbeck addressed in his clever comedic novel *Aufschwung*, in which Edgar Rothenburg, a former professor of Marxist historical philosophy at East Berlin's Academy of the Sciences, a man who had specialized in the Marxist inevitability of a better and more humane future, loses his position after reunification but ultimately manages to transform his failure into success. He becomes a highly successful entrepreneur at an old business which is nevertheless, in the post-reunification context, new: palmistry or chiromancy, the divination of the future by means of palm-reading. In the uncertain postmodern world of German reunification, the old and supposedly outdated superstitions previously disposed of by the

East German Communist regime acquire a new significance and excite pent-up consumer demand, making the philosopher-turned-chiromancer a huge business success and winning him the Federal Republic's highest civilian award, the "Bundesverdienstkreuz" (federal cross of merit). As Rothenburg writes in his last philosophical treatise, the most up-to-date world has become the natural home for the "age-old arts of prophecy, scientifically reworked . . . : Astrology and iris diagnosis, tarot and palmistry. More than half of the Germans believed in it . . ."[53] The chaos of capitalism fits comfortably with old superstitions. In a world deprived of meaning and significance, old beliefs and superstitions rush in to fill the void. For the former believer in Marxist "scientific" utopias, chiromancy fits the bill quite nicely.

The collapse of utopian visions of the future in 1989/1990 was particularly acute for East German writers. To the extent that writers had chosen to stay in the GDR rather than emigrate to the West, it was because they supported the concept of socialism or of a "third path" between socialism and capitalism. In particular writers such as Heiner Müller, Christa Wolf, Volker Braun, and Christoph Hein chose to stay in the GDR because they believed that for all its problems the eastern part of Germany was nevertheless superior to the capitalist, exploitative West. The events of 1989 put the entire life's work of such writers into question.

One of the most eloquent responses to this crisis was a 1993 poem by Müller entitled "Mommsens Block." This poem dealt with the nineteenth-century German historian Theodor Mommsen – whose bust had recently been reinstalled outside the entrance to East Berlin's Humboldt University – and in particular with the question as to why the distinguished scholar had never finished the fourth volume of his history of Rome, which was to have explained the 500-year-long decline of the Roman Empire after Julius Caesar's death. In this lengthy poem Müller brings three historical periods into an unusual constellation with each other: 1) the decline of the Roman Empire; 2) the second German empire created by Bismarck and experienced by the historian Mommsen; and 3) the end of the Soviet/Communist empire experienced by Müller himself. The mood of the poem is elegiac and resigned. Müller's answer to the riddle of Mommsen's missing fourth volume – the "block" in the poem's title refers to both the marble bust outside the university building and Mommsen's "writer's block" – is that the decline of the

Roman Empire was so disheartening that the great historian preferred to leave it unwritten. "(T)he unwritten text is a wound / Out
of which goes blood stilled by no subsequent glory," writes Müller.[54]
What was left after the decline of the Roman republic and the
triumphs of Julius Caesar was a long and inexorable decay and the
misanthropic recognition that the ordinary Roman people were
actually happier under the brutal dictator Nero than they had been
during a republic that had forced on them the terror and responsibility of freedom. "Why write that / Down just because the crowd
wants to read it / That in the swamps there is more life / Than on
high is known to biology."[55] The great historian has come to the
recognition that the history he has devoted his entire life to
understanding is unedifying, depressing, and above all incomprehen-
sible: that its sequence of cause and effect is no longer susceptible to
rational explanation. "I NOW KNOW / ALAS WHAT I DO NOT KNOW,"[56]
declares Müller's Mommsen: the end of the exploration of history is
not knowledge but ignorance, and the final victory goes not to the
wise or to the good but to "two heroes of the new era," "lemurs of
capital, money-changers and dealers."[57]

One of the most interesting novels published by an East German
author after the collapse of the GDR is Hein's *Das Napoleon-Spiel*
[The Napoleon Game] (1993), which addresses similar themes, but
from a different point of view: not the disgusted historian but one
of Müller's "heroes of the new era." Many of Hein's previous works
express the writer's disillusionment with the socialist system. In
1989 Hein published two works that dealt with the collapse of
GDR socialism: the play *Die Ritter der Tafelrunde* [The Knights of the
Round Table] and the novel *Der Tangospieler* [*The Tango Player*].[58]
Hein's play satirized the GDR Politburo as aged knights of King
Arthur's Round Table who had largely lost faith in the persuasive-
ness of their own Communist ideals; his novel treated with utmost
seriousness the sad fate of an intellectual in the GDR following the
Warsaw Pact invasion of Czechoslovakia in 1968. In *Das Napoleon-
Spiel* Hein departs from his critique of the socialist system and
offers instead an unsparing portrait of one of the "winners" of the
capitalist system. *Das Napoleon-Spiel* is the psychological portrait of
an amoral murderer who, not coincidentally, happens to be a
successful politician, businessman, and lawyer. The novel takes the
form of two letters from the murderer, whose name is Wörle, to his
lawyer Fiarthes. In these letters Wörle reveals not only his crime

but also his entire biography and philosophy of life, which is that
life is fundamentally banal (Wörle's victim is named Bagnall and is
chosen precisely because he is unremarkable) and becomes interesting only when one "plays." "All that remains to us in order to
escape boredom is the game."[59] The *Spiel* of the book's title has
many meanings: billiards, gambling, acting, having fun, hood-
winking someone, advertising oneself, playing a musical instrument.
For Wörle, life itself is worthwhile only as a *Spiel*, a game, a wager.
Whereas ordinary, inferior people seek only boring security,
superior "players" seek enjoyment, amusement, the pleasure of the
"game" itself. According to Wörle, the true point of a game is not
to win but rather to stay in the game. Games are their own raison
d'être; one plays in order to play in order to play again. Politics
itself is nothing but a game, and truly great politicians, such as
Napoleon, are nothing but particularly skilled and ruthless players.
Their invocation of idealism is meant for the stupid masses, not
their fellow players or a higher God. What ultimately bores Wörle
about politics is that it is a highly circumscribed game, largely
determined by outside factors and not by the skill of the players.
Wörle is just as frustrated by the inability of politics in the
postmodern world as all his other fellow politicians. Hence he turns
to murder in order to add more excitement and self-affirmation to
his "game." The logical consequence of Wörle's philosophy is that
life "has nothing to do with morality or immorality,"[60] and that the
normal human state of affairs is selfishness, not altruism. "It is not
the selfish man who is a monster; monstrous, rather, is some
humanitarian jungle doctor or a charitable nurse whose many good
deeds demand from us just as much respect as they get on our
nerves."[61] While Wörle is indeed a disturbing and disgusting
character, his logic is nevertheless flawless and entirely consistent
with the logic of the capitalist system to which he fled from the
GDR many years earlier. Wörle is very much the creature of the
system he chose, and *Das Napoleon-Spiel* is in many ways a description of the triumphant *Realpolitik* of the capitalist system itself. That
Wörle ultimately wins his game goes almost without saying. In a
system without morality, whose only value is monetary success, it is
precisely characters like Wörle who "win." As a character in
Jentzsch's novel *Seit die Götter ratlos sind* reflects, "The world is being
divided up again among gamblers who have nothing but their own
interests in their head and in their guts."[62] Wörle is a post-1989

German yuppie version of Bertolt Brecht's triumphant capitalist murderer Mack the Knife from the late Weimar Republic. Significantly, however, Brecht offered at least the supertextual belief in a Communist system in which murderers like Mack would not thrive; for Hein all such hope seems to have disappeared. And to add insult to injury, Wörle does not even have Mack's brutal animal charm.

Günter Gaus offers a somewhat different but strangely parallel assessment of the triumph of capitalism in his 1990 novella *Wendewut*. In the philosophical dispute that forms the major focus of this novella, Communism becomes an essentially conservative force whose chief historical achievement was the creation of a relatively secure and predictable, if boring, lifestyle for its citizens. If, as Hein's snobbish murderer Wörle believes, security is what most human beings desire, then Communism provided that security and is thus, for them, a humane and just system. It is capitalism, not Communism, that is truly radical and revolutionary in Gaus's philosophy, because it offers little but insecurity and constant, unpredictable change. The tragic irony of history, in Gaus's picture, is that ordinary people are doomed by boredom and envy to rebel against the very system that affords them greatest security, only to be plunged into the marginally more interesting but infinitely less secure capitalist system. For Gaus, it is the totalitarian Communist system that in fact serves the interests of the average human being better than the democratic capitalist system, which in fact serves the interests of privileged and intelligent elites. As Gaus's fictional alter ego muses:

However, the chronicler still did not trust history. He remained insistent in his conviction that the historical era that was approaching would once again find its victims, especially among little people. What human rights do the weak need?[63]

In Gaus's theory the old Communist ideology that declared capitalism the economic system of the elites and socialism the economic system of the masses was in fact correct, but in a way far different from what the Communists had meant: it was capitalism, not Communism, that was truly revolutionary. And ordinary citizens would always ultimately rebel against the very system that offered them what they most desired: stability and security.

II

"Where is Germany?" Schiller's question has puzzled two centuries of German writers.[64] For many of them, the place of the nation was precisely the no-place of literature, that airy realm of dreams and utopias. Precisely because it was frequently so difficult to define the German nation politically, the literary concept of the cultural nation acquired a special importance. The closing words of Richard Wagner's opera *Die Meistersinger von Nürnberg* speaks eloquently to the sense that literature provides a safe haven from the slings and arrows of outrageous political misfortune. At the end of the opera Wagner's poet-hero, the Renaissance shoemaker Hans Sachs, declares:

> Honor your German masters!
> Then you will summon good spirits;
> and should you favor their work,
> if the Holy Roman Empire
> were to dissolve in mist
> there would still remain for us
> Holy German Art![65]

In Sachs's view the specific place of the German nation is not geographical but ideal: the place of Germany is its poets, its masters, Holy German Art, not the Holy Roman Empire.[66] What the Reich or the Empire fails to provide is given by art. If the Empire were to dissolve, what would remain would be art itself. There is a paradox here: it is the intangible world of art and literature that is in fact stronger and more lasting than the tangible world of political power. Wagner's Sachs uses the same word that Hölderlin used half a century earlier: "poets establish what remains." In an influential essay of the 1920s, the great Austrian poet and librettist Hugo von Hofmannsthal likewise spoke of literature itself as the "geistiger Raum der Nation" – the spiritual place of the nation.[67]

Such an idealistic view of literature as the non-political site of the political was of course largely compensatory throughout most of German history. It was precisely because the Holy Roman Empire *had* "dissolved into mist" in 1806 that Wagner, half a century later, was prompted to put the idea of Holy Roman Art in its place. The two empires – the political and the artistic – were correlated negatively: the poet Hans Sachs became for Wagner the secret Holy Roman Emperor only after the abject failure of politics epitomized by Francis II's renunciation of the crown of the Holy Roman Empire during Napoleon's early nineteenth-century conquests. Wagner's opera ends with a ritual coronation of Hans Sachs himself, literally "hailed" by the citizens of Nuremberg as their leader. Because of the negative correlation of politics and culture in this Germanic idealism, it was only logical for Wagner's admirer – and subsequent enemy – Friedrich Nietzsche, after Bismarck's consolidation of the Second Empire in 1871, to voice the fear that the triumph of the all-too-political Reich would ultimately mean the utter destruction of German culture.

As Benedict Anderson has suggested, one of the ways nations guarantee their own existence is as "imagined communities." Throughout German national history, in which political disunity has been the rule and unification the exception, it has been as precisely part of the imaginary that Germany has existed in the minds of its citizens. That national imaginary was largely determined as part of an elite culture that separated Germany from other European nations and hence guaranteed the difference that, in turn, guaranteed identity. Elements included in that elite culture were literature, drama, the visual arts, architecture, and music. But above all Germany was a literary phenomenon: the very national anthem both famous and infamous throughout the world after 1945 was an 1841 poem by the nineteenth-century fighter for German liberty and unity, the poet August Heinrich Hoffmann von Fallersleben: "Deutschland, Deuchtschland über alles . . ." Fallersleben's often-misunderstood phrase was meant not as a blueprint for geopolitical conquest, but rather as a rallying cry for the national imaginary: Germany should occupy first place not on the world's battlefields but in the minds of Germans.

Four years after the dissolution of the Holy Roman Empire of the German Nation, the French writer Germaine de Staël published an influential exploration of Germany in which she devoted careful attention to German literature and German philosophy – and almost no attention to politics. "The Germans," wrote de Staël, "form the advance guard of the army of the human spirit; they are breaking new paths, they are exploring unknown methods. How could one not be curious to find out what they have to tell upon return from their trips into infinity?"[68] The German nation, declared the French visitor, "is in its nature literary and philosophical."[69] To Madame de Staël is also, apocryphally, attributed the most famous description of the Germans as a people: a "Volk der

Dichter und Denker," a "nation of poets and thinkers."[70] What those poets were writing and what the thinkers were thinking was in essence the nation itself; it was through their work and the work of their interpreters in the German academy that the nation came into being: the collective project of many people over many decades, part of what Renan called "the will to perpetuate the value of the heritage" and "a rich legacy of memories" which not only supported but actually constituted the nation.

Over a century after Richard Wagner's death, the fears of Günter Grass and other literary opponents of the second German unification followed this same Germanic logic. During almost half a century of political disunity from 1945 to 1990, authors like Grass could take comfort in the fact that even though their nation was politically separated German literature helped to guarantee the unity of the *Kulturnation*. If Germany was a utopian no-place, then the maps which would guide Germans to their elusive homeland were the dreams of Germany's "Dichter und Denker."

To return to Martin Walser, that champion of German unity whose November 1988 call to reawaken the German question had struck so many West Germans then as anachronistic and dangerous, the course of events only a year later was to prove Walser at least partially right. And yet there is a strange and highly characteristic ambiguity in the words with which Walser, citing his own thoughts of a decade earlier, voiced his rhetorical call to arms:

All of us carry the corpse of the fatherland on our backs, the beautiful, the dirty corpse that they have cut open, so that we are now supposed to live in two abbreviations. But we must not desire to live in them. We should recognize the FRG just as little as we recognize the GDR, I declare, trembling at my own courage. We must keep open the wound called Germany.[71]

If this passage was a direct call to political reunification, then Walser chose a very peculiar metaphor for it. Walser refers to Germany not as a body that is wounded, but rather as a "wound" itself. The writer calls not for the healing of the "wound called Germany," but rather for the keeping open of the wound.[72] Within the terms of Walser's metaphor, this is entirely logical. To heal a wound is to make it disappear. If Germany is indeed a wound, then to heal that wound would be to make Germany itself disappear – not the triumph but the end of the nation: *finis Germaniae*. Moreover, Walser does not call for the political reunification of the FRG and the GDR.

As Bullivant points out, Walser "continued to emphasize that his idea of unification excluded the idea of the Federal Republic swallowing up the GDR."[73] Far from glorifying the political power of West Germany, Walser specifically argues that the non-recognition of the GDR as a state should be extended equally to the FRG. Neither state deserves recognition. Or is it that no state deserves recognition, because all states are merely political entities and hence cannot acquire the dignity of Holy German Art?

Walser's metaphor of Germany as a wound was taken up again with an unusual twist in a 1995 novel entitled *Nox* by the young postmodern German author Thomas Hettche. *Nox* is a sadomasochistic fantasy by a man who dreams that he has been murdered by a woman he picked up the night before, on November 9, the date of the opening of the Berlin Wall. After the knife cuts through his flesh and his body begins the process of decay, the man's spirit goes out into the night and pursues the body of his murderer as she aimlessly moves back and forth against the menacing Berlin nightscape. In the metaphorical language of this novel's imagery, the Berlin Wall is scar tissue that has been ripped wide open, leaving the German wound to fester. In the following passage the spirit of the murdered man reflects on the moment at which his murderer encounters the crowds celebrating the opening of the Wall; the knife-murder and the physical opening of the Wall become part of a single image:

As if she were scraping the knife over stone, it suddenly seemed to her, again she saw me in my blood, and the wound arched and closed over her, voices and lights shoved into her, sky, streets and walls, everything was breathing and bleeding around her, and she was in the middle of it. Like food for maggots, like fly larvae on the open wound, which are boring into the necrotic tissue, everywhere in the light of the torches people were clinging with hammers and hands to the Wall.[74]

During the grotesque sadomasochistic ritual and animalistic rape scene with which the novel reaches its high point, a professor of pathology at East Berlin's Charité Hospital again explicitly compares the opening of the Wall to the forceful tearing of scar tissue:

On a living body, do you understand? They are ripping open the wound that seemed to have healed so well. In this very night, do you understand? One must isolate anew, cut into that which is cancerous, deep into the living tissue.[75]

Such imagery suggests, at the very least, that Walser was not alone in his ambiguous usage of the metaphor of a German "wound," and in the recognition that German reunification could not be a straightforward process of "healing."

And yet it is precisely as such a process of healing and normalization that German reunification initially appeared. The reunification of Germany on October 3, 1990, far from being Walser's nonrecognition of the Federal Republic, incorporated the GDR into the political, social, economic, and legal structure of the FRG. Opponents of reunification referred to this event as an "Anschluß," unfairly painting reunification with the same brush as Hitler's annexation of Austria in 1938. Supporters of reunification preferred the word "Beitritt" (accession). Both words indicated that what was happening was not a joining of equals: rather, one country was becoming incorporated into the other. If prior to October 3, 1990 Germany had been a "wound" or a no-place, nowhere, after that date the "wound" was at least superficially healed and Germany became another European state on the global map. To many citizens of the problematic fatherland, this seemed the final step on Germany's long and tortuous road to postwar normalization. If German reunification meant the closing and not the opening of Walser's "wound called Germany," then the political-cultural equation that Germany had been living with during the postwar years was thrown off balance. That is precisely what many German authors feared. Very quickly, and without anybody expecting it, the German national wound was healed, at least nominally. Germany was transformned from a *Kulturnation* into a *Staatsnation*. It was rendered "possible," to use Walser's terminology, even though the essence of German nature was, for Walser as for so many other writers, its impossibility. Utopia had been located on the map, and it lay between the Rhine and the Oder, the Baltic and the Alps. Its currency, at least for the time being, was the Deutsche Mark. But even the Mark as a sign of national identity was increasingly threatened with the approach of European integration and the advent of the international "Euro" as a unit of currency at the end of the millenium. If German identity no longer lay in its culture or even in the Deutsche Mark, what, after 1990, did it mean to be German? Who were "we Germans?"

Günter Grass sought to provide an answer to this question in his forceful opposition to reunification. His reflections are worth returning to:

We have every reason to be afraid of ourselves as a unit capable of action. Nothing, no national emotion, no matter how idyllically tinted, not even any protestations of the amiability of those born afterwards, can relativize or easily do away with this experience which we as the guilty have had with ourselves, and which the victims have had with us as unified Germans. We will not get around Auschwitz. We should not even attempt such an act of violence, no matter how much we might wish to do so, because Auschwitz belongs to us, it is a permanent scar on our history, and it has, on the positive side, made possible an insight which might run like this: now, finally, we know ourselves.[76]

Grass opposes not just one but two German unifications. The first unification is between the FRG and the GDR, and the second unification is between the *Staatsnation* and the *Kulturnation*. Grass is clearly afraid that the first unification will imply the second unification, eliminating *Kultur* as a function of the national superego capable of understanding "this experience which we as the guilty have had with ourselves." Quite aside from the validity or lack of validity of Grass's other arguments against reunification, what is striking about this passage is its implicit picture of German history and German identity. The use of the word "finally" (endlich) in the last line implies that Germany underwent a long and fruitless search for its own identity prior to the Third Reich; and that for all its horror, the knowledge and fact of Auschwitz as the worst crime in human history have finally, once and for all, put an end to that quest for identity: now "we" know who "we" are, namely people capable of the worst that human beings can imagine. This knowledge requires that "we" be afraid of "ourselves," i.e. a splitting of the national personality into that which judges and that which is condemned. In Grass's sense, Auschwitz may not have been the "final solution to the Jewish Question" that Hitler had hoped for, but it certainly was the final solution to the German Question.

While Grass's argument is rhetorically powerful and filled with the moral seriousness of a writer who has spent all of his professional life fighting with remarkable perseverence for a more democratic Germany, his image of Auschwitz as the ultimate guarantor of German identity is, I believe, inadequate both morally and practically. It is inadequate morally because it implies that ultimately Hitler and the SS were and are the final ground of German identity. Such an implication is an insult to the many Germans who fought against Hitler, not to mention the German Communists, German

Social Democrats, German Jews, German Christians, German homosexuals, and many other Germans murdered in concentration camps. Moreover, Grass's argument ascribes to Hitler a moral truth that cannot but be offensive to Hitler's opponents and victims. From a practical standpoint, it is unclear how any positive political identity can emerge solely on the basis of Auschwitz. That Auschwitz "belongs to us" and is a "permanent scar" is certainly true, but Auschwitz "belongs" not just to Germans or even to Jews; it is, alas, part of human history. No one group can or should entirely "claim" it. What for Walser had been "the wound called Germany" is for Grass the "permanent scar" of Auschwitz; both writers want to keep the wound or the scar open, rather than heal it. Their imagery is not as explicit or perverse as Hettche's, but it is equally troubling, implying that history is a permanent and senseless repetition of sadomasochistic crimes.

Much of the reunification debate, as well as subsequent political and cultural debates in Germany, can be understood as a continuation of the discussion of German identity and the possibility or impossibility of German "normalization." Politically, the "normal" position tends to view full German "normality" as its goal. "Normality" is generally taken to mean that Germany should behave in roughly the same way as France, England, and especially the United States in world political affairs. Those in favor of German "normality" pragmatically claim that Germany is an important economic power, and they proceed from this claim to the suggestion that Germany's political power should equal its economic power. As a member of NATO, the European Union, and the democratic, industrialized West, Germany needs to behave in concert especially with the United States, the normalizers claim. Practically, this means that Germany should not hesitate to use its considerable military strength in concert with the other Western allies, and that it deserves a permanent seat on the United Nations Security Council. Supporters of German normality were particularly happy when, in the spring of 1989, George Bush spoke of the United States and the Federal Republic as "partners in leadership."

The "abnormal" position, not surprisingly, draws the opposite conclusion. Germany is not and cannot be France or England or the United States, this position claims; its history has blocked off this "normal" route for all time. Germany is branded by the historical mark of Cain, and it can never be accepted into the "normal" community of nations. It should, instead, serve as a reminder to all other nations of the horrors of war and totalitarianism – and of the very concept "nation." It is easy to recognize the arguments of a writer like Günter Grass in this "abnormal" position.

My purpose here is not to decide the debate in favor of one or the other position. As a citizen of the United States, I would be foolhardy to do so. Rather, I wish to suggest that German cultural identity after reunification exists as precisely a tension between these two positions, both of which are paradoxical. The first position offers "normality" but tends to disintegrate any kind of unique German identity, while the second position is unflattering to Germany but tends to maintain the possibility of a strong national identity. The Polish writer Andrzej Szczypiorski has criticized the second position as a kind of reverse nationalism, suggesting that "such opinions have a brutal, nationalist background which results from the conviction of German particularity, of German extraordinariness, of German threats, strength, anger, rage, as if one were talking about giants, titans, and not average human beings."[77] And yet given the course of German history in the twentieth century it would probably be rash to speak of Germany as in any significant way "normal." It would, I suspect, be a mistake to expect any definitive "answer" to the question of German identity in the coming years; it is the existence of the problem itself that will be characteristic of German intellectual and cultural life. We will probably have to live with what the French call "les incertitudes allemandes" for the foreseeable future.

However the existence of uncertainty about German identity should not be perceived as yet another version of a German *Sonderweg* or German differentness. On the contrary: the postmodern age is characterized by precisely such uncertainty, not only in Germany but throughout the Western world. In this postmodern age, "the sparrows are whistling from the rooftops" the news of the increasing impotence of the nation-state, as the German-born philosopher Frithjof Bergmann puts it, using the German idiom to describe that which is obvious even to the most limited intelligence.[78] In analyzing the onslaught of economic globalization, Richard Barnet and John Cavanagh have suggested that "as traditional communities disappear and ancient cultures are overwhelmed, billions of human beings are losing the sense of place and sense of self that give life meaning."[79] In a larger sense, it is no longer clear

in the late twentieth century – if it ever was clear – what a "normal"
nation is, or even whether the nation itself is normal. As Wenders
declares,

The world is already the proverbial village, and is becoming so more and
more. What does "country" still mean now that there are no more borders,
or behind the borders everything looks the same? It is especially
anachronistic for a country to understand itself as a nation, and even more
so if it celebrates or fanaticizes this idea: hopeless. "We Germans"
understand this perhaps better than any other . . . nation.[80]

With the advent of globalization and international dependency, it is
probably national insecurity, not the "self-confident nation" of
German conservatives, that is the rule. In the late twentieth century
even a supposedly "normal" nation like the United States, which for
many decades had felt itself unified, is racked by "culture wars" that
point toward what the sociologist Todd Gitlin has called "the
twilight of common dreams." As Gitlin has written about American
identity, "During the war against fascism, Germany was the enemy
that helped unite our states. After the war, the Iron Curtain that tore
Germany asunder helped hold America together."[81] Now that Iron
Curtain has fallen, and Germany is no longer torn asunder; the glue
that helped to hold America together for so long has disappeared.
The same global forces that helped to bring Germany back together
again are also tearing Germany and all other nations apart. Hence
Germany as a "postnational" identity – a nation in which more than
anywhere else the very concept of the nation is subject to question –
is perhaps for the first time in its national history, not too late, but
rather too early: in not knowing precisely where, when, or what the
fatherland is, Germany is paradoxically ahead of its neighbors and
rivals, all of whom now face the harsh winds of economic globalization and increasing self-questioning. Perhaps Andreas Kilb was more
correct than he knew when he declared at the moment of reunification that Germans had become "the first people in the world . . . to
be living in after-history, posthistory." In 1989, as the GDR was
collapsing, Martin Ahrends had suggested that because of its
economic slowness the GDR, although behind other nations and
certainly behind West Germany, was nevertheless further ahead in
developing the kind of renunciation of material values necessary if
the world was to survive ecologically: "Awakened from Sleeping
Beauty's slumber, the last here may really be the first."[82] Ahrends'
suggestion that in fact it is sometimes the slow tortoise who wins the

race against the speedy hare in a non-contemporaneous world is similar to Theodor Adorno's suggestion, with respect to Germany as a whole, that "qualitatively modern intentions . . . live on backwardness in the process of economic consumption."[83] As Adorno wrote in 1950, "The more remorselessly the world spirit triumphs, the more it becomes possible for that which has lagged behind it not simply to stand in for what has been lost, for a romantically transfigured past, but to prove its worth as a refuge and escape for something better to come in the future."[84] In the New World Order of globalization, the late and insecure German nation may, paradoxically, be further along the path toward national renunciation than any other modern Western nation. It could well be true, as former Chancellor Kohl and so many other conservatives have suggested, that the German *Sonderweg* is over, and that Germany is, for the first time in its history, a "normal" nation. But it is no longer clear what either "normal" or "nation" means concretely.

Sten Nadolny's character Sir John Franklin, in the 1983 novel *Die Entdeckung der Langsamkeit* [*The Discovery of Slowness*], is perhaps a fitting embodiment of the tortoise's, and the German's, slowness. Nadolny's Franklin is a British explorer of the Canadian polar seas; his extreme slowness separates him not only from his fellow countrymen but also from the processes of modernization and acceleration occurring in England during the first half of the nineteenth century. Franklin's slowness makes him more closely resemble the "real German" who "can't move like other people." John Franklin is able, through hard work and determination, to transform what for others would be a handicap into an asset: his very slowness bestows upon him gifts of observation and deliberation that serve him and his crew well on many occasions – until the final polar disaster in which Sir John's ship and crew are caught and destroyed by ice. Physically, freezing means slowing down so much as to come to a complete stop. Therefore, in the end, Franklin's slowness catches up with him. While the rest of the world moves faster and faster, Sir John moves slower and slower. Nadolny's novel suggests, however, that the fate of the modern world is more likely to be fast and hot than slow and cold. Therefore the world needs slowness and deliberation now more than ever before. John Franklin hates the speed and destruction of war, and while his exploration of the polar regions in an English ship is doubtless part of what the British authorities perceive as a nationalist project, it is, for John, simply an escape into a slower, more predictable world. John's teams are always international and include not just British but also French, a slow German, and Indians and Eskimos with whom John, because of his slowness, is able to communicate admirably. John's explorations of time and space are also explorations into the natural world and the world of the human imagination: the empty whiteness of the polar regions is a space for the projections of the mind, less destructive than the depredations of the various European wars that Sir John has fled. While Nadolny wrote and published his novel in the early 1980s, over half a decade before German reunification, his reflections on slowness have an important bearing on the German situation and on the problem of "discovery," "speed," and "newness" in an industrialized, modernized world. The novel suggests that what needs to be "discovered" in this world is a different attitude toward time and space, a more playful, leisurely, and imaginative way of living and being. "Two friends, one fast, the other slow, get through the entire world," writes the young John Franklin in his diary.[85] It is tempting to interpret his comments as applicable to the relations between fast nations and slow nations in a world of once again increasing speed in which the "cold war" that had "frozen" the European continent for half a century has ended and the "slow" nations of the East must learn to coexist with the "fast" nations of the West. Once again, Germany is itself a microcosm of this process, what Moretti has called "the centre and catalyst of the integrated historical system we call Europe."[86] In the coming together of East and West Germany, the nation in Europe's center is experiencing on the national level what the rest of Europe is experiencing at the continental level and what the entire world is experiencing at the global level. In spite of the West's evident superiority in this process, it may well be that the rest of us really do have something to learn from John Franklin, and that faster nations really do have something to learn, or to relearn, from slower ones. Could it be that Ahrends was right? "Awakened from Sleeping Beauty's slumber, the last here may really be the first."

It would be unrealistic to expect literature to provide definitive interpretations of the current situation in Germany. And yet, as Fritz Rudolf Fries's belated character Dr. Alexander Retard remarks, "on the other hand one has to admit that much of the literary tradition helps prepare us for the battles of the present day."[87] Great literature is almost always belated and slow; it is concerned not with the present but with the past. Because of its slowness and deliberation, it mistakenly appears out of place, awkward, unnecessary in a world in which we like to think of speed and acceleration as self-sufficient qualities. It is not uncommon in Germany to hear declarations about literature like the following statement by the critic Hubert Winkels:

Its help is hardly needed any more for the "education of the heart." What to see, what to think, where to intervene, can be learned better elsewhere. Souls and minds are now formed in electronically well-armed studios, no longer at lonely night-time writing desks.[88]

And yet even Winkels admits that in the electronically dominated world he describes, the printed word has acquired a new subversive and resistant power that it never previously had.[89] Because literature is "historically dysfunctional," Winkels believes that it now has a "unique chance" to act as "a break . . . in the armored covering of the world, disruption of the picture, loss of sound . . . the blind spot in the grand program of world vision."[90] Winkels is joined in this view by no less an ally than the filmmaker Wenders, who declares:

Even though the world of pictures is going completely berserk and even though, via progress and technology, pictures have made themselves more and more independent, so that they are now already out of control and will only get even more out of control in the future – there is nevertheless another culture, a counterculture in which nothing has changed and nothing ever will change: the telling of stories, writing and reading, the *word*.[91]

Wenders is of course wrong to view the world of books and of reading as beyond history – the opposite is in fact the case – but his vision of the importance of the written word is nevertheless as powerfully suggestive as Andreas Neumeister's suggestion that the "end of history" will be followed by the advent of "stories." Wenders' vision of language as the fundamental guarantor of Germanness is consistent not only with German tradition but also with a belief that writers, as the primary agents of language, have privileged access to that identity:

In this land, in Germany, the telling of stories never broke off; here, unlike in America, pictures can no longer generate identity. . . Pictures have here been discredited once and for all. Instead, in this country, it is storytelling that has always had an impact.[92]

Precisely because the history of German susceptibility to propagandistic "pictures" in the Third Reich has now made Germans suspicious of idolatry to a world of images, in Germany the printed word still has an almost sacred power, according to Wenders. "Our salvation (Heil) in this land that is now so unholy (heillos) is our German language," he declares. "It is everything that this country no longer is, is not yet again, and perhaps may never again be."[93] If one of Germany's best known filmmakers believes so strongly in the power of the written word, it is hard to give credence to the idea that language and literature have completely lost their integrative, identificatory power in his country. No matter what the sparrows may whistle from the rooftops, it would be unwise to declare prematurely the death of either the nation-state or national literature. The one thing we know for sure about conventional wisdom is that it is frequently wrong. One could fill a vast cultural-political graveyard with all the institutions and practices that have been declared dead many times over in the course of the twentieth century but are still among us, part of our thought and practice, that compose the warp and woof of how we live. Sparrows are perhaps not the most authoritative experts on such matters. Instead, perhaps one should ask a successful entrepreneur. "We produce hopes, dreams, and illusions. What would that be for a company," asks the Marxist chiromancer Edgar Rothenburg on a trip to Pittsburgh, the postmodern home of the modern American industrial revolution. Rothenburg's conversation partner, a successful German-American businessman, answers that it is not the steel of Andrew Carnegie or the banks of Andrew Mellon that will be of primary importance in the future, but rather dreams and illusions: "They will be the most important products of the future! More important than steel, oil, and electricity. Even the electronics of the next millenium will be above all a part of the illusion industry. You should be clear on this: you are in the most significant growth branch!"[94] Once again it is the anachronistic postmodern tortoise who wins out over the up-to-date modern hare.

We do not quite know what era we are living in; we know only that the postwar era came to an end in 1989. We will probably have to wait until the end of the current era before we can name it and classify it, and before we can expect any major expression of it in literature. As the German philosopher Hegel, so beloved of proponents of the "end of history," wrote in his 1820 preface to *The Philosophy of Right*, "the owl of Minerva spreads its wings only with the falling of the dusk."[95] It is only at the end of an era that one can begin to comprehend that era. Such understanding is one of the basic tasks of literature. This is a very old truth, from Homer to Tolstoy and beyond: the great chronicles always, of necessity come after the fact; wisdom is the gift not of youth but of old age. The essence of literature is its belatedness, its historicity. What this means for the present is that it is naive and unrealistic to expect any time soon the "great German novel" about the events of 1989–1990. Matthias Zschokke makes fun of this widespread expectation by picturing a frustrated middle-aged writer who declares that "of course things have occurred recently, historical events, that have moved all of us deeply," and that throughout the city of Berlin, Germany's once and future capital, writers are getting ready to begin the great marathon race to be the first to transform history into story:

It is veritably the talk of the town that Berlin must be, wants to be, and will be written anew, and the pencils have been sharpened, there is nothing but shuffling and scraping when one walks through the streets, everywhere the sharpened pencils are crowding into the starting gates, no question about it, and believe me, I will get it under control, force it to its knees, this . . . this . . . this mare Babylon . . .[96]

But here, too, the race is not to the swift. As eager as he is to get to the starting gate, Zschokke's "fat poet," like Müller's Mommsen, is suffering from writer's block. His great novel about the new Germany and the new Berlin will never be written. Instead of waiting like the "fat poet" for the definitive novel about current events in Germany, it would be more realistic to expect both literature and literary criticism in Germany to address themselves wholeheartedly to the bygone era: the cold war, the era of German division, the Federal Republic of Germany and the German Democratic Republic. Since that era is now over, it is possible to write about it with an insight never previously possible. If we think back to the history of German epic literature in the twentieth century, we see that the primary works of each period tend to sum up the essence of the previous period. Thus masterpieces like Thomas Mann's *Der Zauberberg* [*The Magic Mountain*] and Robert Musil's *Der Mann ohne Eigenschaften* [*The Man Without Qualities*] summed up the bygone era prior to the First World War; and the great works of postwar German literature, both East and West, from Günter Grass's *Die Blechtrommel* to Christa Wolf's *Kindheitsmuster* and Uwe Johnson's

Jahrestage, responded in different ways to the calamities of the Third Reich. We can expect a repeat of this phenomenon in the new era, which will define itself on the basis of continuity or discontinuity with the old era. In the works of Walser, Maron, Grass, Hilbig, Drawert, Hein, and many others, we can already see the outlines of such summing up. It is partly through literature and through literary criticism that Germans in the present and future will understand the historical period that came to an end in 1989; and the present period will at least in part be the reflection of its own understanding of the previous period. "Germany cannot be expunged from my historical consciousness," Walser declared toward the end of the 1970s. "They can print new maps, but they cannot recreate my consciousness. I have been a reader too long for that to happen."[97] In an era of seemingly endless German division, Walser was declaring that the location of his nation was in the minds of readers and writers who imagined and created it by telling and retelling, reading and rereading stories of its past. Writers and readers created the historical and imaginative space for the problematic nation. Over two decades later, in an era when a previously unthinkable reunification has come to seem commonplace, there is every indication that literature continues to serve a role similar to what Walser envisioned. Hence it is in helping to shape our understanding of the German past that literature will help to shape the German future.

Notes

INTRODUCTION: LOCATING THE NATION

1 Keith Bullivant, *The Future of German Literature* (Oxford: Berg, 1994), p. 70.
2 Ibid., p. 71.
3 Ibid., p. 79.
4 Russell Berman, "Three Comments on Future Perspectives on German Cultural History," *New German Critique* 65 (1995), 115–124 (p. 119).
5 Helmut L. Müller, *Die literarische Republik: Westdeutsche Schriftsteller und die Politik* (Basel: Beltz, 1982), p. 289. Unless otherwise indicated, translations are my own.
6 Ibid., p. 16.
7 David Bathrick, *The Powers of Speech: The Politics of Culture in the GDR* (Lincoln: University of Nebraska Press, 1995), p. 35.
8 Ibid., pp. 43–44.
9 Wolfgang Emmerich, *Kleine Literaturgeschichte der DDR: Erweiterte Neuausgabe* (Berlin: Gustav Kiepenheuer, 1996), p. 456.
10 Bullivant, *Future*, p. 86.
11 Bathrick, *Powers*, p. 35.
12 David Bathrick, "Crossing Borders: The End of the Cold War Intellectual?" *German Politics and Society* 27 (1992), 77–87 (p. 83).
13 Helmut Peitsch, *Vom Faschismus zum Kalten Krieg – auch eine deutsche Literaturgeschichte: Literaturverhältnisse, Genres, Themen* (Berlin: Sigma, 1996), pp. 17–20, 24.
14 Volker Wehdeking, *Die deutsche Einheit und die Schriftsteller: Literarische Verarbeitung der Wende seit 1989* (Stuttgart: W. Kohlhammer, 1995).
15 Throughout this book, I use the word "unification" to refer to the political conjoining of German states in 1870/71 and "reunification" for the event of 1990. For more on these terms, see Erik J. Macki, "Semantics and the Ideological Lexicon of German (Dis)Unity," in Jörg Roche and Thomas Salumets (eds.), *Germanics under Construction: Intercultural and Interdisciplinary Prospects* (Munich: Iudicium, 1996), pp. 123–141.
16 Wolfgang Emmerich, "Do We Need to Rewrite German Literary

History Since 1945? A German Perspective," trans. Peter C. Pfeiffer, in Friederike Eigler and Peter C. Pfeiffer (eds.), *Cultural Transformations in the New Germany: American and German Perspectives* (Columbia, S.C.: Camden House, 1993), pp. 117–131 (pp. 126, 128).

17 Emmerich, "Rewrite?" p. 126.
18 Emmerich himself acknowledges this point in "Rewrite?" p. 127.
19 Oskar Negt (ed.), *Der Fall Fonty: "Ein weites Feld" von Günter Grass im Spiegel der Kritik* (Göttingen: Steidel, 1996).
20 Peitsch, *Vom Faschismus*, p. 19.
21 Robert A. Pois, *Friedrich Meinecke and German Politics in the Twentieth Century* (Berkeley: University of California Press, 1972).
22 Friedrich Meinecke, *Cosmopolitanism and the National State*, trans. Robert B. Kimber (Princeton University Press, 1970), p. 27.
23 Rogers Brubaker, *Citizenship and Nationhood in France and Germany* (Cambridge, MA: Harvard University Press, 1992), p. 52.
24 Quoted in Meinecke, *Cosmopolitanism*, p. 46.
25 Ibid., p. 74.
26 Aleida Assmann, *Arbeit am nationalen Gedächtnis: Eine kurze Geschichte der deutschen Bildungsidee* (Frankfurt: Campus, 1993), p. 40.
27 Berman, "Three Comments," p. 116.
28 Anton Kaes, "Literatur und nationale Identität: Kontroversen um Goethe 1945–49," in Albrecht Schöne (ed.), *Kontroversen, alte und neue* (*Akten des VII. Internationalen Germanisten-Kongresses Göttingen 1985*, vol. 10) (Göttingen: Niemeyer, 1986), pp. 199–206 (p. 199).
29 Theodor W. Adorno, "Auferstehung der Kultur in Deutschland?" in *Kritik: Kleine Schriften zur Gesellschaft* (Frankfurt: Suhrkamp, 1971), pp. 20–33 (p. 23).
30 Bullivant, *Future*, p. 14.
31 Thomas Mann, "Ansprache im Goethejahr 1949," in *Gesammelte Werke in Zwölf Bänden*, vol. 11: *Reden und Aufsätze 3* (Frankfurt: S. Fischer, 1960), pp. 481–497 (p. 488).
32 Ernest Renan, "What is a nation?" trans. Martin Thom, in Homi K. Bhabha (ed.), *Nation and Narration* (London: Routledge, 1993), pp. 8–22 (p. 19).
33 Ibid., p. 19.
34 Ibid., p. 11.
35 Ibid., p. 12.
36 Cited in Peter Peters, "'We are One Book': Perspectives and Developments of an All-German Literature," in *The Individual, Identity and Innovation: Signals from Contemporary Literature and the New Germany*, ed. Arthur Williams and Stuart Parkes (Bern: Peter Lang, 1994), pp. 297–314 (p. 298).
37 K. Stuart Parkes, *Writers and Politics in West Germany* (New York: St. Martin's Press, 1986), p. 235.
38 Thomas Mann, "Die Lager," in *Gesammelte Werke in Zwölf Bänden*, vol.

12: *Reden und Aufsätze 4* (Frankfurt: S. Fischer, 1960), pp. 951–953 (p. 951).

39 Ernst Wiechert, *Rede an die Deutsche Jugend 1945* (Munich: Zinnen, 1945), p. 33.

40 Franz Werfel, "An das deutsche Volk," *Bayerische Landeszeitung*, 25 May 1945, repr. in Bernhard Zeller (ed.), *"Als der Krieg zu Ende war":* *Literarisch-politische Publizistik 1945–1950* (Munich: Kösel, 1973), p. 24.

41 Andrei S. Markovits and Simon Reich, *The German Predicament: Memory and Power in the New Europe* (Ithaca: Cornell University Press, 1997), p. 190.

42 Sigmund Freud, *Civilization and its Discontents* (New York: London, 1989), p. 84.

43 Ibid., p. 106.

44 Ernst Nolte, "Vergangenheit, die nicht vergehen will: Eine Rede, die geschrieben, aber nicht gehalten werden konnte," in Rudolf Augstein, et. al., *"Historikerstreit": Die Dokumentation der Kontroverse um die Einzigartigkeit der nationalsozialistischen Judenvernichtung* (Munich: Piper, 1987), pp. 39–47 (p. 41).

45 Michael Stürmer, "Geschichte in geschichtslosem Land," in Augstein, et. al., *"Historikerstreit,"* pp. 36–38 (p. 36).

46 Serge Schmemann, "Kohl, the Man for the German Moment," *The New York Times*, 1 July 1990, pp. 1, 4.

47 Bertolt Brecht, "Children's Anthem," trans. Edith Roseveare, in *Poems 1913–1956*, ed. John Willett and Ralph Manheim (London: Methuen, 1987), p. 423.

48 Wolf Biermann, "Reden über das eigene Land: Deutschland," in *Klartexte im Getümmel*, ed. Hannes Stein (Cologne: Kiepenheuer & Witsch, 1990), pp. 235–257 (p. 238).

49 Ibid., p. 256.

50 Müller, *Republik*, pp. 166, 167.

51 Peitsch, *Vom Faschismus*, pp. 403–404.

52 Ibid., p. 402.

53 Hinrich Seeba, "Critique of Identity Formation: Toward an Intercultural Model of German Studies," *The German Quarterly* 62: 2 (spring 1989), 144–154 (p. 151).

54 Ibid., p. 149.

55 Russell A. Berman, "Beyond Localism and Universalism: Nationhood and Solidarity," *Telos* 105 (1995), 43–56 (p. 51).

56 Seeba, "Critique," p. 153.

57 George Steiner, *The Death of Tragedy* (New Haven: Yale University Press, 1996), p. 307.

58 Peter Bürger, *Theorie der Avantgarde* (Frankfurt: Suhrkamp, 1974), p. 15.

59 György Lukács, *Theory of the Novel* (Cambridge, MA: MIT Press, 1971).

60 Benedict Anderson, *Imagined Communities* (London: Verso, 1991).

61 Frank Trommler, "What Should Remain? Exploring the Literary

Contributions to Postwar German History" in Keith Bullivant (ed.), *Beyond 1989: Re-reading German Literature since 1945* (Providence: Berghahn, 1997), pp. 153–176 (pp. 162–163).

1 SEARCHING FOR GERMANY IN THE 1980S

1 Franco Moretti, *Signs Taken for Wonders* (London: Verso, 1988), p. 251.
2 Manfred Jäger, *Kultur und Politik in der DDR: Ein historischer Abriß* (Cologne: Wissenschaft und Politik, 1982), p. 34.
3 Jan Tinbergen, "Do Communist and Free Economies Show a Converging Pattern?" *Soviet Studies* 12: 4 (April 1961), 333–341 (pp. 333, 337).
4 For a pre-1989 summary of convergence theory, see Michael Ellman, *Collectivisation, Convergence and Capitalism: Political Economy in a Divided World* (London: Academic Press, 1984); for a post-1989 critique, see Bruno Dallago, Horst Brezinski and Wladimir Andreff (eds.), *Convergence and System Change: The Convergence Hypothesis in the Light of Transition in Eastern Europe* (Aldershot: Dartmouth, 1991).
5 Andrei D. Sakharov, *Progress, Coexistence & Intellectual Freedom* (New York: W. W. Norton, 1968), pp. 76, 83.
6 Alfred Andersch, *Öffentlicher Brief an einen sowjetischen Schriftsteller, das Überholte betreffend: Reportagen und Aufsätze* (Zurich: Diogenes, 1977), p. 208.
7 Erich Honecker, "Zu aktuellen Fragen bei der Verwirklichung der Beschlüsse unseres VIII. Parteitages," *Neues Deutschland*, 18 December 1971, 3–5 (p. 5).
8 On Christa Wolf's response to the eleventh plenum, see Karl-Heinz J. Schoeps, "Intellectuals, Unification, and Political Change 1990: The Case of Christa Wolf," in Walter Pape (ed.), *1870/71–1989/90: German Unifications and the Change of Literary Discourse* (Berlin: Walter de Gruyter, 1993), pp. 251–277, especially pp. 257–262. On the eleventh plenum itself, see Günter Agde (ed.), *Kahlschlag: Das 11. Plenum des ZK der SED 1965: Studien und Dokumente* (Berlin: Aufbau, 1991).
9 Peitsch specifies 1977 as the crucial year; Schmidt would place the change somewhat earlier. See Ulrich Schmidt, *Zwischen Aufbruch und Wende. Lebensgeschichten der sechziger und siebziger Jahre* (Tübingen: Niemeyer, 1993).
10 Emmerich, *Literaturgeschichte*, pp. 239–240. For another reading of the same period, see J. H. Reid, *Writing Without Taboos: The New East German Literature* (New York: Berg, 1990). Reid also stresses an increasing modernization of East German literature.
11 Peitsch (*Vom Faschismus*, p. 20), even seems to imply that it was Brandt who invented the concept of the *Kulturnation*.
12 Alexander von Bormann, "Kulturelle Affinität oder Diskulturalität? Wechselwirkungen der Literaturentwicklung beider deutscher Staaten," *Aus Politik und Zeitgeschichte*, 3 October 1987, 15–26 (p. 15).

13 Fritz J. Raddatz, "Mein Name sei Tonio K.," in Angela Drescher (ed.), *Dokumentation zu Christa Wolf "Nachdenken über Christa T."* (Hamburg: Luchterhand, 1991), pp. 121–123 (p. 123).

14 Thomas von Vegesack, "Jetzt bittet der Verleger für sie um Verzeihung," in Drescher (ed.), *Dokumentation*, pp. 131–133 (p. 132).

15 Marcel Reich-Ranicki, "Christa Wolfs unruhige Elegie," in Drescher (ed.), *Dokumentation*, pp. 104–107 (p. 106).

16 Christa Wolf, *Accident: A Day's News*, trans. Heike Schwarzbauer and Rick Takvorian (New York: Farrar, Straus, Giroux, 1989), p. 105.

17 See particularly Peter Bender, *Das Ende des ideologischen Zeitalters: die Europäisierung Europas* (Berlin: Severin & Siedler, 1981).

18 On the gradual disappearance of the GDR production play as a sign of literary convergence, see Jürgen Link, "Von der Spaltung zur Wiedervereinigung der deutschen Literatur? (Überlegungen am Beispiel des Produktionsstücks)," in Paul Gerhard Klussmann and Heinrich Mohr (eds.), *Literatur im geteilten Deutschland* (Bonn: Bouvier, 1980), pp. 59–77.

19 David Roberts, "Surface and Depth: Christoph Hein's *Drachenblut*," *The German Quarterly* 63: 3/4 (1990), 478–489 (p. 483).

20 Hans Mayer, "Stationen der deutschen Literatur: Die Schriftsteller und die Restauration, die zwei Deutschlands und die Konvergenz," *Frankfurter Allgemeine Zeitung*, 16 June 1979, in the unpaginated glossy insert "Bilder und Zeiten."

21 Frank Trommler, "Auf dem Wege zu einer kleineren Literatur: Ästhetische Perioden und Probleme seit 1945," in Thomas Koebner (ed.), *Tendenzen der deutschen Gegenwartsliteratur* (Stuttgart: Alfred Kröner, 1984), pp. 1–106 (p. 29).

22 Ibid., p. 17.

23 Heinrich Mohr, "Entwicklungslinien der Literatur im geteilten Deutschland," in Klussmann and Mohr (eds.), *Literatur*, pp. 1–58 (pp. 54 and 50).

24 See Klaus Ehring and Martin Dallwitz, *Schwerter zu Pflugscharen: Friedensbewegung in der DDR* (Reinbek: Rowohlt, 1982), especially pp. 209–214.

25 The proceedings of the two meetings were published as *Berliner Begegnung zur Friedensförderung: Protokolle des Schriftstellertreffens am 13./14. Dezember 1981* (Darmstadt: Luchterhand, 1982); and *Zweite Berliner Begegnung: Den Frieden erklären – Protokolle des zweiten Schriftstellertreffens am 22./23. April 1983 – Der vollständige Text aller Beiträge aus Ost und West* (Darmstadt: Luchterhand, 1983); see also Ingrid Krüger (ed.), *Mut zur Angst: Schriftsteller für den Frieden* (Darmstadt: Luchterhand, 1982); and Bernt Engelmann, et. al., *"Es geht, es geht – ": zeitgenössische Schriftsteller und ihr Beitrag zum Frieden: Grenzen und Möglichkeiten* (Munich: Goldman, 1982).

26 Parkes, *Writers*, p. 118.

27 Ibid., p. 119; Peitsch, *Vom Faschismus*, pp. 423–425.

28 Cited in Thomas Steinfeld and Heidrun Suhr, "Die Wiederkehr des Nationalen: Zur Diskussion um das deutschlandpolitische Engagement in der Gegenwartsliteratur," *The German Quarterly* 62: 3 (1989), 345–356 (p. 355).

29 Cited in Seeba, "Critique," p. 150.

30 Alexander von Bormann ("Affinität," p. 24) refers to this kind of thinking as a theory of "negative convergence."

31 Andrei S. Markovits, "On Anti-Americanism in West Germany," *New German Critique* 34 (1985), 3–27.

32 Erich Fried, "Gespräch zweier großer Staatsmänner im Himmel oder in der Hölle," in *Gesammelte Werke* (Berlin: Klaus Wagenbach, 1993), vol. 3, p. 198.

33 *Judith* 9:12, *The Holy Bible* (New York: Douay Bible House, 1941), p. 468.

34 Rolf Hochhuth, *Judith* (Reinbek: Rowohlt, 1988), p. 206.

35 *Schiller's Works*, ed. J. G. Fischer, vol. 1 (Philadelphia: George Barrie, 1883), p. 156. For the German, "Am Antritt des Neuen Jahrhunderts," see *Schillers Werke (Nationalausgabe)*, vol. 2, part 1, *Gedichte*, ed. Norbert Oellers (Weimar: Hermann Böhlaus Nachfolger, 1983), pp. 362–363.

36 Peter Schneider, *The Wall Jumper*, trans. Leigh Hafrey (New York: Pantheon, 1983), pp. 127, 126; in the original, *Der Mauerspringer* (Hamburg: Luchterhand, 1982), p. 108. Peitsch (*Vom Faschismus*, p. 416) criticizes this passage as a flight from political responsibility.

37 Schneider, *Jumper*, p. 109; in German, p. 93.

38 Schneider, *Jumper*, p. 119; in German, p. 102.

39 Martin Walser, *No Man's Land*, trans. Leila Vennewitz (New York: Henry Holt, 1989), pp. 133–4; in the original, *Dorle und Wolf* (Frankfurt: Suhrkamp, 1987), pp. 147–8. In the original, all of this is part of a single paragraph; in the translation, the last sentence begins a new paragraph.

40 Steinfeld and Suhr, "Wiederkehr," p. 350.

41 Plato, *Symposium*, trans. Tom Griffith (Berkeley: University of California Press, 1989), p. 191d.

42 Walser, *No Man's Land*, p. 47; in the original, p. 54.

43 Ibid., p. 47; in the German original, p. 55.

44 For this reason, critics who "maintained that Walser could not convince readers that Germans were still suffering from the country's split" are slightly off the mark. Walser's point is that Germans are suffering, but that they do not know they are suffering. See Heike A. Doane, "The Cultivation of Personal and Political Loss: *Die Verteidigung der Kindheit*," in Frank Pilipp (ed.), *New Critical Perspectives on Martin Walser* (Columbia, S.C.: Camden House, 1994), pp. 156–175 (p. 170).

45 Botho Strauß, *Diese Erinnerung an einen, der nur einen Tag zu Gast war* (Munich: Hanser, 1985), pp. 47–48.

46 Biermann, "Reden," p. 247.

47 Andreas Neumeister, *Ausdeutschen* (Frankfurt: Suhrkamp, 1994), p. 34.

48 Günter Gaus, *Texte zur deutschen Frage: Mit den wichtigsten Dokumenten zum*

Verhältnis der beiden deutschen Staaten (Darmstadt: Luchterhand, 1981), pp. 31, 26.

49 Ibid., p. 33.
50 Ibid., p. 32.
51 Ibid., p. 31.
52 Strauß, *Erinnerung*, p. 47.
53 Karl Heinz Bohrer, "Why We are Not a Nation – And Why We Should Become One," trans. Stephen Brockmann, *New German Critique* 52 (1991), 72–83.
54 Irene Dische, *Ein fremdes Gefühl, oder Veränderungen über einen Deutschen*, trans. Reinhard Kaiser (Berlin: Rowohlt, 1993), p. 67. Dische, an American living in Berlin since 1980, originally wrote the novel in English under the title "A Violent Chord," but the only published version exists in German translation. Since her creative writing appears almost exclusively in German and is intended for a German reading public, Dische can be considered part of the German literary scene.
55 Peter von Becker, *Die andere Zeit* (Frankfurt: Suhrkamp, 1994), p. 86.
56 Christoph Hein, *The Distant Lover*, trans. Krishna Winston (New York: Pantheon, 1989), p. 76; in the original, *Der fremde Freund* (Berlin: Aufbau, 1986), p. 90.
57 Martin Walser, "Über Deutschland reden (Ein Bericht)," in *Über Deutschland reden* (Frankfurt: Suhrkamp, 1988), pp. 76–100 (p. 96).
58 Ibid., p. 98.
59 Ibid., p. 89. These words were cited from a speech Walser had given over a decade earlier, in August 1977. See Walser, "Über den Leser – soviel man in einem Festzelt darüber sagen soll," in *Wer ist ein Schriftsteller: Aufsätze und Reden* (Frankfurt: Suhrkamp, 1979), pp. 94–101 (pp. 100 and 101). Walser cited these words yet again in an equally controversial speech he made in October 1998 calling for a less politicized approach to the Nazi past. See Martin Walser, "Die Banalität des Guten: Erfahrungen beim Verfassen einer Sonntagsrede aus Anlaß der Verleihung des Friedenspreises des Deutschen Buchhandels," *Frankfurter Allgemeine Zeitung*, 13 October 1998, p. 15.
60 Walser, "Deutschland," p. 89. This phrase was also a citation from the 1977 speech, p. 101.

2 A THIRD PATH?

1 Bernd Wagner, *Paradies* (Berlin: Ullstein, 1997), p. 143. This passage is a play on the verb "rasen," which can mean either "to be crazy" or "to speed."
2 Peter Schneider, "If the Wall Came Tumbling Down," *The New York Times Magazine*, 25 June 1989, 22–70.
3 Ibid., 70.

4 Harold James and Marla Stone (eds.), *When the Wall Came Down: Reactions to German Unification* (New York: Routledge, 1992), p. 126.
5 Ibid., p. 126.
6 Ibid., p. 129. This slogan was a play on the peace movement's early 1980s slogan: "Imagine there's a war, and no one turns up."
7 Fritz Rudolf Fries, *Die Nonnen von Bratislava* (Munich: Piper, 1994), p. 44.
8 Bathrick, *Powers*, p. 30.
9 John Erpenbeck, *Aufschwung* (Berlin: Eulenspiegel, 1996), p. 35.
10 On the events surrounding the fall of the Berlin Wall, see Hans-Hermann Hertle, *Der Fall der Mauer: Die unbeabsichtigte Selbstauflösung des SED-Staates* (Wiesbaden: Westdeutscher Verlag, 1996). For an English-language account of the GDR's demise, see Charles S. Maier, *Dissolution: The Crisis of Communism and the End of East Germany* (Princeton University Press, 1997).
11 Reinhold had argued: "The GDR is thinkable only as an antifascist and socialist state, as a socialist alternative to the FRG. What right to existence can a capitalist GDR have next to a capitalist Federal Republic? None, of course." See "Die Flut ist nicht zu stoppen," *Der Spiegel*, 6 November 1989 (no. 45), 20–29 (p. 29).
12 Günter Grass, *Ein weites Feld* (Göttingen: Steidl, 1995), p. 409.
13 Wolf Biermann, "Nur wer sich ändert, bleibt sich treu," in *Über das Geld und andere Herzensdinge: Prosaische Versuche über Deutschland* (Cologne: Kiepenheuer & Witsch, 1991), pp. 51–71 (p. 60).
14 The appeal, translated by reporter David Binder, was printed in *The New York Times* under the somewhat facetious title "The G.D.R. Forever" on 8 December 1989, A39. For the original German, see Christa Wolf, *Reden im Herbst* (Berlin: Aufbau, 1990), pp. 170–171.
15 Stefan Heym, "Ash Wednesday in the GDR," trans. Stephen Brockmann, *New German Critique* 52 (1991), 31–35 (p. 31).
16 Ibid., p. 34.
17 Wolf Biermann, *Alle Lieder* (Cologne: Kiepenheuer & Witsch, 1991), p. 410.
18 Ibid., p. 418.
19 Monika Maron, "Writers and the People," trans. Stephen Brockmann, *New German Critique* 52 (1991), 36–41.
20 Gottfried Benn, "Answer to the Literary Emigrants," trans. E. B. Ashton, in *Primal Vision: Selected Writings of Gottfried Benn*, ed. E. B. Ashton (New York: New Directions, n.d.), pp. 46–53 (pp. 48, 46–47).
21 *The Complete Fairy Tales of the Brothers Grimm*, trans. Jack Zipes (New York: Bantam, 1992), p. 187.
22 Ibid., p. 189.
23 Martin Ahrends, "The Great Waiting, or The Freedom of the East: An Obituary for Life in Sleeping Beauty's Castle," trans. Stephen Brockmann, *New German Critique* 52 (1991), 41–49 (p. 43).
24 Günter Grass, *Schreiben nach Auschwitz* (Frankfurt: Luchterhand, 1990),

p. 42. For an alternative English translation, see Grass, *Two States – One Nation?*, trans. Krishna Winston with A. S. Wensinger (San Diego: Harcourt Brace Jovanovich, 1990), p. 123.

25 Grass, *Schreiben*, p. 41.

26 Grass, "What Am I Talking For? Is Anybody Still Listening?" trans. Stephen Brockmann, *New German Critique* 52 (1991), 66–72 (p. 68).

27 Jürgen Habermas, "Yet Again: German Identity – A Unified Nation of Angry DM-Burghers?" trans. Stephen Brockmann, *New German Critique* 52 (1991), 84–101.

28 Markovits and Reich make the same point when they write that "Ironically, the Germans have become the very 'mercenary creatures' or *Krämerseelen* – one of the worst epithets associated with allegedly venal England and the Jews – that they formerly despised." See *Predicament*, p. 48.

29 Hans Magnus Enzensberger, "Europe in Ruins," trans. Martin Chalmers, in *Civil Wars: From L. A. to Bosnia* (New York: The New Press, 1994), pp. 73–99 (pp. 98–99).

30 Cited in Fritz Stern, *The Politics of Cultural Despair* (Berkeley: University of California Press, 1961), p. 32.

31 Günter Grass, "Kurze Rede eines vaterlandslosen Gesellen," in *Nichts wird mehr so sein, wie es war: Zur Zukunft der beiden deutschen Republiken*, ed. Frank Blohm and Wolfgang Herzberg (Leipzig: Reclam, 1990), pp. 226–231 (p. 229).

32 Bohrer, "Nation," p. 81.

33 Günter Gaus, "Nationale Identität in Europa," *Neues Deutschland*, 18 May 1990, 9.

34 Walter Benjamin, "The Work of Art in the Age of Mechanical Reproduction," in *Illuminations*, trans. Harry Zohn (New York: Schocken, 1985), pp. 217–251 (pp. 241–242).

35 Gisela Elsner, "Über die sogenannte deutsche Revolution," *Neues Deutschland*, 6 April 1990, 8 and 14/15 April, 14.

36 Helmut Hanke, "Was wird bleiben?" *Neues Deutschland*, 23 May 1990, 8.

37 See the open letter by two GDR artists, "Die Geschichte der DDR geht zu Ende," *Neues Deutschland*, 23 May 1990, 8.

38 Friedrich Nietzsche, *Unzeitgemäße Betrachtungen* (Leipzig: Alfred Kröner, 1930), p. 3.

39 Serge Schmemann, "Germans Move to Unite Economies, as Kohl Leads and Modrow Follows," *The New York Times*, 14 February 1990, A10.

40 Markovits and Reich, *Predicament*, pp. 191–192.

3 LITERATURE AND POLITICS

1 Friedrich Hölderlin, "Remembrance" [Andenken], in *Hymns and Fragments*, trans. Richard Sieburth (Princeton University Press, 1984), pp. 106–109 (pp. 108, 109).

2 Christa Wolf, "What Remains," in Wolf, *What Remains and Other Stories*, trans. Heike Schwarzbauer and Rick Takvorian (New York: Farrar, Straus, Giroux, 1993), pp. 229–295 (p. 233); German original; *Was bleibt* (Berlin: Aufbau, 1990), p. 8.

3 For a useful reading of *Was bleibt* as a diary text, and for parallels between *Was bleibt* and *Kassandra*, see Georgina Paul, "Text and Context – *Was bleibt* 1979–1989," in Axel Goodbody and Dennis Tate (eds.,) *Geist und Macht: Writers and the State in the GDR* (*German Monitor*, no. 29) (Amsterdam: Rodopi, 1992), pp. 117–128.

4 Wolf, "What Remains," p. 234.

5 For an attempt to place *Was bleibt* in its historical and literary context, see Gisela Roethke, "*Was bleibt* – 'Nun ja! Das nächste Leben geht aber heute an' – Zur politisch-literarischen Gratwanderung von Christa Wolf im Jahre 1979," *German Life and Letters* 48: 1 (1995), 86–95.

6 Ulrich Greiner, "Mangel an Feingefühl," *Die Zeit*, 1 June 1990, 63. This contribution to the debate and many others were later collected in Thomas Anz (ed.), *"Es geht nicht um Christa Wolf: Der Literaturstreit im vereinten Deutschland* (Munich: Spangenberg, 1991).

7 For a useful summary of that debate, see Reinhold Grimm, "Innere Emigration als Lebensform," in Reinhold Grimm and Jost Hermand (eds.), *Exil und Innere Emigration* (Frankfurt: Athenäum, 1972), pp. 31–73.

8 Albert O. Hirschman, "Exit, Voice, and the Fate of the German Democratic Republic: An Essay in Conceptual History," *World Politics*, 45: 2 (January 1993), 173–202 (p. 202).

9 Parkes, *Writers*, p. 239.

10 T. J. Reed, "Another Piece of the Past," in Pape (ed.), *1870/71*, pp. 233–250 (p. 248).

11 Karl Heinz Bohrer, *Nach der Natur: Über Politik und Ästhetik* (Munich: Carl Hanser, 1988), p. 144.

12 Ibid., p. 155.

13 Frank Schirrmacher, "Abschied von der Literatur der Bundesrepublik," *Frankfurter Allgemeine Zeitung*, 2 October 1990: L1–2.

14 Max Weber, *Politics as a Vocation*, trans. H. H. Gerth and C. Wright Mills (Philadelphia: Fortress Press, 1965), pp. 46–55.

15 Karl Heinz Bohrer, "Die Ästhetik am Ausgang ihrer Unmündigkeit," *Merkur*: 500 (1990), 851–865.

16 Helmut Schelsky, *Die Arbeit tun die anderen* (Munich: Deutscher Taschenbuch Verlag, 1977).

17 Arnold Gehlen, *Moral und Hypermoral: Eine pluralistische Ethik* (Frankfurt: Athenäum, 1969), pp. 150–151.

18 Ibid., pp. 151–152.

19 Parkes, *Writers*, p. 171.

20 For accounts in English of the *Historikerstreit*, see Charles S. Maier, *The Unmasterable Past: History, Holocaust, and German National Identity* (Cambridge, MA: Harvard University Press, 1988); Richard J. Evans, *In*

Hitler's Shadow: West German Historians and the Attempt to Escape from the Nazi Past (New York: Pantheon, 1989); the special issue on the *Historikerstreit* published by *New German Critique* 44 (Spring/Summer 1988); and my own "The Politics of German History," *History and Theory*, 29: 2 (1990), 178–189.

21 Claudia Mayer-Iswandy, "Ästhetik und Macht: Zur diskursiven Unordnung im vereinten Deutschland," *German Studies Review* 19: 3 (1996), 501–523 (p. 512).

22 See also Irene Heidelberger-Leonhard, "Der Literaturstreit – ein Historikerstreit im gesamtdeutschen Kostüm?" in Karl Deiritz and Hannes Krauss (eds.), *Der deutsch-deutsche Literaturstreit oder "Freunde, es spricht sich schlecht mit gebundener Zunge"* (Hamburg: Luchterhand, 1991), pp. 69–77.

23 H. J. Hahn, "'Es geht nicht um Literatur': Some Observations on the 1990 'Literaturstreit' and its Recent Anti-Intellectual Implications," *German Life and Letters* 50: 1 (1997), 65–81; see especially pp. 69–71. In view of the previous work of Bullivant, Huyssen, Heidelberger-Leonhard, Mayer-Iswandy, and others, Hahn's assertion (p. 65) that "no serious attempt has been made to relate [the *Literaturstreit*] to the wider intellectual debate" in Germany is both bizarre and groundless.

24 Nolte, "Vergangenheit," p. 41.

25 Ibid., p. 39.

26 Alfred Döblin, *Die literarische Situation* (Baden-Baden: P. Keppler, 1947), p. 44.

27 On the problem of historicization with respect to the Third Reich and the *Historikerstreit*, see Dan Diner (ed.), *Ist der Nationalsozialismus Geschichte?: Zu Historisierung und Historikerstreit* (Frankfurt: Fischer, 1987).

28 I developed this argument in "The Politics of German Literature," *Monatshefte* 84: 1 (1992), 46–58.

29 Jochen Vogt, *'Erinnerung ist unsere Aufgabe': Über Literatur, Moral und Politik 1945–1990* (Opladen: Westdeutscher Verlag, 1991).

30 Andreas Huyssen, "After the Wall: The Failure of German Intellectuals," *New German Critique* 52 (1991), 109–143 (p. 143).

31 Emmerich, *Literaturgeschichte*, p. 462.

4 LITERATURE AND THE STASI

1 Rainer Schedlinski, *die rationen des ja und des nein* (Frankfurt: Suhrkamp, 1990), p. 150.

2 Erich Loest, *Der Zorn des Schafes: Aus meinem Tagewerk* (Kunzelsau: Linden, 1990).

3 Reiner Kunze (ed.), *Deckname "Lyrik": Eine Dokumentation* (Frankfurt: Fischer, 1990).

4 Wolf, "What Remains," pp. 260–261; in the German original, *Was bleibt*, p. 38.

5 Sascha Anderson, "jeder satellit hat einen killersatelliten," *Jeder Satellit hat einen Killersatelliten* (Berlin: Rotbuch, 1982), p. 50.

6 Sascha Anderson and Elke Erb (eds.), *Berührung ist nur eine Randerscheinung: Neue Literatur aus der DDR* (Cologne: Kiepenheuer & Witsch, 1985), p. 216.

7 Wolf Biermann, "Der Lichtblick im gräßlichen Fatalismus der Geschichte," in *Der Sturz des Dädalus, oder: Eizes für die Eingeborenen der Fidschi-Inseln über den IM Judas Ischariot und den Kuddelmuddel in Deutschland seit dem Golfkrieg* (Cologne: Kiepenheuer & Witsch, 1992), pp. 48–63; especially p. 56.

8 "Conspiratorial" meetings with the Stasi were kept secret from anyone else; nonconspiratorial meetings were not a secret. Since the Stasi preferred complete secrecy, the distinction was very important. On Müller's and Wolf's Stasi contacts, see Emmerich, *Literaturgeschichte*, pp. 473–475.

9 For a detailed study of the Stasi and its literary conspiracies, see Joachim Walther, *Sicherungsbereich Literatur: Schriftsteller und Staatssicherheit in der Deutschen Demokratischen Republik* (Berlin: LinksDruck, 1996).

10 Klaus Schlesinger, "Ich war ein Roman: Blick auf eine Kolportage," *Die Zeit*, 24 April 1992, 13–14.

11 Jane Kramer, "Stasi," in *The Politics of Memory: Looking for Germany in the New Germany* (New York: Random House, 1996), pp. 153–212 (p. 164).

12 Henryk M. Broder, "Eine schöne Revolution," *Die Zeit*, 17 January 1992, 15.

13 Henryk M. Broder, "Die Unfähigkeit zu feiern," *Der Spiegel*, 2 October 1995 (no. 40), 236–246 (p. 246).

14 Kerstin Jentzsch, *Seit die Götter ratlos sind* (2nd edn, Munich: Wilhelm Heyne, 1996), p. 533.

15 Michel Foucault, "What Is an Author?", in Josué V. Harari (ed.), *Textual Strategies: Perspectives in Post-Structuralist Criticism* (Ithaca: Cornell University Press, 1979), pp. 141–160 (p. 158).

16 Wolf Biermann, "Die Stasi-Ballade," *Alle Lieder*, pp. 204–207 (p. 204), loosely translated.

17 Klaus Pohl, *Karate-Billi kehrt zurück / Die schöne Fremde* (Frankfurt: Verlag der Autoren, 1993).

18 Uwe Saeger, *Die Nacht danach und der Morgen* (Munich: Piper, 1991).

19 Andreas Sinakowski, *Das Verhör* (Berlin: BasisDruck, 1991).

20 Wolfgang Hilbig, "*ICH*" (Frankfurt: Fischer, 1993).

21 Kerstin Hensel, *Tanz am Kanal* (Frankfurt: Suhrkamp, 1994).

22 Brigitte Burmeister, *Unter dem Namen Norma* (Stuttgart: Klett-Cotta, 1994).

23 Jentzsch, *Götter*, p. 329.

24 Jürgen Fuchs, "Landschaften der Lüge," *Der Spiegel*, 18 November–16 December 1991 (nos. 47–51).

25 Cited in Frank Schirrmacher, "Verdacht und Verrat: Die Stasi Vergangenheit verändert die literarische Szene," in Peter Böthig and Klaus

Michael (eds.), *MachtSpiele: Literatur und Staatssicherheit* (Leipzig: Reclam, 1993), p. 306.

26 The important documents related to Wolf's Stasi connection and the debate surrounding it appear in Hermann Vinke (ed.), *Akteneinsicht Christa Wolf: Zerrspiegel und Dialog* (Hamburg: Luchterhand, 1993).

27 Wolf, "What Remains," p. 287; in the German original, *Was bleibt*, p. 67.

28 Rainer Schedlinski, "Die Unzuständigkeit der Macht," *Neue deutsche Literatur* 474 (1992), 75–105 (p. 76).

29 Wolf, "What Remains," p. 259; German original, p. 37. The sentence is phrased in the negative, but the context makes it clear that Jürgen M. is a competitor.

30 Wolf, "What Remains," p. 259; German original, p. 37. I have offered a reading of this work in "Preservation and Change in Christa Wolf's *Was bleibt*," *The German Quarterly* 67: 1 (1994), 73–85.

31 *A Derrida Reader: Between the Blinds*, ed. Peggy Kamuf (New York: Columbia University Press, 1991), p. 52.

32 Saeger, *Nacht*, p. 99.

33 Ibid., p. 126.

34 Ibid., p. 199.

35 See Marshall McLuhan, *Understanding Media: The Extensions of Man* (New York: McGraw Hill, 1964).

36 "Kulturnik 7423/91," *Der Spiegel*, 21 October 1991 (no. 43), 336–337.

37 On the controversy surrounding de Man, see David Lehmann, *Signs of the Times: Deconstruction and the Fall of Paul de Man* (New York: Poseidon, 1991).

38 Kurt Drawert, "Niemand braucht sie, sie brauchen niemand: Über das Volk und die Intellektuellen in Deutschland," *Monatshefte* LXXXII: 4 (1990), 399–402 (p. 400).

39 Anderson and Erb (eds.), *Berührung*, p. 15.

40 Ibid., p. 40.

41 Ibid.

42 Ibid., p. 37.

43 Drawert, "Niemand," p. 400.

44 Jan Faktor, "Sechzehn Punkte zur Prenzlauer-Berg-Szene," in Böthig and Michael (eds.), *MachtSpiele*, pp. 91–111 (p. 98).

45 For a useful introduction to the Prenzlauer Berg scene in English, see Philip Brady, "'Wir hausen im Prenzlauer Berg.' On the Very Last Generation of GDR Poets," in Pape (ed.), *1870/71*, pp. 278–301.

46 Marshall McLuhan and Quentin Fiore, *The Medium is the Massage* (New York: Touchstone, 1989), no page number.

47 Bathrick, *Powers*, p. 239.

48 Schedlinski, *rationen*, pp. 146, 135.

49 Kurt Drawert, *Spiegelland: Ein deutscher Monolog* (Frankfurt: Suhrkamp, 1992), p. 27.

50 Ibid., p. 144.
51 *A Derrida Reader*, p. 412.
52 Drawert, *Spiegelland*, p. 148.
53 Ibid., p. 120.
54 Sascha Anderson, "mann kann watzmann geheissen haben mit zet & en en," in *Satellit*, pp. 16–17 (p. 17).
55 Bathrick, *Powers*, p. 241.
56 Wolf, "What Remains," p. 237; German original, p. 12. There is a paragraph break before the last sentence.
57 Drawert, *Spiegelland*, pp. 114–115.
58 Wolf, "Remains," pp. 231, 295; German original, pp. 5, 76.
59 Wolf, *Kassandra*, p. 153.
60 See Wolf, "Remains," pp. 245–246: I have modified the translation somewhat in order to render more precisely the meaning of "nicht Vorhandenem" and "eigenschaftslos." Cf. German original, pp. 21–22.
61 Anderson, "wer ich bin werden wir," in *Satellit*, p. 24. Karen Leeder offers a more extensive interpretation of this poem, and of the problem of subjectivity in late GDR poetry, in *Breaking Boundaries: A New Generation of Poets in the GDR* (Oxford: Clarendon, 1996), pp. 77–107, especially p. 98.
62 Anderson, "die zusammenhänge sind einfach," in *Satellit*, p. 30.
63 Sascha Anderson, "jeder, der spricht, stirbt," in Egmont Hesse (ed.), *Sprache & Antwort: Stimmen und Texte einer anderen Literatur aus der DDR* (Frankfurt: Fischer, 1998), pp. 55–64 (pp. 56–57).
64 Saeger, *Nacht*, p. 126.
65 Anderson, "wenn ich über grün spreche," in *Satellit*, p. 66.
66 Thomas Brussig, *Helden wie wir* (Berlin: Volk & Welt, 1995), p. 169. For an alternative English translation, see Brussig, *Heroes Like Us*, trans. John Brownjohn (New York: Farrar, Straus, Giroux, 1997), pp. 136–137. I have used my own more literal translation of the German because the published English version somewhat diminishes the force of the narrator's self-negation.
67 Brussig, *Helden*, p. 113. Cf. *Heroes*, p. 91.
68 Hilbig, "*ICH*," p. 25. For further information on Hilbig, whom Wehdeking (*Einheit*, p. 41) calls the "most eloquent witness and heir to a questionable and increasingly dehumanized 'socialism from above,'" see *Text+Kritik* 123 (1994), which is devoted to Hilbig; and Wehdeking, *Einheit*, pp. 40–63.
69 Hilbig, "*ICH*," p. 62.
70 Ibid., p. 64.
71 Ibid., p. 65.
72 Ibid., p. 132.
73 Ibid., p. 112.
74 Ibid., p. 284.
75 Ibid., p. 190.
76 Ibid., p. 289.

77 Ibid., p. 173.
78 Ibid., p. 232.
79 Ibid., p. 290.
80 Ibid., p. 24.
81 Wolf, "What Remains," p. 241; German original, p. 16.
82 Wolf, "What Remains," p. 256; German original, p. 34.
83 Goethe, *Faust*, Part I, in *The Harvard Classics*, vol. 19 (New York: P. F. Collier & Son, 1909), p. 70.
84 Heinrich Böll, "Bekenntnis zur Trümmerliteratur," in *Erzählungen Hörspiele Aufsätze* (Cologne: Kiepenheuer & Witsch, 1961), pp. 339–343 (p. 342).
85 Hilbig, "*ICH*," p. 21.
86 Schneider, *Wall*, p. 139; in the original German, *Mauerspringer*, p. 118.
87 Goethe, *Faust*, Part I, p. 9.

5 THE REBIRTH OF TRAGEDY?

1 Jürgen Habermas, *The New Conservatism: Cultural Criticism and the Historians' Debate*, trans. Shierry Weber Nicholsen (Cambridge, MA: MIT Press, 1989), p. 227.
2 Ibid., pp. 256–257.
3 Ansgar Graw, "(Historiker-)Streit unter Adenauers Enkeln," in Rainer Zitelmann, Karlheinz Weißmann, and Michael Grossheim (eds.), *Westbindung: Chancen und Risiken für Deutschland* (Frankfurt: Propyläen, 1993), pp. 365–389 (pp. 366–367).
4 Arnulf Baring, *Deutschland, was nun?* (Berlin: Siedler bei Goldmann, 1991), p. 16.
5 Elisabeth Noelle-Neumann and Renate Köcher, *Die verletzte Nation: Über den Versuch der Deutschen, ihren Charakter zu ändern* (Stuttgart: Deutsche Verlags-Anstalt, 1987). See also Noelle-Neumann, *Eine demoskopische Deutschstunde* (Zurich: Edition Interforum, 1983), pp. 90–93.
6 Jurek Becker, "Die Wiedervereinigung der deutschen Literatur," *The German Quarterly* 63: 3/4 (1990), 359–366 (p. 364).
7 On literary pictures of the German capital, see Katherine Roper, "Imagining the German Capital: Berlin Writers on the Two Unification Eras," in Pape (ed.), *1870/71*, pp. 171–194.
8 Patrick Süskind, "Deutschland, eine Midlife-crisis," in Ulrich Wickert (ed.), *Angst vor Deutschland* (Hamburg: Hoffmann und Campe, 1990), pp. 111–122 (p. 122).
9 Baring, *Deutschland*, pp. 15–16.
10 Michael Mertes and Hubertus von Morr, "Linke, rechts drehend," *Frankfurter Allgemeine Zeitung*, 20 April 1994, 35.
11 Stefan Ulbrich, "1000 gute Gründe," in Ulbrich (ed.), *Gedanken zu Großdeutschland* (Vilsbiburg: Arun, 1990), pp. 225–239 (p. 234).
12 Theodor W. Adorno, "Was ist deutsch?" in Hermann Glaser, ed.,

Bundesrepublikanisches Lesebuch (Munich: Carl Hanser, 1978), pp. 335–346 (p. 343).

13　Ibid., p. 344.

14　Karl Marx and Friedrich Engels, *Basic Writings on Politics and Philosophy*, ed. Lewis S. Feuer (Garden City: Doubleday Anchor, 1959), p. 12.

15　Ibid., p. 247.

16　Eva Geulen, "Nationalisms: Old, New and German," *Telos* 105 (fall 1995), 2–20 (p. 16).

17　See, for example, Martin Broszat, Elke Fröhlich, and Falk Wiesemann (eds.), *Bayern in der NS-Zeit*, 6 vols. (Munich: Oldenbourg, 1977–1983); Martin Broszat, Klaus-Dietmar Henke, and Hans Woller (eds.), *Von Stalingrad zur Währungsreform: Zur Sozialgeschichte des Umbruchs in Deutschland* (Munich: Oldenbourg, 1988); Rainer Zitelmann, *Hitler: Selbstverständnis eines Revolutionärs* (Hamburg: Berg, 1991); and Rainer Zitelmann and Eckhard Jesse (eds.), *Nationalsozialismus und Modernisierung* (Darmstadt: Wissenschaftliche Buchgesellschaft, 1991). In English, see David Schoenbaum, *Hitler's Social Revolution: Class and Status in Nazi Germany, 1933–1939* (Garden City: Doubleday, 1966) and Jeffrey Herf, *Reactionary Modernism* (Cambridge University Press, 1984).

18　This is one of Ernst Nolte's fundamental points in his controversial book *Der europäische Bürgerkrieg, 1917–1945: Nationalsozialismus und Bolschewismus* (Berlin: Propyläen, 1987). It is worth pointing out that the right-wing Nolte is in agreement with left-wing historians on Hitler's profound enmity toward the Soviet Union.

19　Hans Jürgen Syberberg, *Vom Unglück und Glück der Kunst in Deutschland nach dem letzten Kriege* (Munich: Matthes & Seitz, 1990), p. 114.

20　Ibid., pp. 90–91.

21　Four years later Syberberg seemed to admit that his hopes for a transformation of the Federal Republic had been dashed: "We live in a revolutionary phase of history; but the world has done the wrong thing. Instead of rethinking and changing the structure of all things and actions, we have transported our false principles into the decline of the East – a revolution that leads not to explosions but rather to an implosion, an inward fall into the emptiness of the desert . . ." Hans Jürgen Syberberg, *Der verlorene Auftrag* (Vienna: Karolinger, 1994), p. 51.

22　Hans Jürgen Syberberg, *Hitler, A Film from Germany*, trans. Joachim Neugroschel (New York: Farrar, Straus, Giroux, 1982), p. 6; in the German original, *Hitler, ein Film aus Deutschland* (Reinbek bei Hamburg: Rowohlt, 1978), p. 14.

23　Karl Heinz Bohrer, "Die permanente Theodizee: Über das verfehlte Böse im deutschen Bewußtsein," in *Natur*, pp. 133–161 (pp. 154–155).

24　Jan Ross, "Schwellendes Philistertum: Gegen politisch korrekte Westbindung und Metaphysikverbot," *Frankfurter Allgemeine Zeitung*, 9 May 1994, 35.

25 Claus Leggewie, *Der Geist steht rechts: Ausflüge in die Denkfabrike der Wende* (Berlin: Rotbuch, 1987), p. 27.
26 Karlheinz Weißmann, "Die Nation denken," *Frankfurter Allgemeine Zeitung*, 22 April 1994, 33.
27 Rainer Zitelmann, *Wohin treibt unsere Republik?* (Frankfurt: Ullstein, 1994), p. 192.
28 Frank Hauke, "Der rote Faden," in Roland Bubik (ed.), *Wir '89er: Wer wir sind und was wir wollen* (Frankfurt: Ullstein, 1995), pp. 51–68 (p. 53).
29 Zitelmann, *Republik*, p. 40.
30 Ibid., p. 165.
31 Syberberg, *Auftrag*, p. 86.
32 Cited in Jochen Buchsteiner, ". . . und kein bißchen bissig," *Die Zeit*, 28 February 1997, 21–22 (p. 21).
33 Aachim Schmillen, "Wir sind besser als die Alten!" *Die Zeit*, 28 February 1997, 21–22 (p. 21).
34 Leeder, *Boundaries*, p. 51.
35 Jochen Buchsteiner, ". . . bissig," p. 22.
36 *Rocky Dutschke, '68: Dokumentarfotos (2)* (Berlin: Volksbühne am Rosa-Luxemburg Platz, 1996).
37 Ulrich Woelk, *Rückspiel* (Munich: Piper, 1993), p. 54.
38 Ibid.
39 Ibid., p. 292.
40 Cited in Leggewie, *Der Geist steht rechts*, p. 214.
41 Karl Richter, "Barbarossa erwacht," in Ulbrich (ed.), *Gedanken*, pp. 63–117 (p. 82).
42 Syberberg, *Auftrag*, p. 14.
43 Marcus Bauer, "Plädoyer für ein Neues Deutschland," in Ulbrich (ed.), *Gedanken*, pp. 11–42 (p. 30).
44 Roland Bubik, "Trotzdem rechts," in Bubik (ed.), *'89er*, pp. 107–124 (p. 122).
45 Heimo Schwilk, "Der eigene deutsche Weg," *Junge Freiheit*, 3 November 1995, 13.
46 Richter, "Barbarossa," pp. 89–90.
47 Ibid., p. 90.
48 Stefan Ulbrich, "Verdammt viele Thesen: Warum Multikulturalismus ein Konzept der Neuen Rechten ist," in Stefan Ulbrich (ed.), *Multikultopia: Gedanken zur multikulturellen Gesellschaft* (Vilsbiburg: Arun, 1991), pp. 299–344 (p. 304).
49 Syberberg, *Auftrag*, p. 81.
50 Geulen, "Nationalisms," p. 15.
51 See Peter Wehling, "Multikulti von rechts: Die Neue Rechte entdeckt die Vorzüge der 'multikulturellen Gesellschaft,'" *Kommune*, January 1992, pp. 68–69, a skeptical and negative review of Ulbrich's *Multikultopia*.
52 Jentzsch, *Götter*, p. 329.
53 Richter, "Barbarossa," p. 82.
54 Botho Strauß, *Schlußchor* (Munich: Hanser, 1991).

55 Botho Strauß, *Das Gleichgewicht* (Munich: Hanser, 1993), p. 53.

56 Ibid., p. 27. For a useful essay on Strauß's recent work, see Arthur Williams, "Botho Strauß: The Janus-Head Above the Parapet – Final Choruses and Goat Songs Without Beginnings," in Arthur Williams and Stuart Parker (eds.), *The Individual, Identity and Innovation: Signals from Contemporary Literature and the New Germany* (Bern: Peter Lang, 1994), pp. 315–344.

57 Sigrid Berka, "Botho Strauß und die Debatte um den 'Bocksgesang': Zu diesem Heft," *Weimarer Beiträge* 40: 2 (1994), 165–178 (p. 167). Berka also includes a selective bibliography of the many contributions to the debate about Strauß's essay; the other articles in the same special issue of *Weimarer Beiträge* are all attempts to draw conclusions from Strauß's essay. Because the large amount of material included in the debate about the essay precludes exhaustive coverage here, I will focus exclusively on the essay itself, and refer readers who desire more information on the debate about Strauß to Berka's essay and bibliography.

58 Friedrich Nietzsche, "The Birth of Tragedy out of the Spirit of Music", in *The Birth of Tragedy and The Case of Wagner*, trans. Walter Kaufmann, (New York: Vintage, 1967), pp. 29–144 (p. 61).

59 Botho Strauß, "Anschwellender Bocksgesang," *Der Pfahl* VII (1993), 9–25 (p. 14).

60 Ibid., p. 14.

61 Ibid., p. 19.

62 Ibid., p. 24.

63 Nietzsche, "Birth of Tragedy," p. 76.

64 See Stephen Brockmann, Julia Hell, and Reinhilde Wiegmann, "The Greens: Images of Survival in the Early 1980s," in Reinhold Grimm and Jost Hermand (eds.), *From the Greeks to the Greens: Images of the Simple Life* (Madison: University of Wisconsin Press, 1989), pp. 127–144.

65 Strauß, "Bocksgesang," p. 15.

66 Alain de Benoist, "Zwang zur deutschen Geburt," interview in Ulbrich (ed.), *Gedanken*, p. 219. For more on de Benoist and his role in the European New Right, see Pierre-Andre Taguieff, *Sur la Nouvelle Droite: Jalons d'une analyse critique* (Paris: Descartes & Cie, 1994).

67 Strauß, "Bocksgesang," p. 23.

68 Dan Diner, "Feinde des Westens," *Frankfurter Allgemeine Zeitung*, 11 May 1994, p. 33.

69 Mathias Wedel, *Einheitsfrust* (Berlin: Rowohlt, 1994), p. 12.

70 Cited in Zitelmann, *Republik*, p. 10.

6 THE DEFENSE OF CHILDHOOD AND THE GUILT
OF THE FATHERS

1 Martin Walser, *Die Verteidigung der Kindheit* (Frankfurt: Suhrkamp, 1991), p. 198.

2 Ibid., p. 337.

3 Ibid., p. 520.

4 Stuart Parkes, "Looking Forward to the Past: Identity and Identification in Martin Walser's *Die Verteidigung der Kindheit*," in Williams and Parkes (eds.), *Individual*, pp. 57–74 (p. 72).

5 Doane, "Cultivation," pp. 172, 170.

6 Hans Magnus Enzensberger, "Landessprache," trans. Enzensberger and Michael Hamburger, in *Selected Poems* (Newcastle: Bloodaxe, 1994), pp. 16–25 (p. 17).

7 Syberberg, *Unglück*, p. 15.

8 Ibid., p. 38.

9 Ibid., p. 39. Trudi Montag, the central figure in Ursula Hegi's popular American novel *Stones from the River* (New York: Scribner, 1995; first pub. 1994), is also a dwarf.

10 Schirrmacher, "Abschied," p. L2.

11 Ibid., p. L1.

12 Alfred Andersch, "Notwendige Aussage zum Nürnberger Prozeß," *Der Ruf* 1: 1 (August 1946); reprinted in Hans Schwab-Felisch (ed.), *Der Ruf: Eine deutsche Nachkriegszeitschrift* (Munich: Deutscher Taschenbuch Verlag, 1962), pp. 26–29 (p.26).

13 Alfred Andersch, *Deutsche Literatur in der Entscheidung: Ein Beitrag zur Analyse der literarischen Situation* (Karlsruhe: Volk und Zeit, [1948]), p. 24.

14 On "father literature," see Michael Schneider, "Fathers and Sons, Retrospectively: The Damaged Relationship Between Two Generations," trans. Jamie Owen Daniel, *New German Critique* 31 (1984), 3–51.

15 Alexander and Margarete Mitscherlich, *The Inability to Mourn: Principles of Collective Behavior*, trans. Beverley R. Placzek (New York: Grove Press, 1975), p. 221. In German, *Die Unfähigkeit zu trauern: Grundlagen kollektiven Verhaltens* (Munich: Piper, 1991), p. 262.

16 Bohrer, *Natur*, p. 156.

17 Mitscherlich, *Inability*, pp. 50–51.

18 Hans-Joachim Maaz, *Der Gefühlsstau: Ein Psychogramm der DDR* (2nd edn, Munich: Knauer, 1992). Published in a significantly abridged English version as *Behind the Wall: The Inner Life of Communist Germany*, trans. Margot Bettauer Dembo (New York: W. W. Norton, 1995).

19 Hans-Joachim Maaz, *Die Entrüstung: Deutschland Deutschland Stasi Schuld und Sündenblock* (Berlin: Argon, 1992), p. 49.

20 Maaz, *Das gestürzte Volk: Die unglückliche Einheit* (Berlin: Argon, 1991), pp. 54–55.

21 Ibid., p. 55.

22 Alison Lewis, "Unity Begins Together: Analyzing the Trauma of German Unification," *New German Critique* 64 (1995), 135–159 (p. 152).

23 Maaz, *Gefühlsstau*, p. 189. This passage, along with about forty other pages of text belonging to the book's last two sections, is eliminated in Dembo's English translation.

24 Mitscherlich, *Inability*, p. 45.
25 Maaz, *Behind*, p. 186.
26 Ibid., p. 187.
27 Maaz, *Entrüstung*, p. 56.
28 Maaz, *Behind*, p. 148; in the original, *Gefühlsstau*, p. 139.
29 Maaz, *Entrüstung*, p. 57.
30 Ibid., p. 56.
31 Ibid., p. 19.
32 Ibid., p. 54.
33 Gabriele Eckart, "Brief an den Vater," *europäische ideen* 81 (1993), 19–25 (p. 21).
34 Ibid., p. 24.
35 Ibid., p. 21.
36 Ibid., p. 25.
37 Drawert, *Spiegelland*, p. 156.
38 Ibid., p. 14.
39 Anna K. Kuhn, "Berlin as Locus of Terror: Gegenwartsbewältigung in Berlin Texts since the Wende," in Barbara Becker-Cantarino (ed.), *Berlin in Focus: Cultural Transformations in Germany* (Westport: Praeger, 1996), pp. 159–185 (p. 170).
40 Rosalind Polkowski is also the heroine of Maron's previous novel, *Die Überläuferin* (Frankfurt: Fischer, 1986).
41 Monika Maron, *Stille Zeile Sechs* (Frankfurt: Fischer, 1991), p. 182. I have modified the English translation which appears in *Silent Close No. 6*, trans. David Newton Marinelli (Columbia, Louisiana: Readers International, 1993), p. 153. For a useful analysis of Maron's development as a writer in the 1980s and 1990s, see Brigitte Rossbacher, "The Status of State and Subject: Reading Monika Maron from *Flugasche* to *Animal triste*," in Robert Weninger and Brigitte Rossbacher (eds.), *Wendezeiten Zeitenwende: Positionsbestimmungen zur deutschsprachigen Literatur 1945–1995* (Tübingen: Stauffenberg, 1997), pp. 193–214.
42 Maron, *Stille*, p. 118; I have modified the translation which appears in *Silent*, p. 97.
43 Maron, *Silent*, p. 174.
44 Maron, *Stille*, p. 34; I have modified the translation which appears in *Silent*, p. 27.
45 Maron, *Silent*, p. 180.
46 Cited in Wehdeking, *Einheit*, p. 37.
47 Monika Maron, *Animal triste* (Frankfurt: Fischer, 1996), p. 68.
48 Alison Lewis, "Re-Membering the Barbarian: Memory and Repression in Monika Maron's *Animal Triste*," *The German Quarterly* 71: 1 (1998), 30–46 (p. 36).
49 Maron, *Animal*, p. 74.
50 Christa Wolf, *Medea*, trans. John Cullen (New York: Doubleday, 1998), p. 186; in the German original, *Medea: Stimmen* (Hamburg: Luchter-

hand, 1996), p. 236. For more on this novel, see Marianne Hoch-geschurz (ed.), *Christa Wolfs* Medea: *Voraussetzungen zu einem Text – Mythos und Bild* (Berlin: Gerhard Wolf Janus Press, 1998).

51 Ingo Schramm, *Fitchers Blau* (Berlin: Volk & Welt, 1996), p. 247. For the original fairy tale, see "Fitcher's Bird," in *The Complete Fairy Tales of the Brothers Grimm*, trans. Jack Zipes (New York: Bantam, 1992) pp. 167–171.

52 Schramm, *Fitchers*, pp. 355–356.

53 Ibid., p. 91.

54 Brussig, *Helden*, p. 8; in John Brownjohn's translation, this phrase is rendered as "the story of my dick" (*Heroes*, p. 5).

55 Brussig, *Heroes*, p. 7; German original, *Helden*, p. 10.

56 Ibid., p. 31; in the German original, *Helden*, pp. 39–40.

57 Ibid., p. 217; German original, *Helden*, p. 268.

58 Brussig, *Helden*, p. 7; in the Brownjohn translation (*Heroes*, p. 5): "The story of the Wall's end is the story of my penis."

59 Schneider, *Wall*, p. 119.

60 With respect to their influence on Alfred, the narrator of Walser's novel notes: "The agreement between parents so divided was remarkable." Walser, *Verteidigung*, p. 346. Moreover, "To be against the father is easy. But one cannot be against the mother. That is the curse," p. 511. Citing these passages, Alexander Mathäs suggests that "Alfred's mother functions as the internalized voice of the father," because Alfred "replaces the father with the mother," and that hence "the mother-father dichotomy represents only two parts of the same personality." See Alexander Mathäs, "Copying Kafka's Signature: Martin Walser's *Die Verteidigung der Kindheit*," *The Germanic Review* 69: 2 (1994), 79–91 (p. 84, 87). It is probably not sufficient to reduce Alfred's mother to nothing but the voice of the father; however, the point that the mother becomes a representative of the superego even more demanding than the father is well taken.

61 Carl Gustav Jung, "Nach der Katastrophe," *Neue Schweizer Rundschau* 13: 6 (1945/1946), 67–88.

62 Karl Jaspers, *Die Schuldfrage* (Heidelberg: Lambert Schneider, 1946), p. 69; my translation. An alternative translation is available as *The Question of German Guilt*, trans. E. B. Ashton (New York: The Dial Press, 1947), p. 77.

63 Jaspers, *Schuldfrage*, p. 71. Ashton has: "We have to bear the guilt of our fathers," p. 79.

64 Jaspers, *Schuldfrage*, p. 71.

65 Ibid., pp. 71–72.

66 Bohrer, "Nation," p. 79.

67 Ibid., p. 80.

68 Philipp Jenninger, "Von der Verantwortung für das Vergangene: Fünfzig Jahre nach der 'Reichskristallnacht,'" *Die Zeit*, 25 November 1988, 4–6 (p. 6). The German version of the penultimate sentence runs:

"Unsere Vergangenheit wird nicht ruhen, sie wird auch nicht vergehen." The play on words between "Vergangenheit" (the past) and
"vergehen" (to pass away) was a reference back to Nolte's 1986 turn of
phrase which had started the *Historikerstreit*. The conservative Jenninger
was clearly positioning himself *against* the conservative Nolte and *for* the
liberal Habermas in the debate.

69 Moser, *Politik*, p. 49.
70 Horst-Eberhard Richter, *Die Chance des Gewissens: Erinnerungen und Assoziationen* (Hamburg: Hoffmann und Campe, 1986), especially pp. 14–15
and 270–271. See also Moser, *Politik*, p. 65.

7 THE TIME AND THE PLACE OF THE NATION

1 Sten Nadolny, *The Discovery of Slowness*, trans. Ralph Freedman (New
York: Viking, 1987), p. 206; translation slightly modified. For the
original German, see *Die Entdeckung der Langsamkeit* (Munich: Piper,
1983), p. 230.
2 Thomas Mann, "Deutschland und die Deutschen," in *Gesammelte Werke
in Zwölf Bänden*, vol. 11: *Reden und Aufsätze 3* (Frankfurt: S. Fischer, 1960),
pp. 1126–1148 (pp. 1140–1141).
3 Süskind, "Deutschland," pp. 118–119.
4 Jakob Arjouni, *Magic Hoffmann* (Zurich: Diogenes, 1996), p. 51.
5 Neumeister, *Ausdeutschen*, p. 11.
6 Walser, "Deutschland," p. 87.
7 Ibid., p. 79.
8 Günter Gaus, *Wendewut* (Hamburg: Hoffmann und Campe, 1990),
p. 89. "Wende" actually means transformation or turn, and "Wut" can
mean not only anger but an unhealthy enthusiasm, i.e. the opposite of
anger. The title thus has a dual meaning perhaps best captured by the
English "fever."
9 von Becker, *Zeit*, p. 377.
10 Woelk, *Rückspiel*, pp. 208–209.
11 Helmuth Plessner, *Die verspätete Nation: Über die politische Verführbarkeit
bürgerlichen Geistes* (Frankfurt: Suhrkamp, 1994). Originally published as
Das Schicksal des deutschen Geistes im Ausgang seiner bürgerlichen Epoche
(Zurich: M. Niehans, 1935) and then republished in 1959 under the
more famous title.
12 Cited in Zitelmann, *Republik*, p. 54.
13 Adorno, "Auferstehung?" p. 32.
14 Godfrey Carr and Georgina Paul also note that "it may seem ironic
that the renewed debate about the nature of German culture, identity,
and nationhood should come at a time when the validity of the nation-
state was itself being called into question by historical and economic
developments." "Unification and its Aftermath: The Challenge of

History," in Rob Burns (ed.), *German Cultural Studies: An Introduction* (Oxford University Press, 1995), pp. 325–348 (p. 345).

15 Walser, "Deutschland," pp. 77, 78.

16 Süskind, "Deutschland," pp. 116, 118.

17 Hanns-Josef Ortheil, *Abschied von den Kriegsteilnehmern* (Munich: Piper, 1992), p. 107.

18 Ibid., p. 240.

19 Wim Wenders, "Reden über Deutschland," in *The Act of Seeing: Texte und Gespräche* (Frankfurt: Verlag der Autoren, 1992), pp. 187–198 (p. 189); for an alternative translation, see Wenders, "Talking about Germany," in Roger F. Cook and Gerd Gemünden (eds.), *The Cinema of Wim Wenders: Image, Narrative, and the Postmodern Condition* (Detroit: Wayne State University Press, 1997), pp. 51–59 (p. 52).

20 Leggewie, *Geist*, p. 217.

21 Dische, *Gefühl*, p. 16.

22 Cited in Zitelmann, *Republik*, p. 132.

23 Arjouni, *Magic*, p. 75.

24 von Becker, *Zeit*, p. 375.

25 "Neue Heimat," *Die Zeit*, 12 October 1990, p. 21.

26 Hans Magnus Enzensberger, "The Great Migration," trans. Martin Chalmers, in *Civil Wars: From L. A. to Bosnia*, pp. 101–144 (p. 131).

27 Monika Maron, "Ich war ein antifaschistisches Kind," in Michael Naumann (ed.), *Die Geschichte ist offen* (Reinbek: Rowohlt, 1990), pp. 117–135 (p. 128).

28 Ernst Bloch, *Heritage of Our Time*, trans. Neville and Stephen Plaice (Berkeley: University of California Press, 1990), p. 109; in the German original *Erbschaft dieser Zeit* (Frankfurt: Suhrkamp, 1985), p. 117. The book was first published in 1935.

29 Bloch, *Heritage*, p. 108.

30 Alvin Toffler, *Future Shock* (New York: Random House, 1970).

31 Adorno, "Auferstehung?" p. 23.

32 Freud, *Civilization*, pp. 20, 18.

33 Wolf, *Medea*, pp. 2, 1; German original, pp. 10, 9.

34 Leon Trotsky, *History of the Russian Revolution*, trans. Max Eastman (London: Pluto Press, 1977), p. 1156.

35 Benjamin R. Barber, *Jihad vs. McWorld* (New York: Times Books, 1995), p. 32.

36 John Lukacs, *The End of the Twentieth Century and the End of the Modern Age* (New York: Ticknor & Fields, 1993), p. 253.

37 *Deutschland Nachrichten*, 27 September 1996, 6.

38 Jurek Becker, "Wiedervereinigung," pp. 359, 360.

39 Edward Abbey, *The Monkey Wrench Gang* (Philadelphia: Lippincott, 1975); and Andrew Macdonald, *The Turner Diaries* (Washington: National Alliance, 1980).

40 Grass, *Feld*, p. 275.

41 Ibid., p. 249.
42 Fries, *Nonnen*, p. 26. In the aftermath of reunification Heiner Müller also spoke of a positive East German "retardation." See Carr and Paul, "Unification," p. 342.
43 Woelk, *Rückspiel*, p. 212.
44 Helmut Krausser, "Durach," in *Die Zerstörung der europäischen Städte* (Munich: List, 1994), pp. 107–185 (p. 130).
45 Matthias Zschokke, *Der dicke Dichter* (Cologne: Bruckner & Thünker, 1995).
46 Jentzsch, *Götter*, pp. 328–329.
47 Grass, "Talking?" pp. 67–68.
48 Dische, *Gefühl*, p. 24.
49 *Deutschland Nachrichten*, 19 January 1995, 6.
50 Cited by Carr and Paul, "Unification," p. 328.
51 Francis Fukuyama, "The End of History?" *The National Interest* (summer 1989), 3–18 (p. 4). These ideas were later incorporated into Fukuyama's book *The End of History and the Last Man* (New York: Free Press, 1992).
52 Neumeister, *Ausdeutschen*, p. 68.
53 Erpenbeck, *Aufschwung*, p. 34.
54 Heiner Müller, "Mommsens Block," *Sinn und Form* 45: 2 (1993), 206–211 (p. 211).
55 Müller, "Mommsens," p. 208.
56 Ibid., p. 207.
57 Ibid., pp. 210, 211.
58 Christoph Hein, *Die Ritter der Tafelrunde: Eine Komödie* (Frankfurt: Luchterhand, 1989); and *Der Tangospieler* (Darmstadt: Luchterhand, 1989); English translation by Philip Boehm published as *The Tango Player* (New York: Farrar, Straus, Giroux, 1992).
59 Hein, *Das Napoleon-Spiel* (Berlin: Aufbau, 1993), p. 109.
60 Ibid., p. 133.
61 Ibid., p. 134.
62 Jentzsch, *Götter*, p. 329.
63 Gaus, *Wendewut*, p. 81.
64 "Germany? But where is it? I don't know where to find the land." Friedrich Schiller, "Das Deutsche Reich," in *Schillers Werke (Nationalausgabe)*, vol. 1, *Gedichte*, ed. Julius Petersen and Friedrich Beißner (Weimar: Hermann Böhlaus Nachfolger, 1943), p. 320.
65 Richard Wagner, *Die Meistersinger von Nürnberg* (Stuttgart: Reclam, 1997), pp. 104–105. I have opted for my own unpoetic literal translation here. English translations tend to eliminate the specifically national element of this passage. See for instance *The Mastersingers of Nuremberg*, trans. Frederick Jameson with revisions by Norman Feasey and Gordon Kember (London: John Calder, 1983), p. 125, where one finds "Honour your noble Masters" and "The fame of ancient Rome" rather than the

specific reference Wagner makes to the Holy Roman Empire and to "German masters."

66 Sachs's thinking exactly parallels that of Schiller in the 1801 reflections on "German greatness."

67 Hugo von Hofmannsthal, "Das Schrifttum als geistiger Raum der Nation," in *Die Berührung der Sphären* (Berlin: S. Fischer, 1931), p. 432.

68 Germaine de Staël, *Über Deutschland*, trans. Friedrich Buchholz, Samuel Heinrich Catel, and Julius Eduard Hitzig (Frankfurt: Insel, 1985), pp. 141–142. Originally published in 1810 as *De l'Allemagne*; first German edition in 1814.

69 Ibid., p. 28.

70 On the cultural consequences of this description, see Helmuth Plessner, "Ein Volk der Dichter und Denker," in Plessner, *Diesseits der Utopie* (Düsseldorf: Eugen Diederichs, 1966), pp. 66–73.

71 Martin Walser, "Deutschland," p. 89.

72 Therefore I believe that Bullivant's translation, "keep the German wound open," misses the point that it is Germany itself which exists *as* a wound. This does not, however, affect the correctness of Bullivant's other conclusions. See Keith Bullivant, "The End of the Dream of the 'Other Germany': The 'German Question' in West German Letters," in Pape (ed.), *1870/71*, pp. 302–319 (p. 306, footnote 12). Alexander Mathäs seems much further from the mark when he misquotes the crucial words as "Germany's wound," suggesting that this wound had been "unacceptable" to Walser "long before unification." See Mathäs, "Copying," p. 90.

73 Bullivant, *Future*, p. 107.

74 Thomas Hettche, *Nox* (Frankfurt: Suhrkamp, 1995), pp. 96–97.

75 Ibid., p. 128.

76 Grass, *Schreiben*, p. 42. Grass's reference to those literally "born afterwards" (nachgeboren) is of course a critique of Kohl's "grace of late birth."

77 Andrzej Szczypiorski, "Einige Gedanken über Deutschland," in *Reden über Deutschland* (Munich: Bertelsmann, 1990), pp. 87–97 (pp. 96–97).

78 Erika Martens, " 'Das Gold in den Köpfen heben,' " *Die Zeit*, 14 March 1997, 11.

79 Richard J. Barnet and John Cavanagh, *Global Dreams: Imperial Corporations and the New World Order* (New York: Touchstone, 1995), p. 22.

80 Wim Wenders, "Reden," p. 189; for an alternative translation, see Wenders, "Talking," p. 53.

81 Todd Gitlin, *The Twilight of Common Dreams: Why America is Wracked by Culture Wars* (New York: Metropolitan Books, 1995), p. 66.

82 Ahrends, "Waiting," p. 49.

83 Adorno, "Deutsch?" p. 343.

84 Adorno, "Auferstehung?" pp. 23–24.

85 Nadolny, *Discovery*, p. 31; German original, *Entdeckung*, p. 39.

86 Moretti, *Signs*, p. 251.
87 Fries, *Nonnen*, p. 383.
88 Hubert Winkels, "Buch und Mensch – ein Unglückspaar," *Die Zeit*, 15 November 1996, 25–26 (p. 26).
89 This does not imply that literature did not previously have subversive power but simply that it has acquired a qualitatively new power in the new electronic context. It is telling that in his reflections on a rewriting of postwar German literary history, Wolfgang Emmerich, citing Foucault's definition of literary discourse as characterized by "radical 'intransitivity,'" emphasizes the fact that literary "reality . . . cannot be grasped in an unidimensional way" and can thus take on a subversive power – not only in the GDR context. See Emmerich, "Rewrite?" pp. 125, 123.
90 Winkels, "Buch und Mensch," p. 26.
91 Wenders, "Reden," p. 197; alternative English translation in "Talking," p. 59.
92 Wenders, "Reden," pp. 197–198; cf. "Talking," p. 59.
93 Wenders, "Reden," p. 198; cf. "Talking," p. 59.
94 Erpenbeck, *Aufschwung*, p. 91.
95 Georg Wilhelm Friedrich Hegel, *The Philosophy of Right*, trans. T. M. Knox in *The Philosophy of Right; The Philosophy of History* (Chicago: Encyclopaedia Britannica, 1952), p. 7.
96 Zschokke, *Dichter*, pp. 127–128.
97 Walser, "Leser," p. 100.

Works cited

Abbey, Edward, *The Monkey Wrench Gang*, Philadelphia: Lippincott, 1975.

Adorno, Theodor W., "Auferstehung der Kultur in Deutschland?" in *Kritik: Kleine Schriften zur Gesellschaft*, Frankfurt: Suhrkamp, 1971, pp. 20–33.

"Was ist deutsch?" in Hermann Glaser (ed.), *Bundesrepublikanisches Lesebuch*, Munich: Carl Hanser, 1978, pp. 335–346.

Agde, Günter (ed.), *Kahlschlag: Das 11. Plenum des ZK der SED 1965: Studien und Dokumente*, Berlin: Aufbau, 1991.

Ahrends, Martin, "The Great Waiting, or The Freedom of the East: An Obituary for Life in Sleeping Beauty's Castle," trans. Stephen Brockmann, *New German Critique* 52 (1991), 41–49.

Andersch, Alfred, *Deutsche Literatur in der Entscheidung: Ein Beitrag zur Analyse der literarischen Situation*, Karlsruhe: Volk und Zeit, [1948].

Öffentlicher Brief an einen sowjetischen Schriftsteller, das Überholte betreffend: Reportagen und Aufsätze, Zurich: Diogenes, 1977.

Anderson, Benedict, *Imagined Communities*, London: Verso, 1991.

Anderson, Sascha, *Jeder Satellit hat einen Killersatelliten*, Berlin: Rotbuch, 1982.

Anderson, Sascha and Elke Erb (eds.), *Berührung ist nur eine Randerscheinung: Neue Literatur aus der DDR*, Cologne: Kiepenheuer & Witsch, 1985.

Anz, Thomas (ed.), *"Es geht nicht um Christa Wolf": Der Literaturstreit im vereinten Deutschland*, Munich: Spangenberg, 1991.

Arjouni, Jakob, *Magic Hoffmann*, Zurich: Diogenes, 1996.

Assmann, Aleida, *Arbeit am nationalen Gedächtnis: Eine kurze Geschichte der deutschen Bildungsidee*, Frankfurt: Campus, 1993.

Augstein, Rudolf, et. al., *"Historikerstreit": Die Dokumentation der Kontroverse um die Einzigartigkeit der nationalsozialistischen Judenvernichtung*, Munich: Piper, 1987.

Barber, Benjamin R., *Jihad vs. McWorld*, New York: Times Books, 1995.

Baring, Arnulf, *Deutschland, was nun?* Berlin: Siedler bei Goldmann, 1991.

Barnet, Richard J. and John Cavanagh, *Global Dreams: Imperial Corporations and the New World Order*, New York: Touchstone, 1995.

Bathrick, David, "Crossing Borders: The End of the Cold War Intellectual?" *German Politics and Society* 27 (1992), 77–87.

The Powers of Speech: The Politics of Culture in the GDR, Lincoln: University of Nebraska Press, 1995.

Becker, Jurek, "Die Wiedervereinigung der deutschen Literatur," *The German Quarterly* 63: 3/4 (1990), 359–366.

Becker, Peter von, *Die andere Zeit*, Frankfurt: Suhrkamp, 1994.

Becker-Cantarino, Barbara (ed.), *Berlin in Focus: Cultural Transformations in Germany*, Westport: Praeger, 1996.

Bender, Peter, *Das Ende des ideologischen Zeitalters: die Europäisierung Europas*, Berlin: Severin & Siedler, 1981.

Benn, Gottfried, "Answer to the Literary Emigrants," trans. E. B. Ashton, in *Primal Vision: Selected Writings of Gottfried Benn*, ed. E. B. Ashton, New York: New Directions, n.d., pp. 46–53.

Berliner Begegnung zur Friedensförderung: Protokolle des Schriftstellertreffens am 13./ 14. Dezember 1981, Darmstadt: Luchterhand, 1982.

Benjamin, Walter, "The Work of Art in the Age of Mechanical Reproduction," in *Illuminations*, trans. Harry Zohn, New York: Schocken, 1985, pp. 217–251.

Berka, Sigrid, "Botho Strauß und die Debatte um den 'Bocksgesang': Zu diesem Heft," *Weimarer Beiträge* 40: 2 (1994), 165–178.

Berman, Russell A., "Beyond Localism and Universalism: Nationhood and Solidarity," *Telos* 105 (1995), 43–56.

"Three Comments on Future Perspectives on German Cultural History," *New German Critique* 65 (1995), 115–124.

Biermann, Wolf, "Reden über das eigene Land: Deutschland," in *Klartexte im Getümmel*, ed. Hannes Stein, Cologne: Kiepenheuer & Witsch, 1990, pp. 235–257.

Alle Lieder, Cologne: Kiepenheuer & Witsch, 1991.

"Nur wer sich ändert, bleibt sich treu," in *Über das Geld und andere Herzensdinge: Prosaische Versuche über Deutschland*, Cologne: Kiepenheuer & Witsch, 1991, pp. 51–71.

"Der Lichtblick im gräßlichen Fatalismus der Geschichte," in *Der Sturz des Dädalus, oder: Eizes für die Eingeborenen der Fidschi-Inseln über den IM Judas Ischariot und den Kuddelmuddel in Deutschland seit dem Golfkrieg*, Cologne: Kiepenheuer & Witsch, 1992, pp. 48–63.

Bloch, Ernst, *Heritage of Our Time*, trans. Neville and Stephen Plaice, Berkeley: University of California Press, 1990.

Bohrer, Karl Heinz, *Nach der Natur: Über Politik und Ästhetik*, Munich: Carl Hanser, 1988.

"Die Ästhetik am Ausgang ihrer Unmündigkeit," *Merkur*, 44: 500 (1990), 851–865.

"Why We are Not a Nation – And Why We Should Become One," trans. Stephen Brockmann, *New German Critique* 52 (1991), 72–83.

Böll, Heinrich, "Bekenntnis zur Trümmerliteratur," in *Erzählungen Hörspiele Aufsätze*, Cologne: Kiepenheuer & Witsch, 1961, pp. 339–343.

Bormann, Alexander von, "Kulturelle Affinität oder Diskulturalität? Wechselwirkungen der Literaturentwicklung beider deutscher Staaten," *Aus Politik und Zeitgeschichte*, 3 October 1987, 15–26.

Böthig, Peter and Klaus Michael (eds.), *MachtSpiele: Literatur und Staatssicherheit*, Leipzig: Reclam, 1993.

Brecht, Bertolt, "Children's Anthem," trans. Edith Roseveare, in *Poems 1913–1956* (ed.) John Willett and Ralph Manheim, London: Methuen, 1987, p. 423.

Brockmann, Stephen, "The Politics of German History," *History and Theory*, 29: 2 (1990), 178–189.

"The Politics of German Literature," *Monatshefte* 84: 1 (1992), 46–58.

"Preservation and Change in Christa Wolf's *Was bleibt*," *The German Quarterly* 67: 1 (1994), 73–85.

Brockmann, Stephen, Julia Hell and Reinhilde Wiegmann, "The Greens: Images of Survival in the Early 1980s," in Reinhold Grimm and Jost Hermand (eds.), *From the Greeks to the Greens: Images of the Simple Life*, Madison: University of Wisconsin Press, 1989, pp. 127–144.

Broder, Henryk M., "Eine schöne Revolution," *Die Zeit* (American edition), 17 January 1992, 15.

"Die Unfähigkeit zu feiern," *Der Spiegel*, 2 October 1995 (no. 40), 236–246.

Broszat, Martin, Elke Fröhlich and Falk Wiesemann (eds.), *Bayern in der NS-Zeit*, 6 vols, Munich: Oldenbourg, 1977–1983.

Broszat, Martin, Klaus-Dietmar Henke and Hans Woller (eds.), *Von Stalingrad zur Währungsreform: Zur Sozialgeschichte des Umbruchs in Deutschland*, Munich: Oldenbourg, 1988.

Brubaker, Rogers, *Citizenship and Nationhood in France and Germany*, Cambridge, MA: Harvard University Press, 1992.

Brussig, Thomas, *Helden wie wir*, Berlin: Volk & Welt, 1995. English translation: *Heroes Like Us*, trans. John Brownjohn, New York: Farrar, Straus, Giroux, 1997.

Bubik, Roland (ed.), *Wir '89er: Wer wir sind und was wir wollen*, Frankfurt: Ullstein, 1995.

Buchsteiner, Jochen, ". . .und kein bißchen bissig," *Die Zeit* (American edition), 28 February 1997, 21–22.

Bullivant, Keith (ed.), *Beyond 1989: Re-reading German Literature since 1945*, Providence: Berghahn, 1997.

Bullivant, Keith, *The Future of German Literature*, Oxford: Berg, 1994.

Bürger, Peter, *Theorie der Avantgarde*, Frankfurt: Suhrkamp, 1974.

Burmeister, Brigitte, *Unter dem Namen Norma*, Stuttgart: Klett-Cotta, 1994.

Carr, Godfrey and Georgina Paul, "Unification and its Aftermath: The Challenge of History," in Rob Burns (ed.), *German Cultural Studies: An Introduction*, Oxford University Press, 1995, pp. 325–348.

The Complete Fairy Tales of the Brothers Grimm, trans. Jack Zipes, New York: Bantam, 1992.

Dallago, Bruno, Horst Brezinski and Wladimir Andreff (eds.), *Convergence and System Change: The Convergence Hypothesis in the Light of Transition in Eastern Europe*, Aldershot: Dartmouth, 1991.

Deiritz, Karl and Hannes Krauss (eds.), *Der deutsch-deutsche Literaturstreit oder "Freunde, es spricht sich schlecht mit gebundener Zunge,"* Hamburg: Luchterhand, 1991.

Derrida, Jacques, *A Derrida Reader: Between the Blinds* (ed.) Peggy Kamuf, New York: Columbia University Press, 1991.

"Die Flut ist nicht zu stoppen," *Der Spiegel*, 6 November 1989 (no. 45), 20–29.

"Die Geschichte der DDR geht zu Ende," *Neues Deutschland*, 23 May 1990, 8.

Diner, Dan, "Feinde des Westens," *Frankfurter Allgemeine Zeitung*, 11 May 1994, 33.

Diner, Dan (ed.), *Ist der Nationalsozialismus Geschichte?: Zu Historisierung und Historikerstreit*, Frankfurt: Fischer, 1987.

Dische, Irene, *Ein fremdes Gefühl, oder Veränderungen über einen Deutschen*, trans. Reinhard Kaiser, Berlin: Rowohlt, 1993.

Doane, Heike A., "The Cultivation of Personal and Political Loss: *Die Verteidigung der Kindheit*," in Frank Pilipp (ed.), *New Critical Perspectives on Martin Walser*, Columbia, SC: Camden House, 1994, pp. 156–175.

Döblin, Alfred, *Die literarische Situation*, Baden-Baden: P. Keppler, 1947.

Drawert, Kurt, "Niemand braucht sie, sie brauchen niemand: Über das Volk und die Intellektuellen in Deutschland," *Monatshefte* LXXXII: 4 (1990), 399–402.

Spiegelland: Ein deutscher Monolog, Frankfurt: Suhrkamp, 1992.

Drescher, Angela (ed.), *Dokumentation zu Christa Wolf "Nachdenken über Christa T."* Hamburg: Luchterhand, 1991.

Eckart, Gabriele, "Brief an den Vater," *europäische ideen* 81 (1993), 19–25.

Ehring, Klaus and Martin Dallwitz, *Schwerter zu Pflugscharen: Friedensbewegung in der DDR*, Reinbek: Rowohlt, 1982.

Elsner, Gisela, "Über die sogenannte deutsche Revolution," *Neues Deutschland*, 6 April 1990, 8 and 14/15 April 1990, 14.

Ellman, Michael, *Collectivisation, Convergence and Capitalism: Political Economy in a Divided World*, London: Academic Press, 1984.

Emmerich, Wolfgang, "Do We Need to Rewrite German Literary History Since 1945? A German Perspective," trans. Peter C. Pfeiffer, in Friederike Eigler and Peter C. Pfeiffer (eds.), *Cultural Transformations in the New Germany: American and German Perspectives*, Columbia, SC: Camden House, 1993, pp. 117–131.

Kleine Literaturgeschichte der DDR: Erweiterte Neuausgabe, Berlin: Gustav Kiepenheuer, 1996.

Engelmann, Bernt, et. al., *"Es geht, es geht – ": zeitgenössische Schriftsteller und ihr Beitrag zum Frieden: Grenzen und Möglichkeiten*, Munich: Goldman, 1982.

Enzensberger, Hans Magnus, *Civil Wars: From L. A. to Bosnia*, trans. Martin Chalmers, New York: The New Press, 1994.

Selected Poems, Newcastle: Bloodaxe, 1994.

Erpenbeck, John, *Aufschwung*, Berlin: Eulenspiegel, 1996.

Evans, Richard J., *In Hitler's Shadow: West German Historians and the Attempt to Escape from the Nazi Past*, New York: Pantheon, 1989.

Foucault, Michel, "What Is an Author?" in Josué V. Harari (ed.), *Textual Strategies: Perspectives in Post-Structuralist Criticism*, Ithaca: Cornell University Press, 1979, pp. 141–160.

Freud, Sigmund, *Civilization and its Discontents*, New York: London, 1989.

Fried, Erich, "Gespräch zweier großer Staatsmänner im Himmel oder in der Hölle," in *Gesammelte Werke*, Berlin: Klaus Wagenbach, 1993, vol. 3, p. 198.

Fries, Fritz Rudolf, *Die Nonnen von Bratislava*, Munich: Piper, 1994.

Fuchs, Jürgen, "Landschaften der Lüge," *Der Spiegel*, 18 November–16 December 1991 (nos. 47–51).

Fukuyama, Francis, "The End of History?" *The National Interest* (Summer 1989), 3–18.

The End of History and the Last Man, New York: Free Press, 1992.

Gaus, Günter, *Texte zur deutschen Frage: Mit den wichtigsten Dokumenten zum Verhältnis der beiden deutschen Staaten*, Darmstadt: Luchterhand, 1981.

"Nationale Identität in Europa," *Neues Deutschland*, 18 May 1990, 9.

Wendewut, Hamburg: Hoffmann und Campe, 1990.

Gehlen, Arnold, *Moral und Hypermoral: Eine pluralistische Ethik*, Frankfurt: Athenäum, 1969.

Geulen, Eva, "Nationalisms: Old, New and German," *Telos* 105 (1995), 2–20.

Gitlin, Todd, *The Twilight of Common Dreams: Why America is Wracked by Culture Wars*, New York: Metropolitan Books, 1995.

Goethe, *Faust*, Part I, in *The Harvard Classics*, vol. 19, New York: P. F. Collier & Son, 1909.

Grass, Günter, *Die Blechtrommel*, Dramstadt: Luchterhand, 1959. English translation: *The Tin Drum*, trans. Ralph Mannheim, London: Secker and Warburg, 1962.

Kopfgeburten oder Die Deutschen sterben aus, Darmstadt: Luchterhand, 1980. English translation: *Headbirths, or The Germans Are Dying Out*, trans. Ralph Mannheim, New York: Harcourt Brace Jovanovich, 1982.

Die Rättin, Darmstadt: Luchterhand, 1986. English translation: *The Rat*, trans. Ralph Mannheim, San Diego: Harcourt Brace Jovanovich, 1987.

"Kurze Rede eines vaterlandslosen Gesellen," in *Nichts wird mehr so sein, wie es war: Zur Zukunft der beiden deutschen Republiken*, ed. Frank Blohm and Wolfgang Herzberg, Leipzig: Reclam, 1990, pp. 226–231.

Schreiben nach Auschwitz, Frankfurt: Luchterhand, 1990. English translation: "Writing after Ausschwitz," in *Two States – One Nation?* trans. Krishna Winston with A. S. Wensinger, San Diego: Harcourt Brace Jovanovich, 1990, pp. 94–123.

"What Am I Talking For? Is Anybody Still Listening?" trans. Stephen Brockmann, *New German Critique* 52 (1991), 66–72.

Ein weites Feld, Göttingen: Steidl, 1995. English translation: *Too Far Afield*, trans. Krishna Winston, New York: Harcourt Brace Jovanovich, forthcoming.

Greiner, Ulrich, "Mangel an Feingefühl," *Die Zeit* (American edition), 1 June 1990, 63.

Grimm, Reinhold, "Innere Emigration als Lebensform," in Reinhold Grimm and Jost Hermand (eds.), *Exil und Innere Emigration*, Frankfurt: Athenäum, 1972, pp. 31–73.

Habermas, Jürgen, *The New Conservatism: Cultural Criticism and the Historians' Debate*, trans. Shierry Weber Nicholsen, Cambridge, MA: MIT Press, 1989.

"Yet Again: German Identity – A Unified Nation of Angry DM-Burghers?" trans. Stephen Brockmann, *New German Critique* 52 (1991), 84–101.

Hahn, H. J., " 'Es geht nicht um Literatur': Some Observations on the 1990 'Literaturstreit' and its Recent Anti-Intellectual Implications," *German Life and Letters* 50: 1 (1997), 65–81.

Hanke, Helmut, "Was wird bleiben?" *Neues Deutschland*, 23 May 1990, 8.

Hegel, Georg Wilhelm Friedrich, *The Philosophy of Right*, trans. T. M. Knox, in *The Philosophy of Right; The Philosophy of History*, Chicago: Encyclopaedia Britannica, 1952.

Hegi, Ursula, *Stones from the River*, New York: Scribner, 1995.

Hein, Christoph, *Der fremde Freund*, Berlin: Aufbau, 1986. English translation: *The Distant Lover*, trans. Krishna Winston, New York: Pantheon, 1989.

Die Ritter der Tafelrunde: Eine Komödie, Frankfurt: Luchterhand, 1989.

Der Tangospieler, Darmstadt: Luchterhand, 1989. English translation: *The Tango Player*, trans. Philip Boehm, New York: Farrar, Straus, Giroux, 1992.

Das Napoleon-Spiel, Berlin: Aufbau, 1993.

Hensel, Kerstin, *Tanz am Kanal*, Frankfurt: Suhrkamp, 1994.

Herf, Jeffrey, *Reactionary Modernism*, Cambridge University Press, 1984.

Hertle, Hans-Hermann, *Der Fall der Mauer: Die unbeabsichtigte Selbstauflösung des SED-Staates*, Wiesbaden: Westdeutscher Verlag, 1996.

Hesse, Egmont (ed.), *Sprache & Antwort: Stimmen und Texte einer anderen Literatur aus der DDR*, Frankfurt: S. Fischer, 1988.

Hettche, Thomas, *Nox*, Frankfurt: Suhrkamp, 1995.

Heym, Stefan, "Ash Wednesday in the GDR," trans. Stephen Brockmann, *New German Critique* 52 (1991), 31–35.

Hilbig, Wolfgang, "*ICH*," Frankfurt: Fischer, 1993.

Hirschman, Albert O., "Exit, Voice, and the Fate of the German Democratic Republic: An Essay in Conceptual History," *World Politics* 45: 2 (1993), 173–202.

Hochhuth, Rolf, *Judith*, Reinbek: Rowohlt, 1988.

Hochgeschurz, Marianne (ed.), *Christa Wolfs Medea: Voraussetzungen zu einem Text – Mythos und Bild*, Berlin: Gerhard Wolf Janus Press, 1998.

Hofmannsthal, Hugo von, *Die Berührung der Sphären*, Berlin: S. Fischer, 1931.

Hölderlin, Friedrich, "Remembrance" [Andenken], in *Hymns and Fragments*, trans. Richard Sieburth, Princeton University Press, 1984, pp. 106–109.

Honecker, Erich, "Zu aktuellen Fragen bei der Verwirklichung der Beschlüsse unseres VIII. Parteitages," *Neues Deutschland*, 18 December 1971, 3–5.

Huyssen, Andreas, "After the Wall: The Failure of German Intellectuals," *New German Critique* 52 (1991), 109–143.

Jäger, Manfred, *Kultur und Politik in der DDR: Ein historischer Abriß*, Cologne: Wissenschaft und Politik, 1982.

James, Harold and Marla Stone (eds.), *When the Wall Came Down: Reactions to German Unification*, New York: Routledge, 1992.

Jaspers, Karl, *Die Schuldfrage*, Heidelberg: Lambert Schneider, 1946. English translation: *The Question of German Guilt*, trans. E. B. Ashton, New York: The Dial Press, 1947.

Jenninger, Philipp, "Von der Verantwortung für das Vergangene: Fünfzig Jahre nach der 'Reichskristallnacht," *Die Zeit* (American edition), 25 November 1988, 4–6.

Jentzsch, Kerstin, *Seit die Götter ratlos sind*, Munich: Wilhelm Heyne, 1996.

Jerzwekski, Roland (ed.), *Literarische Texte zur deutschen Frage nach 1945*, Berlin: Langenscheidt, 1986.

Jung, Carl Gustav, "Nach der Katastrophe," *Neue Schweizer Rundschau*, 13: 6 (1945/1946) 67–88.

Kaes, Anton, "Literatur und nationale Identität: Kontroversen um Goethe 1945–49," in Albrecht Schöne (ed.), *Kontroversen, alte und neue (Akten des VII. Internationalen Germanisten-Kongresses Göttingen 1985*, vol. 10), Göttingen: Niemeyer, 1986, pp. 199–206.

[Klein, Joe], *Primary Colors: A Novel of Politics*, New York: Warner Books, 1996.

Klussmann, Paul Gerhard and Heinrich Mohr (eds.), *Literatur im geteilten Deutschland*, Bonn: Bouvier, 1980.

Kramer, Jane, *The Politics of Memory: Looking for Germany in the New Germany*, New York: Random House, 1996.

Krausser, Helmut, *Die Zerstörung der europäischen Städte*, Munich: List, 1994.

Krüger, Ingrid (ed.), *Mut zur Angst: Schriftsteller für den Frieden*, Darmstadt: Luchterhand, 1982.

"Kulturnik 7423/91," *Der Spiegel*, 21 October 1991 (no. 43), 336–337.

Kunze, Reiner (ed.), *Deckname "Lyrik": Eine Dokumentation*, Frankfurt: Fischer, 1990.

Leggewie, Claus, *Der Geist steht rechts: Ausflüge in die Denkfabrike der Wende*, Berlin: Rotbuch, 1987.

Lehmann, David, *Signs of the Times: Deconstruction and the Fall of Paul de Man*, New York: Poseidon, 1991.

Lewis, Alison, "Unity Begins Together: Analyzing the Trauma of German Unification," *New German Critique* 64 (1995), 135–159.

"Re-Membering the Barbarian: Memory and Repression in Monika Maron's *Animal Triste*," *The German Quarterly* 71: 1 (1998), 30–46.

Leeder, Karen, *Breaking Boundaries: A New Generation of Poets in the GDR*, Oxford: Clarendon, 1996.

Loest, Erich, *Der Zorn des Schafes: Aus meinem Tagewerk*, Kunzelsau: Linden, 1990.

Lukács, György, *Theory of the Novel*, Cambridge, MA: MIT. Press, 1971.

Lukacs, John, *The End of the Twentieth Century and the End of the Modern Age*, New York: Ticknor & Fields, 1993.

Maaz, Hans-Joachim, *Das gestürzte Volk: Die unglückliche Einheit*, Berlin: Argon, 1991.

Der Gefühlsstau: Ein Psychogramm der DDR, 2nd edn, Munich: Knauer, 1992. Abridged English translation: *Behind the Wall: The Inner Life of Communist Germany*, trans. Margot Bettauer Dembo, New York: W. W. Norton, 1995.

Die Entrüstung: Deutschland Deutschland Stasi Schuld und Sündenblock, Berlin: Argon, 1992.

Macdonald, Andrew, *The Turner Diaries*, Washington: National Alliance, 1980.

Macki, Erik J., "Semantics and the Ideological Lexicon of German (Dis)Unity," in Jörg Roche and Thomas Salumets (eds.), *Germanics under Construction: Intercultural and Interdisciplinary Prospects*, Munich: Iudicium, 1996, pp. 123–141.

Maier, Charles S., *Dissolution: The Crisis of Communism and the End of East Germany*, Princeton University Press, 1997.

The Unmasterable Past: History, Holocaust, and German National Identity, Cambridge, MA: Harvard University Press, 1988.

Mann, Thomas, *Gesammelte Werke in Zwölf Bänden*, Frankfurt: S. Fischer, 1960.

Markovits, Andrei S., "On Anti-Americanism in West Germany," *New German Critique* 34 (1985) 3–27.

Markovits, Andrei S. and Simon Reich, *The German Predicament: Memory and Power in the New Europe*, Ithaca: Cornell University Press, 1997.

Maron, Monika, *Die Überläuferin*, Frankfurt: Fischer, 1986. English translation: *The Defector*, trans. David Newton Marinelli, London: Readers International, 1988.

"Ich war ein antifaschistisches Kind," in Michael Naumann (ed.), *Die Geschichte ist offen*, Reinbek: Rowohlt, 1990, pp. 117–135.

Stille Zeile Sechs, Frankfurt: Fischer, 1991. English translation: *Silent Close No. 6*, trans. David Newton Marinelli, Columbia, LA: Readers International, 1993.

"Writers and the People," trans. Stephen Brockmann, *New German Critique* 52 (1991), 36–41.

Animal triste, Frankfurt: Fischer, 1996.

Martens, Erika, "'Das Gold in den Köpfen heben,'" *Die Zeit* (American edition), 14 March 1997, 11.

Marx, Karl and Friedrich Engels, *Basic Writings on Politics and Philosophy* (ed.) Lewis S. Feuer, Garden City: Doubleday Anchor, 1959.

Mathäs, Alexander, "Copying Kafka's Signature: Martin Walser's *Die Verteidigung der Kindheit*," *The Germanic Review* 69: 2 (spring 1994), 79–91.

Mayer, Hans, "Stationen der deutschen Literatur: Die Schriftsteller und die Restauration, die zwei Deutschlands und die Konvergenz," *Frankfurter Allgemeine Zeitung*, 16 June 1979.

Mayer-Iswandy, Claudia, "Ästhetik und Macht: Zur diskursiven Unordnung im vereinten Deutschland," *German Studies Review* 19: 3 (October 1996), 501–523.

McLuhan, Marshall, *Understanding Media: The Extensions of Man*, New York: McGraw Hill, 1964.

McLuhan, Marshall and Quentin Fiore, *The Medium is the Massage*, New York: Touchstone, 1989.

Meinecke, Friedrich, *Cosmopolitanism and the National State*, trans. Robert B. Kimber, Princeton University Press, 1970.

Mertes, Michael and Hubertus von Morr, "Linke, rechts drehend," *Frankfurter Allgemeine Zeitung*, 20 April 1994, 35.

Mitscherlich, Alexander and Margarete, *Die Unfähigkeit zu trauern: Grundlagen kollektiven Verhaltens*, Munich: Piper, 1991. English translation: *The Inability to Mourn: Principles of Collective Behavior*, trans. Beverley R. Placzek, New York: Grove Press, 1975.

Moretti, Franco, *Signs Taken for Wonders*, London: Verso, 1988.

Moser, Tilmann, *Politik und seelischer Untergrund*, Frankfurt: Suhrkamp, 1993.

Müller, Heiner, "Mommsens Block," *Sinn und Form* 45: 2 (March/April 1993), 206–211.

Müller, Helmut L., *Die literarische Republik: Westdeutsche Schriftsteller und die Politik*, Basel: Beltz, 1982.

Nadolny, Sten, *Die Entdeckung der Langsamkeit*, Munich: Piper, 1983. English translation: *The Discovery of Slowness*, trans. Ralph Freedman, New York: Viking, 1987.

Negt, Oskar (ed.), *Der Fall Fonty: "Ein weites Feld" von Günter Grass im Spiegel der Kritik*, Göttingen: Steidel, 1996.

Neumeister, Andreas, *Ausdeutschen*, Frankfurt: Suhrkamp, 1994.

Nietzsche, Friedrich, *The Birth of Tragedy and The Case of Wagner*, trans. Walter Kaufmann, New York: Vintage, 1967.

Unzeitgemäße Betrachtungen, Leipzig: Alfred Kröner, 1930.

Noelle-Neumann, Elisabeth, *Eine demoskopische Deutschstunde*, Zurich: Edition Interforum, 1983.

Noelle-Neumann, Elisabeth and Renate Köcher, *Die verletzte Nation: Über den Versuch der Deutschen, ihren Charakter zu ändern*, Stuttgart: Deutsche Verlags-Anstalt, 1987.

Nolte, Ernst, *Der europäische Bürgerkrieg, 1917–1945: Nationalsozialismus und Bolschewismus*, Berlin: Propyläen, 1987.

Ortheil, Hanns-Josef, *Abschied von den Kriegsteilnehmern*, Munich: Piper, 1992.

Pape, Walter (ed.), *1870/71–1989/90: German Unifications and the Change of Literary Discourse*, Berlin: Walter de Gruyter, 1993.

Parkes, K. Stuart, *Writers and Politics in West Germany*, New York: St. Martin's Press, 1986.

Paul, Georgina, "Text and Context – *Was bleibt* 1979–1989," in Axel Goodbody and Dennis Tate (eds.), *Geist und Macht: Writers and the State in the GDR (German Monitor*, no. 29), Amsterdam: Rodopi, 1992, pp. 117–128.

Peitsch, Helmut, *Vom Faschismus zum Kalten Krieg – auch eine deutsche Literaturgeschichte: Literaturverhältnisse, Genres, Themen*, Berlin: Sigma, 1996.

Plato, *Symposium*, trans. Tom Griffith, Berkeley: University of California Press, 1989.

Plessner, Helmuth, *Diesseits der Utopie*, Düsseldorf: Eugen Diederichs, 1966.

  Die verspätete Nation: Über die politische Verführbarkeit bürgerlichen Geistes, Frankfurt: Suhrkamp, 1994.

Pohl, Klaus, *Karate-Billi kehrt zurück / Die schöne Fremde*, Frankfurt: Verlag der Autoren, 1993.

Pois, Robert A., *Friedrich Meinecke and German Politics in the Twentieth Century*, Berkeley: University of California Press, 1972.

Reid, J. H., *Writing Without Taboos: The New East German Literature*, New York: Berg, 1990.

Renan, Ernest, "What is a nation?" trans. Martin Thom, in Homi K. Bhabha (ed.), *Nation and Narration*, London: Routledge, 1993, pp. 8–22.

Richter, Horst-Eberhard, *Die Chance des Gewissens: Erinnerungen und Assoziationen*, Hamburg: Hoffmann und Campe, 1986.

Roberts, David, "Surface and Depth: Christoph Hein's *Drachenblut*," *The German Quarterly* 63: 3/4 (1990), 478–489.

Rocky Dutschke, '68: Dokumentarfotos (2), Berlin: Volksbühne am Rosa-Luxemburg Platz, 1996.

Roethke, Gisela, "*Was bleibt* – 'Nun ja! Das nächste Leben geht aber heute an' – Zur politisch-literarischen Gratwanderung von Christa Wolf im Jahre 1979," *German Life and Letters* 48: 1 (1995), 86–95.

Ross, Jan, "Schwellendes Philistertum: Gegen politisch korrekte Westbindung und Metaphysikverbot," *Frankfurter Allgemeine Zeitung*, 9 May 1994, 35.

Saeger, Uwe, *Die Nacht danach und der Morgen*, Munich: Piper, 1991.

Sakharov, Andrei D., *Progress, Coexistence & Intellectual Freedom*, New York: W. W. Norton, 1968.

Schedlinski, Rainer, *die rationen des ja und des nein*, Frankfurt: Suhrkamp, 1990.

  "Die Unzuständigkeit der Macht," *Neue deutsche Literatur* 474 (1992) 75–105.

Schelsky, Helmut, *Die Arbeit tun die anderen*, Munich: Deutscher Taschenbuch Verlag, 1977.

Schiller, Friedrich, *Schillers Werke (Nationalausgabe)*, Weimar: Hermann Böhlaus Nachfolger, 1943.

Schiller's Works (ed.) J. G. Fischer, Philadelphia: George Barrie, 1883.

Schirrmacher, Frank, "Abschied von der Literatur der Bundesrepublik," *Frankfurter Allgemeine Zeitung*, 2 October 1990, L1–2.

Schlesinger, Klaus, "Ich war ein Roman: Blick auf eine Kolportage," *Die Zeit* (American edition), 24 April 1992, 13–14.

Schmemann, Serge, "Germans Move to Unite Economies, as Kohl Leads and Modrow Follows," *The New York Times*, 14 February 1990, A10.

"Kohl, the Man for the German Moment," *The New York Times*, 1 July 1990, 1, 4.

Schmidt, Ulrich, *Zwischen Aufbruch und Wende. Lebensgeschichten der sechziger und siebziger Jahre*, Tübingen: Niemeyer, 1993.

Schmillen, Achim, "Wir sind besser als die Alten!" *Die Zeit* (American edition), 14 March 1997, 22.

Schneider, Michael, "Fathers and Sons, Retrospectively: The Damaged Relationship Between Two Generations," trans. Jamie Owen Daniel, *New German Critique* 31 (1984), 3–51.

Schneider, Peter, *Der Mauerspringer*, Hamburg: Luchterhand, 1982. English translation: *The Wall Jumper*, trans. Leigh Hafrey, New York: Pantheon, 1983.

'If the Wall Came Tumbling Down," *The New York Times Magazine*, 25 June 1989, 22–70.

Schoenbaum, David, *Hitler's Social Revolution: Class and Status in Nazi Germany, 1933–1939*, Garden City: Doubleday, 1966.

Schramm, Ingo, *Fitchers Blau*, Berlin: Volk & Welt, 1996.

Schwab-Felisch, Hans (ed.), *Der Ruf: Eine deutsche Nachkriegszeitschrift*, Munich: Deutscher Taschenbuch Verlag, 1962.

Schwilk, Heimo, "Der eigene deutsche Weg," *Junge Freiheit*, 3 November 1995, 13.

Seeba, Hinrich, "Critique of Identity Formation: Toward an Intercultural Model of German Studies," *The German Quarterly* 62: 2 (1989), 144–154.

Sinakowski, Andreas, *Das Verhör*, Berlin: BasisDruck, 1991.

Staël, Germaine de, *Über Deutschland*, trans. Friedrich Buchholz, Samuel Heinrich Catel, and Julius Eduard Hitzig, Frankfurt: Insel, 1985.

Steiner, George, *The Death of Tragedy*, New Haven: Yale University Press, 1996.

Steinfeld, Thomas and Heidrun Suhr, "Die Wiederkehr des Nationalen: Zur Diskussion um das deutschlandpolitische Engagement in der Gegenwartsliteratur," *The German Quarterly* 62: 3 (1989), 345–356.

Stern, Fritz, *The Politics of Cultural Despair*, Berkeley: University of California Press, 1961.

Strauß, Botho, *Diese Erinnerung an einen, der nur einen Tag zu Gast war*, Munich: Hanser, 1985.

Schlußchor, Munich: Hanser, 1991.

"Anschwellender Bocksgesang," *Der Pfahl* 7 (1993), 9–25.

Das Gleichgewicht, Munich: Hanser, 1993.

Süskind, Patrick, "Deutschland, eine Midlife-crisis," in Ulrich Wickert (ed.), *Angst vor Deutschland*, Hamburg: Hoffmann und Campe, 1990, pp. 111–122.

Syberberg, Hans Jürgen, *Hitler, ein Film aus Deutschland*, Reinbek bei Hamburg: Rowohlt, 1978. English translation: *Hitler, A Film from Germany*, trans. Joachim Neugroschel, New York: Farrar, Straus, Giroux, 1982.

Vom Unglück und Glück der Kunst in Deutschland nach dem letzten Kriege, Munich: Matthes & Seitz, 1990.

Der verlorene Auftrag, Vienna: Karolinger, 1994.

Szczypiorski, Andrzej, "Einige Gedanken über Deutschland," in *Reden über Deutschland*, Munich: Bertelsmann, 1990, pp. 87–97.

Taguieff, Pierre-Andre, *Sur la Nouvelle Droite: Jalons d'une analyse critique*, Paris: Descartes & Cie, 1994.

Tinbergen, Jan, "Do Communist and Free Economies Show a Converging Pattern?" *Soviet Studies* 12: 4 (April 1961), 333–341.

Toffler, Alvin, *Future Shock*, New York: Random House, 1970.

Trommler, Frank, "Auf dem Wege zu einer kleineren Literatur: Ästhetische Perioden und Probleme seit 1945," in Thomas Koebner (ed.), *Tendenzen der deutschen Gegenwartsliteratur*, Stuttgart: Alfred Kröner, 1984, pp. 1–106.

Trotsky, Leon, *History of the Russian Revolution*, trans. Max Eastman, London: Pluto Press, 1977.

Ulbrich, Stefan (ed.), *Gedanken zu Großdeutschland*, Vilsbiburg: Arun, 1990.

(ed.), *Multikultopia: Gedanken zur multikulturellen Gesellschaft*, Vilsbiburg: Arun, 1991.

Vinke, Hermann, (ed.), *Akteneinsicht Christa Wolf: Zerrspiegel und Dialog*, Hamburg: Luchterhand, 1993.

Vogt, Jochen, *'Erinnerung ist unsere Aufgabe': Über Literatur, Moral und Politik 1945–1990*, Opladen: Westdeutscher Verlag, 1991.

Wagner, Bernd, *Paradies*, Berlin: Ullstein, 1997.

Wagner, Richard, *Die Meistersinger von Nürnberg*, Stuttgart: Reclam, 1997.

Walser, Martin, "Über den Leser – soviel man in einem Festzelt darüber sagen soll," in *Wer ist ein Schriftsteller: Aufsätze und Reden*, Frankfurt: Suhrkamp, 1979, pp. 94–101.

"Über Deutschland reden (Ein Bericht)," in *Über Deutschland reden*, Frankfurt: Suhrkamp, 1988, pp. 76–100.

Dorle und Wolf, Frankfurt: Suhrkamp, 1987. English translation: *No Man's Land*, trans. Leila Vennewitz, New York: Henry Holt, 1989.

Die Verteidigung der Kindheit, Frankfurt: Suhrkamp, 1991.

Walther, Joachim, *Sicherungsbereich Literatur: Schriftsteller und Staatssicherheit in der Deutschen Demokratischen Republik*, Berlin: LinksDruck, 1996.

Weber, Max, *Politics as a Vocation*, trans. H. H. Gerth and C. Wright Mills, Philadelphia: Fortress Press, 1965.

Wedel, Mathias, *Einheitsfrust*, Berlin: Rowohlt, 1994.

Wehdeking, Volker, *Die deutsche Einheit und die Schriftsteller: Literarische Verarbeitung der Wende seit 1989*, Stuttgart: W. Kohlhammer, 1995.

Wehling, Peter, "Multikulti von rechts: Die Neue Rechte entdeckt die Vorzüge der 'multikulturellen Gesellschaft,'" *Kommune*, January 1992, 68–69.

Weißmann, Karlheinz, *Rückruf in die Geschichte: Die deutsche Herausforderung: Alte Gefahren–Neue Chancen*, Berlin: Ullstein, 1993.

"Die Nation denken," *Frankfurter Allgemeine Zeitung*, 22 April 1994, 33.

Wenders, Wim, "Reden über Deutschland," in *The Act of Seeing: Texte und Gespräche*, Frankfurt: Verlag der Autoren, 1992, pp. 187–198. English translation: "Talking about Germany," in Roger F. Cook and Gerd Gemünden (eds.), *The Cinema of Wim Wenders: Image, Narrative, and the Postmodern Condition*, Detroit: Wayne State University Press, 1997, pp. 51–59.

Weninger, Robert and Brigitte Rossbacher (eds.), *Wendezeiten Zeitenwende: Positionsbestimmungen zur deutschsprachigen Literatur 1945–1995*, Tübingen: Stauffenberg, 1997.

Wiechert, Ernst, *Rede an die Deutsche Jugend 1945*, Munich: Zinnen, 1945.

Williams, Arthur and Stuart Parkes (eds.), *The Individual, Identity and Innovation: Signals from Contemporary Literature and the New Germany*, Bern: Peter Lang, 1994.

Winkels, Hubert, "Buch und Mensch – ein Unglückspaar," *Die Zeit* (American edition), 15 November 1996, 25–26.

Woelk, Ulrich, *Rückspiel*, Munich: Piper, 1993.

Wolf, Christa, *Nachdenken über Christa T.*, Halle: Mitteldeutscher Verlag, 1968. English translation: *The Quest for Christa T.*, trans. Christopher Middleton, New York: Farrar, Straus, Giroux, 1970.

Der geteilte Himmel, Munich: Deutscher Taschenbuch Verlag, 1973. English translation: *Divided Heaven*, trans. Joan Becker, New York: Farrar, Straus, Giroux, 1984.

Kindheitsmuster, Darmstadt: Luchterhand, 1977. English translation: *Patterns of Childhood*, trans. Ursule Molinaro and Hedwig Rappolt, New York: Farrar, Straus, Giroux, 1984. (English translation originally published as *A Model Childhood*, 1980.)

Kein Ort. Nirgends, Darmstadt: Luchterhand, 1979. English translation: *No Place on Earth*, trans. Jan van Heurck, New York: Farrar, Straus, Giroux, 1982.

Kassandra, Darmstadt: Luchterhand, 1983. English translation in: *Cassandra: A Novel and Four Essays*, trans. Jan von Heurck, New York: Farrar, Straus, Giroux, 1984.

Störfall: Nachrichten eines Tages, Darmstadt: Luchterhand, 1987. English translation: *Accident: A Day's News*, trans. Heike Schwarzbauer and Rick Takvorian, New York: Farrar, Straus, Giroux, 1989.

"The G.D.R. Forever," *The New York Times*, 8 December 1989, A39.

Reden im Herbst, Berlin: Aufbau, 1990.

Was bleibt, Berlin: Aufbau, 1990. English translation in: *What Remains and Other Stories*, trans. Heike Schwarzbauer and Rick Takvorian, New York: Farrar, Straus, Giroux, 1993.

Medea: Stimmen, Hamburg: Luchterhand, 1996. English translation: *Medea*, trans. John Cullen, New York: Doubleday, 1998.

Zeller, Bernhard (ed.), *"Als der Krieg zu Ende war": Literarisch-politische Publizistik 1945–1950*, Munich: Kösel, 1973.

Zitelmann, Rainer, *Hitler: Selbstverständnis eines Revolutionärs*, Hamburg: Berg, 1991.

Wohin treibt unsere Republik?, Frankfurt: Ullstein, 1994.

Zitelmann, Rainer and Eckhard Jesse (eds.), *Nationalsozialismus und Modernisierung*, Darmstadt: Wissenschaftliche Buchgesellschaft, 1991.

Zitelmann, Rainer, Karlheinz Weißmann and Michael Grossheim (eds.), *Westbindung: Chancen und Risiken für Deutschland*, Frankfurt: Propyläen, 1993.

Zschokke, Matthias, *Der dicke Dichter*, Cologne: Bruckner & Thünker, 1995.

Zweite Berliner Begegnung: Den Frieden erklären – Protokolle des zweiten Schriftstellertreffens am 22./23. April 1983 – Der vollständige Text aller Beiträge aus Ost und West, Darmstadt: Luchterhand, 1983.

Index

Abbey, Edward, 173
Adenauer, Konrad, 110, 119, 121
Adorno, Theodor W., 8, 93, 115–116, 171, 193
aestheticism, 71, 72, 74–76, 78, 92, 107
Ahrends, Martin, 55, 56, 192, 194
Alexanderplatz, 48, 50, 54, 66
alienation, 29, 47–48, 60, 118–119, 127, 129,145
Americanization, 41, 55, 60, 117–119, 128–130
anachronisms, 165
Andersch, Alfred, 24, 141
Anderson, Benedict, 20, 185
Anderson, Sascha, 81, 91, 97, 99–101
anti-Americanism, 33–35, 117–119, 128–130
anticapitalism, 114–119
anti-Communism, 45, 117, 121
antifascism, 45, 52, 64, 73, 123, 133
anti-imperialism, 130
anti-Semitism, 120, 146
Aragon, Louis, 72
Aristophanes, 38
Arjouni, Jakob, 163, 168, 176
Arndt, Ernst Moritz, 10
Arnim, Achim von, 7
Artaud, Antonin, 72
Assmann, Aleida, 7
Auschwitz, 57, 86, 127, 161, 189, 190
Austria, 33, 47, 163, 184

baby boomers, 123, 125–126, 167
Barber, Benjamin R., 172
Baring, Arnulf, 110, 112–113, 120, 135
Barnet, Richard J., 191
Bartsch, Kurt, 82
Basic Law, 111–112
Basic Treaty, 41
Bataille, Georges, 128
Bathrick, David, 2, 3, 50, 95, 97–98
Baudelaire, Charles, 71, 120
Bauer, Marcus, 128

Becher, Johannes R., 22, 165
Becker, Jurek, 111, 173
Becker, Peter von, 43, 164, 168
Beethoven, Ludwig van, 131
belated nation, 10, 20, 116, 165–167, 193, 222
Bender, Peter, 203
Benjamin, Walter, 60, 115
Benn, Gottfried, 53–54, 72
Benoist, Alain de, 134
Bergfleth, Gerd, 127–128
Bergmann, Frithjof, 191
Berka, Sigrid, 131, 216
Berlin, 22, 32, 36–37, 48, 52, 55, 65, 81–82, 90, 93, 102–104, 106–108, 110–112, 124, 126, 139, 164, 169,175–176, 179–180, 187, 197, 205, 213, 218
Berlin Wall, 13, 18, 31, 36–37, 41, 47, 50–52, 63, 66, 81, 89, 112, 118, 127, 147–149, 157–158, 164, 175, 187, 206
Berliner Begegnungen zur Friedensförderung, 31–32
Berman, Russell A., 2, 8, 18
Biermann, Wolf, 15, 41, 51, 53, 66, 82, 84, 90, 92
Bismarck, Otto von, 16, 59, 61, 165, 174, 185
Bitburg, 13
Bitterfelder Weg, 26
Bloch, Ernst, 170–171
Böhme, Ibrahim, 80, 83
Bohrer, Karl Heinz, 42–43, 56–57, 60, 71–73, 75–76, 78–79, 107, 120, 142
Böll, Heinrich, 1, 12, 26, 31, 72, 107, 108
Bonn, 37–38, 54–55, 62, 112
Bormann, Alexander von, 25, 204
Brandenburg, 43, 163
Brandt, Willy, 8, 25, 121
Braun, Volker, 87, 91, 180
Brecht, Bertolt, 14, 15, 72, 103, 183
Brentano, Clemens, 7
Breton, André, 72
Broder, Henryk M., 83, 85

Brubaker, Rogers, 7
Brussig, Thomas, 85, 101, 156–158
Bruyn, Günter de, 8
Bubik, Roland, 128
Buchsteiner, Jochen, 124
Bullivant, Keith, 1, 3, 6, 9, 19–20, 187, 223
Bürger, Peter, 19
Burmeister, Brigitte, 85
Bush, George, 172, 176, 190

capitalism, 23–24, 42, 50–51, 56, 59, 61,
　114–115, 117–118, 134, 144–145, 148,
　169–170, 175, 177–180, 182–183
Carnegie, Andrew, 196
Carr, Godfrey, 220
castration anxiety,154–157
Catholicism, 115
Cavanagh, John, 191
Central Europe, see *Mitteleuropa*
Chernobyl, 27
child-rearing, 148; *see also* family, German *and*
　pedagogy
Christian Democratic Union (CDU), 54, 111,
　121
classicism, 40, 119
Clinton, Bill, 174, 177
Cocteau, Jean, 72
cold war, 3, 4, 8, 22, 23, 25, 30, 31, 32, 114,
　122, 146, 178, 194, 197
Coleridge, Samuel Taylor, 114
Communism, 2–3, 35, 42, 45, 48, 50–51, 54,
　67, 69, 70, 78, 87, 93, 96, 117, 120, 122,
　151–152, 157, 159, 169, 178–180, 183,
　189; *see also* Socialist Unity Party
conscience (of the nation), 5, 12, 32, 58, 125,
　127
conservatism, 1, 16, 42, 75–76, 78, 113–117,
　120–123, 128, 131, 133, 135, 161, 172, 183,
　193
Conservative Revolution, 117, 128
constitutional patriotism, 58, 109
consumerism, 46, 52, 60–62, 132, 134,
　144–145, 180
convergence, literary, 4, 25–26, 29–30, 203
convergence theory, 23–25, 29
culture, 5–8, 10–11, 16, 30–31, 59–62, 129,
　132–135, 141, 168, 177, 220
culture wars, 177, 192

Dadaism, 72
deconstruction, 18, 91, 127
denial, psychological, 147–148, 168
Derrida, Jacques, 89, 91, 94–96
détente, 24–25, 29–30, 121
Deutsche Mark (D-Mark), 58, 60, 62, 112, 188

Deutsche Volks-Union (DVU), 121
Diner, Dan, 135, 209
Dische, Irene, 43, 168, 176, 205
Doane, Heike A., 139, 204
Döblin, Alfred, 77
Dostoyevsky, 115
Drawert, Kurt, 91, 93, 96–99, 151, 158–159,
　198
Dresden, 39, 90, 137

East bloc, 23–24, 32–33, 155, 177, 179
Eckart, Gabriele, 150, 153
ecologism, 27, 33, 56, 118, 128, 133–134, 144,
　145, 173
economic miracle, see *Wirtschaftswunder*
ego, 12, 98, 99–101, 103, 107, 133, 159, 161
Elsner, Gisela, 61
Eluard, Paul, 72
Emmerich, Wolfgang, 3–5, 25, 79, 210, 224
Engels, Friedrich, 54, 116, 178
England, 6, 10, 59, 110, 117, 164–165, 190
Enlightenment, 17, 29, 133–134
Enzensberger, Hans Magnus, 59, 139, 140,
　169
Erb, Elke, 91
Erpenbeck, John, 50, 179–180, 196
Euro, 188
European Union, 135, 165, 188, 190
Expressionism, 72, 119

Faktor, Jan, 91, 93
family, German, 42, 142, 148, 150, 152; *see also*
　child-rearing *and* pedagogy
fascism, 46, 60–61, 72, 116, 126, 166, 192
Faust, 102–104, 106, 108
feminism, 15, 29, 33, 75, 154
feudalism, 10, 114
Fichte, Johann Gottlieb, 7, 10
finis Germaniae, 169, 186
First World War, *see* World War One
Fischer, Joschka, 124
Flakhelfer-Generation, 139–141, 155
Flaubert, Gustave, 71, 120
Fontane, Theodor, 174
Foucault, Michel, 83, 224
France, 6, 10, 46, 62, 91, 102, 109–110, 117,
　122, 164, 165, 185, 190, 191
Francis II, 184
Franco-Prussian War, 62
Frankfurt, 9, 74
Frankfurt School, 115–116
Frankfurter Allgemeine Zeitung, 73
French Revolution, 122
Freud, Sigmund, 12, 38, 94, 95, 133, 148, 149,
　158, 160, 171, 172

Fried, Erich, 33
Friedrich Barbarossa, 119
Fries, Fritz Rudolf, 49, 85, 153, 175, 194
Frisch, Max , 26
Fuchs, Jürgen, 86
Fühmann, Franz, 87
Fukuyama, Francis, 177–179, 222

Gauck, Joachim, 82
Gaus, Günter, 41–43, 60, 164, 183
Gehlen, Arnold, 75–76
generation gap, 141–142, 161
generation of 1989, 122
Generation X, 123–124, 126–127
genres, literary, 19–20
GDR anthem, 22, 165
GDR revolution, 22, 48–49, 51–53, 61, 67,
    70, 106, 122, 140, 145
German division, 3, 6, 8, 22, 25, 27, 30,
    36–40, 44, 143, 145–147, 149, 161, 164,
    185, 197–198
German national anthem, 11, 185
German Question, 16, 41, 43, 45–46, 63, 163,
    166, 186, 189
German Reich, 10, 41, 59, 62, 110, 117, 185;
    see also Holy Roman Empire *and* Third
    Reich
German reunification (1990), 1, 3, 5–6, 10,
    16, 22, 28, 30, 46–47, 50–52, 54–55,
    58–59, 63–64, 66, 73–75, 79–80, 101,
    109, 111–114, 120, 122, 127–128,
    130–131, 135–136, 139, 142–145,
    148–149, 151, 158, 160, 162–163, 166,
    171–174, 176, 179, 188, 191–192, 222;
    how to refer to, 122, 165–166, 172, 199,
    220; pre-October 1990 discussions of, 16,
    31, 47, 53–57, 59–61, 119, 186–187, 198
German Studies, 8, 17, 18
German unification (1871), 10, 61, 165, 166,
    174
Germanistik, 17, 18
Geulen, Eva, 116, 129
Gitlin, Todd, 192
globalization, 166, 172, 191, 192, 193
Goethe, Johann Wolfgang von, 9, 40,
    106–108
Gorbachev, Mikhail, 166
Gramsci, Antonio, 123
Grass, Günter, 1–2, 4–5 8, 10, 20, 26, 32–33,
    51, 57–59, 62, 85, 139–141, 160,
    173–176, 186, 188, 191, 197, 198, 223
    Die Blechtrommel, 20, 140–141, 197
    Ein weites Feld, 1, 20, 51, 85, 173–175
    Die Rättin, 32–33
    Schreiben nach Auschwitz, 57, 189

Graw, Ansgar, 110
Great Britain, 1, 46, 109, 193–194
Greens, 15, 16, 121, 124
Greiner, Ulrich, 67, 70, 74–75, 78, 92, 95
Grimm, Brothers, 55–56, 155, 219
Group 47, 72
Grünbein, Durs, 91
Gruppe 47, *see* Group 47
guilt, problem of, 12, 84, 101, 127, 133,
    139–140, 144, 146, 148–149, 158–161,
    168

Habermas, Jürgen, 17, 58–59, 109–110, 165,
    172, 220
Hahn, Hans-Joachim, 76, 209
Halle, 143–144, 146
Handke, Peter, 73
Hanke, Helmut, 61
Hauke, Frank, 123
Havemann, Robert, 30, 52
Hegel, Georg Wilhelm Friedrich, 177, 196
Hegi, Ursula, 217
Heidegger, Martin, 115, 121
Hein, Christoph, 29, 43, 48, 50, 61, 87, 113,
    180–183, 198
    Der fremde Freund, 29, 43
    Das Napoleon-Spiel, 181–183
    Die Ritter der Tafelrunde, 181
    Der Tangospieler, 181
Hensel, Kerstin, 85
Herder, Johann Gottfried von, 7
Hermann, Ludolf, 127
Herzog, Roman, 172
Herzog, Werner, 31
Hettche, Thomas, 187
Heym, Stefan, 35–36, 49–50, 52–54, 56, 68,
    82, 113
Hilbig, Wolfgang, 85, 94, 101–108, 126,
    137–138, 175–176, 198, 212
Hildesheimer, Wolfgang, 26
Hirschman, Albert O., 69
historicization, 78, 209
Historikerstreit, 13, 57, 76–78, 109–110, 127,
    162, 208, 220
history, politics of, 7, 9, 13, 57, 76–78, 130,
    161–162
Hitler, Adolf, 13–14, 16, 23, 33, 45, 74, 84,
    107, 117–118, 143–144, 146, 178, 190,
    214
Hochhuth, Rolf, 34–35, 139
Hocke, Gustav René, 74
Hoffmann von Fallersleben, August
    Heinrich, 11, 185
Hofmannsthal, Hugo von, 184
Hölderlin, Friedrich, 64, 67

Holocaust, 13, 34, 72, 76, 125, 127, 146, 168
Holy Roman Empire, 7, 119, 184–185, 223
Homer, 32, 197
homosexuality, 85–86, 115, 132, 138, 170, 190
Honecker, Erich, 24–25, 47–48, 50, 87, 157, 166
Humboldt University, 151, 180
Huysmanns, Joris Karl, 71
Huyssen, Andreas, 79

idealism, 44, 48, 92, 116–117, 123, 134, 184–185
"Ideas of 1914," 117, 122, 128
identification, 10, 168
identities, subaltern, 18
identity, cultural, 63, 118; East German, 54, 56; formation of, 18–19; individual, 38, 99, 101, 160; German, 5–8, 10–11, 13–21, 32, 36, 40, 44, 47, 56–57, 109–110, 114, 118, 130, 139, 149, 159–161, 172, 188–190, 191, 220; loss of, 98–99, 102, 129; national, 9, 11, 13–18, 20–21, 32, 36, 44, 47, 54, 56, 109–110, 114, 118, 130, 172, 177, 188, 190; postnational, 58, 109–110, 165, 169, 172, 177, 192; West German, 60, 73, 109–110, 135
imperialism, 141
impotence, 96, 106, 126, 156
individualism, 129
inner emigration, 92, 69, 208
Iron Curtain, 111, 192
irrationalism, 17, 119, 120, 132
Italy, 46, 110

Jaspers, Karl, 159–160
Jenninger, Philipp, 13, 161, 219–220
Jens, Walter, 31
Jentzsch, Kerstin, 83, 85, 130, 176, 182
Johnson, Uwe, 26, 140, 197–198
Jung, Carl Gustav, 159
Junge Freiheit, 122, 128
Jünger, Ernst, 71

Kaes, Anton, 8
Kant, Hermann, 70
Kant, Immanuel, 91
Kilb, Andreas, 169, 192
Kinkel, Klaus, 177
Kirsten, Wulf, 43
Klein, Joe, 174
Kleist, Heinrich von, 40, 44
Kohl, Helmut, 13–15, 54, 58–59, 61–62, 112–113, 121, 130, 139–140, 174, 223
Kolbe, Uwe, 91–93
Kolbenhoff, Walter, 139

Königsdorf, Helga, 29
Kramer, Jane, 83, 85
Krausser, Helmut, 175
Krenz, Egon, 50
Kroetz, Franz Xaver, 164
Kuhn, Anna, 151
Kulturnation, 5–10, 12, 15–16, 22, 25, 31–32, 36, 44, 59, 61, 135, 176–177, 184, 186, 188, 189
Kunze, Reiner, 80

Lafontaine, Oskar, 165
Lagarde, Paul de, 59, 115
Langbehn, Julius, 115
le Carré, John, 22
Leeder, Karen, 124, 212
Leggewie, Claus, 121–122, 168
Leibnitz, 120
Leipzig, 39, 53, 55, 61, 80, 90–91, 139, 164
Lenz, Siegfried, 139
Lewis, Alison, 144–145, 148, 153
liberalism, 19, 21, 122, 129, 131, 134–135, 161, 172, 177–179
Link, Jürgen, 203
literary genres, *see* genres, literary
Literaturstreit, 76, 78, 82, 209
Loest, Erich, 80
Lukács, György, 18, 20, 115
Lukacs, John, 172
Luther, Martin, 98

Maaz, Hans-Joachim, 143–149, 160, 217
Macdonald, Andrew, 173
Macki, Erik J., 199
Magdeburg, 164
Maizière, Lothar de, 54, 83
Man, Paul de, 91, 211
Mann, Thomas, 9–11, 23, 94, 115, 163, 166, 197
Markovits, Andrei S., 11, 33, 63, 207
Marlowe, Christopher, 107
Maron, Monika, 53–54, 82, 151–154, 158–159, 169, 176, 198, 218
    Animal triste, 153–154, 158–159, 176
    Stille Zeile Sechs, 151–153, 158–159
    "Writers and the People," 53–54
Maron, Paul, 151
Marx, Karl, 54, 114, 116, 178, 179
Marxism, 51, 61, 70, 115, 118, 134, 154, 179, 196
masturbation, 155–157
materialism, 59–60, 117–119, 124, 130–132, 134
Mathäs, Alexander, 219, 223
Mayer, Hans, 29, 30

Mayer-Iswandy, Claudia, 76
McLuhan, Marshall, 90, 94
Meckel, Christoph, 142
Mecklenburg-Western Pommerania, 39, 42, 163
Meinecke, Friedrich, 6–10, 16, 30
Mellon, Andrew, 196
Mertes, Michael, 113
Mielke, Erich, 87
Ministerium für Staatssicherheit, *see* Stasi
Mitscherlich, Alexander and Margarete, 142–144
Mitteleuropa, 120, 170
Modrow, Hans, 54, 62
Moeller van den Bruck, Arthur, 115
Mohr, Heinrich, 30
Mommsen, Theodor, 180–181, 197
moralism, 56, 71–73, 75, 123
Moretti, Franco, 22, 194
Morgner, Irmtraud, 29
Morr, Hubertus von, 113
Moser, Tilmann, 162
Müller, Heiner, 29, 82, 86, 95, 124–125, 139, 180–181, 197, 222
Müller, Helmut L., 2, 10, 16
multiculturalism, 129–130
Musil, Robert, 197

Nadolny, Sten, 163, 193–194
nation, definition of, 6–8, 9–10, 16
nation-state, 10, 16, 20, 46, 58–59, 165, 168, 171–172, 220
nationalism, 14–15, 17, 19, 46, 57–58, 109–110, 168, 193; *see also* patriotism and renationalization
National Socialism, 11, 23, 27, 29, 35, 45–46, 53, 57, 72–73, 77, 92, 94, 96, 107, 115, 117, 119, 125–127, 130, 141–142, 145, 149, 151, 159–160, 162, 166, 168, 178, 205
naturalism, 89
Nazism, see National Socialism
Negt, Oskar, 4
neo-Nazism, 17, 132, 148
Neumeister, Andreas, 41, 163–164, 178, 195
New Left, 122
New Right, 116, 122–123, 125, 127–130, 134
New Subjectivity, 25, 29
Niekisch, Ernst, 117
Nietzsche, Friedrich, 61–62, 72, 115, 119, 121, 132, 133, 185
Night of Broken Glass, 13
nihilism, 128
1968, cultural revolution of, 122–127, 141
Nischengesellschaft, 41
Noelle-Neumann, Elisabeth, 135

Nolte, Ernst, 13, 76–78, 127, 135, 162, 214, 220
non-contemporaneity, 116, 170–171, 174, 176
normalization, 13–14, 59, 72, 78, 79, 127, 130, 135, 160, 188, 190
North Atlantic Treaty Organization (NATO), 30, 112, 190
nostalgia, 110, 112–113, 164, 170
Novalis, 114
novel (as a literary genre), 19–20
nuclear war, 31, 33
Nuremberg, 141, 184–185, 217, 222

Oedipus, 126, 154
Ortheil, Hanns-Josef, 167–169
Ossis, 176
Ostpolitik, 25, 121

Papenfuß-Gorek, Bert, 91
paranoia, 147, 103
Parkes, K. Stuart, 6, 10, 11, 20, 31, 71, 76, 138
patriarchy, 33, 95, 149–150, 153, 155
patriotism, 14, 15, 37, 40; *see also* constitutional patriotism *and* nationalism
Paul, Georgina, 208, 220
peace movement, 30–31, 34, 130, 206
pedagogy, 151; *see also* child-rearing *and* family, German
Peitsch, Helmut, 3–5, 8, 10, 13, 16–20, 25, 31, 32, 202, 204
Pennsylvania, 170
Persian Gulf War, 57, 172
phallogocentrism, *see* patriarchy
Pittsburgh, 196
Plato, 38
Plessner, Helmuth, 20, 165, 220, 223
Pohl, Klaus, 84–85
Poland, 57, 69
Politburo, 48, 50, 166, 181
political correctness, 121
popular culture, 50, 129
postmodernism and postmodernity, 75, 79, 90, 103, 105, 125, 169, 173, 174, 176–177, 179, 187, 191
potency, 96, 157
Prenzlauer Berg, 93–94, 96–98, 103, 107, 157, 211
projection, psychological, 143, 147–149
Protestantism, 56, 72, 82, 86, 143
Prussia, 6, 118, 174
Pynchon, Thomas, 103

racism, 46, 130
Raddatz, Fritz J., 91
rationalism, 119–120, 134

Rathenow, Lutz, 91
Reagan, Ronald, 13, 33, 178
Reed, Terrence James, 71
Reemtsma, Jan Philipp, 168
Rehmann, Ruth, 142
Reich, Simon, 11, 63, 207
Reichskristallnacht, see Night of Broken Glass
Reich-Ranicki, Marcel , 1–2, 4–5, 26–27
Reid, James Henderson, 202
reification, 18
Reimann, Brigitte , 29
Reinhold, Otto, 50, 52, 206
Renan, Ernest, 9–10, 186
renationalization, 13, 16–17, 30–31
repression, psychological, 15, 39, 92, 101,
    119–120, 143–144, 146–148,
Republikaner, 121
Richter, Hans Werner, 22, 72
Richter, Horst-Eberhard, 162
Richter, Karl, 127–130
Roberts, David, 29
Roethke, Gisela, 208
romanticism, 27, 117, 119
Roper, Katherine, 213
Ross, Jan, 121
Rossbacher, Brigitte, 218
Russia, 41, 109, 117, 128

sadomasochism, 187, 190
Saeger, Uwe, 85, 89–90, 100
Sakharov, Andrei D., 24
Saxony, 6, 43, 163
Schalck-Golodkowski, Alexander, 88
Schedlinski, Rainer, 80–82, 88, 91, 95–96,
    98, 101
Schelsky, Helmut, 75–76
Schiller, Friedrich, 7, 35–36, 184, 222, 223
Schirrmacher, Frank, 73–74, 78–79, 92, 95
Schlesinger, Klaus, 82
Schlingensief, Christoph, 124–125, 127
Schmidt, Helmut, 47–48, 121
Schmidt, Ulrich, 25
Schneider, Michael, 217
Schneider, Peter, 36–38, 46–48, 55, 108, 158
Schnur, Wolfgang, 83
Schopenhauer, Arthur, 115
Schramm, Ingo, 155–156
Schröder, Gerhard, 15
Schwaiger, Brigitte, 142
Schwilk, Heimo, 128
Second Reich, *see* German Reich
Second World War, *see* World War Two
Seeba, Hinrich, 18–19
Shakespeare, William, 134
Simon, Annette, 162

Simonov, Konstantin Mikhailovich, 24
Sinakowski, Andreas, 85
social constructions, 6, 8, 18–19
Social Democratic Party (SPD), 15, 35, 41, 80,
    121, 165, 190
Social-Liberal coalition, 29, 121
socialism, 24–26, 29, 35, 45–46, 48–49,
    51–54, 92, 113–114, 123, 134, 169, 173,
    178–181, 183
socialist realism, 23, 25, 28–29
Socialist Unity Party (SED), 24, 50, 52–53,
    67, 87, 143; *see also* Communism
solipsism, 91, 107
Sonderweg, 13, 109, 111, 130, 135, 191
Soviet Red Army, 35
Soviet Union, 23–24, 30, 113, 117, 134, 179,
    180, 214
Spengler, Oswald, 115, 121
Spiegel, Der, 1–2, 4–5, 21, 26, 52–54
Staatsnation, 7–8, 10, 12, 15, 188–189
Staël, Germaine de, 185–186
Stalin, 23, 78
Stalinism, 45, 48–49, 160, 162
Stasi, 51, 65–67, 79–92, 94–99, 101–107,
    137–138, 148, 153, 156–157, 175, 210
Steiner, George, 19–20
Steinfeld, Thomas, 38
Stern, Fritz, 115
Sternberger, Dolf, 109
Stifter, Adalbert, 43
Stolpe, Manfred, 83
Strauß, Botho, 39–40, 42, 44, 131–134, 169,
    216
    "Anschwellender Bocksgesang," 131–134
    Diese Erinnerung an einen, der nur einen Tag zu
        Gast war, 39–40
    Das Gleichgewicht, 131
    Schlußchor, 131, 169
Sturm und Drang, 119
Stürmer, Michael, 13, 110
Suhr, Heidrun, 38
superego, 12, 57, 72, 94, 99–101, 103, 105,
    107, 123, 133, 148, 158, 161, 189, 219
Süskind, Patrick, 112, 163, 167
Syberberg, Hans Jürgen, 118–120, 123,
    127–129, 132, 140–141, 214
Szczypiorski, Andrzej, 191

Tageszeitung, 122
Tendenzwende, 25
terrorism, 134, 142
theodicy, 72, 120
"third path," 33, 51, 56, 113, 117, 134, 145, 180
Third Reich, 11, 16, 69, 73, 76, 95, 109, 144,
    149, 159–160, 189, 196, 198

Thuringia, 39, 42, 163
Tinbergen, Jan, 23
Toffler, Alvin, 170–171
Tolstoy, Leo, 197,
Tönnies, Ferdinand, 115
tragedy, 19, 131–133
Trommler, Frank, 20, 30
Trotsky, Leon, 171
Troy, 27, 28, 32–33, 65, 87, 90

Ulbrich, Stefan, 114, 127, 129
unemployment, 123
United States of America (USA), 15, 33,
    34–35, 47, 60, 78, 109, 116, 118, 121, 123,
    128, 130, 164–165, 167, 170, 172–173,
    177, 190–192
utilitarianism, 132

Väterliteratur, 142, 150, 217
Vegesack, Thomas von, 26
Vergangenheitsbewältigung, 27, 73, 72, 78, 127,
    142, 144, 160, 162
vigilantism, 173
Vogt, Jochen, 78
Volksbühne, 124–125
Voltaire, François Marie Arouet de, 120

Wagner, Bernd, 205
Wagner, Richard, 115, 119, 184–186, 222–223
Walser, Martin, 37–40, 43–44, 63, 110,
    137–142, 158, 161, 164, 167, 175,
    186–187, 198, 204–205, 219, 223
    Dorle und Wolf, 37–39, 204
    Die Verteidigung der Kindheit, 137–139, 158,
    175
    "Über Deutschland reden," 43–44, 164,
    186–187
Wander, Maxi, 29
Warsaw Pact, 30
Weber, Max, 74–75
Wedel, Mathias, 135
Wegner, Bettina, 82
Wehdeking, Volker, 3–5, 10, 20, 212
Weimar Republic, 183
Weißmann, Karlheinz, 122, 125, 127

Wende, 121, 122, 220; see also *Tendenzwende*
Wenders, Wim, 168, 192, 195
Werfel, Franz, 11
Wessis, 130
West bloc, 23–24, 32–33, 155
West Germany, *see* Federal Republic of
    Germany
Westernization, 79, 122, 135, 109; *see also*
    Americanization
Wicki, Bernhard, 139
Wiechert, Ernst, 11
Wilde, Oscar, 120
Williams, Arthur, 216
Winkels, Hubert, 195
Wirtschaftswunder, 40, 139
Woelk, Ulrich, 125–127, 164–165, 175
Wolf, Christa, 10, 25–29, 32–33, 49–50, 52,
    63–70, 73, 78–82, 84, 86–92, 98–99,
    106, 113, 139, 154–155, 171, 173, 176, 180,
    197, 208
    Der geteilte Himmel, 26–27
    Kassandra, 26–27, 32–33, 65, 87, 90, 99,
    154
    Kein Ort. Nirgends, 26–27
    Kindheitsmuster, 26–27, 197
    Medea, 154–155, 171, 176
    Nachdenken über Christa T., 25–26
    Störfall, 26–28, 65
    Was bleibt, 63–68, 80–81, 84, 87–90, 98,
    106, 155, 208, 211
World War One, 59, 117, 122, 146, 197
World War Two, 12, 31, 41, 45–46, 64, 72, 74,
    84, 115, 135, 137, 139, 146, 148, 152–153,
    159, 166

xenophobia, 132, 148

Yalta, 16, 122
Yugoslavia, 57

Zeit, Die, 67, 169, 195
"zero hour," 8–9, 11, 46, 64, 78, 112, 130, 141,
    160, 166, 169
Zitelmann, Rainer, 123, 125
Zschokke, Matthias, 175–176, 197